MERE ESCHATOLOGY

A BIBLICAL STUDY OF THE SECOND COMING

THE END OF THE AGE

ROBERT E. PICIRILLI

randall house
114 Bush Rd – Nashville, TN 37217
randallhouse.com

Published by D6 Family Ministry
114 Bush Road
Nashville, TN 37217
Visit d6family.com

ISBN: 9781614841814

Printed in the United States of America

TABLE OF CONTENTS

Preface

Perhaps it is fitting that in the *last* days of my life I should write about eschatology, which is the study of biblical teaching about the end of this age or "*last* things." I am aware that I will soon be moving on if the Lord does not come first. Wouldn't it be wonderful if He did! "Even so, come quickly, Lord Jesus!"

Throughout my ministry I have tended to neglect eschatology. Perhaps *avoided* would be a better word. I am part of a denomination that does not take a confessional stance on the subject, apart from a few, brief generalities. Of "The Second Coming of Christ," for example, we affirm only that the Lord Jesus, "who ascended on high and sits at the right hand of God, will come again to close the Gospel dispensation, glorify His saints, and judge the world." Following this are two equally brief affirmations about "The Resurrection" and "The Judgment and Retribution." They affirm that both resurrection and judgment will be the experience of all, both saved and lost; but they avoid defining the times involved.

This neutrality was intentional, reflecting long-standing differences of opinion among us about eschatological frameworks. Like the Christian Church in general, we have room for those with various views, so long as we all take seriously the biblical teaching that Jesus is coming back and that we will be judged and spend eternity in God's presence or separated from Him in Hell.

At one stage of my adult life I gave such matters some attention. While teaching Bible at Free Will Baptist Bible College (now Welch College), I was asked to teach Revelation (the book). In those younger (naïve?) days I would tackle almost anything. I got a well-known commentary on Revelation from the library—the work of J. A. Seiss[1]—and proceeded to teach Revelation according to Seiss. Soon I felt guilty about that, so I asked a friend, Wade Jernigan, to recommend a good book on Revelation that took a different (amillennial) approach. He recommended Ray Summers's *Worthy Is the Lamb*,[2] and then I started taking students through Revelation two times, presenting Seiss and Summers.

Finally, I didn't have to teach Revelation any more. The truth is that the more I became familiar with Revelation the less sure I was about its meaning. No doubt that was another reason I entered a long period of avoiding the subject. I still read Revelation now and again, in my devotional reading, but I tended to shrug it off. I gave up hope of figuring it out.

Until recently, that is. I began to feel that I ought to give eschatology some serious attention, but in a different sort of way. I wanted to focus on the second coming of Jesus more than anything else, and in doing so to emphasize the things we agree on more than the things we differ about. After all, the New Testament has a lot to say about the return of Jesus to this earth. He Himself spoke of it often. Angels taught it. The inspired apostles gave instruction on the subject. It is clear that they meant for us to take it seriously and to live in such a way that Jesus' impending appearance makes a dramatic difference in who and what we are. We are obviously meant to be excited about it, to look with expectancy and longing for it. We can't afford to allow differences of opinion about the future to dampen our enthusiasm for His promised return. There's too much we agree on for the disagreements to divide us and rob us of joy in the prospect of seeing Him. It's clear that the New Testament focuses on the big picture and does so in a positive way that appeals—or ought to appeal—to us all.

So I decided to study the subject for an extended period of time. This book is the result of that study. I began by reading through the entire New Testament and making a list of everything said about the future. I am attempting to include as many of these references as possible. Above all, we must be biblical. If nothing else, studying God's Word as it speaks about the Second Coming ought to whet our appetites for that glorious event.

The other part of what I mean when I say "in a different sort of way" is that I am giving virtually no attention to what other interpreters have to say. In this respect, this book is different from most others I have written. For the most part, I am offering my own conclusions about the text. It is the text of Scripture itself that guides me in everything included here. This is a Bible study. My emphasis on the Second Coming itself is obvious from the fact that the first part of the book will be about that. In that part, at least, there will not be so much that brings up differences of opinion.

Not that I will avoid debatable matters entirely. While the major part of the book deals with the four Gospels and the Epistles, one cannot ignore the book of Revelation. Part of the book, then, will represent my attempt to give Revelation a fresh look, grappling with the text itself and trying to remain uninfluenced, as much as possible, by the various views of Revelation that are "out there." My approach will require that I offer some suggestions about what may precede and what may follow Jesus' return, but I won't mind if readers differ after I explain why I take the approach I do. I will not do much arguing for my view, or against the views of others. It will become clear, I suppose, that I take the position that there will be a "Messianic kingdom" of Jesus on earth following the Second Coming, and Revelation plays a part in my adopting this view—which is much like "historic premillennialism" and is not like the dispensational premillennialism that has been popular among those in the line of Darby and Scofield—the view I first learned. At the end of my study of Revelation, I decided that I apparently take a sort of diachronic-futurist approach—by which I mean that it speaks of events that are both "across time" and future. The nature of this view should become clear to the reader in the process of going through the several chapters.

A chapter near the end will take a brief look at a matter that reflects especially the Old Testament: namely, whether there will be any sort of Jewish restoration involved in Jesus' kingdom. I am open to that possibility, which depends largely—though not entirely—on the way we read some important Old Testament prophetic pronouncements.

Regardless of the differences that may arise in my analysis, the reader will not find me to be dogmatic in my interpretation; as I said, I will not be argumentative. I hope that any Christian whose eschatology is like mine or different from mine will find the book to be helpful. My approach to Revelation is not exactly like any I have ever read; I offer it for the consideration of others and for further development by any interpreters who should find it helpful.

I acknowledge, with appreciation, the helpful comments of Billy Hanna, Jackson Watts, and Jeff Blair. These remain friends, I believe, even though none of them will closely agree with me.

A companion Mere Eschatology Study Guide is available for purchase at D6.family/store.

Endnotes

[1] J. A., Seiss, *The Apocalypse: Lectures on the Book of Revelation* (Grand Rapids: Zondervan, 1950).

[2] Ray Summers, *Worth Is the Lamb: An Interpretation of Revelation* (Nashville: Broadman, 1951).

Part One

THE SECOND COMING OF JESUS AND ATTENDANT CIRCUMSTANCES

As I have suggested in the Preface, the second coming of Jesus to earth is, for me, the most important truth in the theology of last things we call eschatology. If I'm reading the Bible right, it ought to be one of the most important truths for all believers to know about and hold close to their chests. I fear, however, that many people in our churches give little if any thought to that fact, and that's not the way our faith is supposed to focus. The Second Coming should take center stage in our view of Christian teaching. We ought to think of it every day with longing. I do not say that harshly; I know from personal experience that it is far too easy for us to get so caught up in the concerns of this life that we scarcely cast a glance at the return of our Lord and what will transpire then.

Even for Christians who are conscious of the importance of this truth, many have very little in their eschatology except for the general idea that Jesus is coming back, we will all be judged, and all will spend eternity either in Heaven or in Hell—in whatever ways those two destinies may be defined. But the biblical treatment of the Second Coming is far more developed than that; and most of what it says isn't controversial at all.

In the New Testament, that Jesus will return to earth is a pervasive and essential theme. Not counting the book of Revelation, there are more than forty specific references to His coming in the New Testament, and that doesn't include many more indirect references like those to "the day of the Lord" or "entering the kingdom of God" or other indications of what will transpire—like resurrection and judgment—when He returns.

Theology, including eschatology, is intended by God to make a difference in our lives. I hope the first part of this book will reawaken our interest in the Second Coming and make a revolutionary change in our lives.

Chapter 1

The Second Coming of Jesus and the End of the Age

At the heart of biblical eschatology is this momentous promise: Jesus is going to come back to this earth. There were things He purposed to do in this world but did not schedule for His first visit, when He became flesh and dwelled—literally, "tabernacled" (Greek *eskēnōsen*)—among us (John 1:14). He will return to finish His work, to bring His purposes to full and final consummation. *That return will mark the end of this age.*

Jesus' second coming is prominent in the biblical narrative, as in the account of His ascension, forty days following His resurrection from the dead, for example. He had soared into the skies before some of His disciples' very eyes and disappeared in a cloud. Understandably shaken, they were frozen in place, staring with awe and mixed emotions—perhaps a measure of distress—into the heavens where they had watched until they could see Him no longer. Instantly, two angel-messengers in glistening white stood by them and gave them the startling, encouraging promise: "This same Jesus, who was taken up from you into heaven, will so come in like manner as you saw Him go into heaven" (Acts 1:11).

The Certainty of Jesus' Coming

Theologians, commentators, and preachers typically emphasize the certainty of the promise of Jesus' return by pointing out that this was affirmed and reaffirmed at many different levels.

Jesus Himself promised to return. Perhaps the most well-known passage demonstrating this promise is John 14:1–6. Jesus sensed that His disciples were troubled by His saying that He was going to leave them and return to His

Father, and He wanted to reassure them. He was going home to His Father to prepare a place there for them. He said, "And if I go and prepare a place for you, I will come again and receive you to Myself; that where I am, there you may be also" (verse 3).

This was not the only time He talked about His return. Later, I will give more attention to various things Jesus said about the Second Coming.

Angels bore witness to His promised return. Just above, I have cited Acts 1:11, when at Jesus' ascension into Heaven the angels in attendance spoke directly to His yearning followers and assured them that He would come as they had seen Him go.

The other writers of the New Testament, including the apostles, under the inspiration of the Spirit of God, confirmed that Jesus will come back. Taking the apostles first, in canonical order, here is the evidence for this claim. For Paul, see 1 Thessalonians 4:13–18, which includes this: "For the Lord Himself will descend from heaven with a shout, with the voice of an archangel, and with the trumpet of God" (verse 16). Paul speaks of this glorious event many more times, and Chapters 10–11 will focus on several passages.

For Peter, consider 2 Peter 1:16–18. There Peter must have felt it necessary to assure his readers that he had not spoken to them in fables when he "made known" to them "the power and coming of our Lord Jesus Christ" (verse 16). Indeed, he went on to affirm that he (with James and John) had personally eye-witnessed the glory that Jesus will have when He returns, having seen Him transformed on the Mount of Transfiguration.

The apostle John urged his readers, as his dear children in the faith: "Abide in Him, that when He appears, we may have confidence and not be ashamed before Him at His coming" (1 John 2:28).

Evidently there were two other inspired authors of New Testament epistles who were not original apostles. One was the unknown writer of Hebrews 10:36–37, who said: "You have need of endurance, so that … you may receive the promise: 'For yet a little while, and He who is coming will come and will not tarry.'" There was also James, the brother of Jesus, who wrote: "Therefore be patient, brethren, until the coming of the Lord.... Establish your hearts, for the coming of the Lord is at hand" (James 5:7–8).

Other passages will be cited in a subsequent chapter. In summary, the promise of the second coming of Jesus is a recurring theme throughout the New Testament and one of the cardinal doctrines of the Christian faith. It is at the heart of the Christian's beliefs and behavior.

The Purpose of Jesus' Coming

For now, it is enough to look at the purpose of the Second Coming in a broad and summary way. Subsequent chapters in this work will add detail.

1. *Jesus is coming to gather and receive His followers into His permanent presence.* In John 14:3, already cited, Jesus said to His disciples, "I will come again and receive you to Myself, that where I am there you may be also." Also cited was 1 Thessalonians 4:16, promising that the Lord Jesus will descend from Heaven, and that the dead in Christ will be brought back to life. Verses 17 and 18 follow to say that all followers of His who are living at the time will be forcefully caught up with those resurrected ones to meet Him—on His way down, perhaps—in the air, "And thus [in this way] we shall always be with the Lord." The word *with* (Greek *sun*), in this context, means *together with.*

Nothing could be more obvious or biblical than that the hearts' desire of the Lord Jesus and His followers is to be together forever. The Second Coming will bring that dream to life. In John 14:3 the word *receive* is not the simple verb but a compound (Greek *paralambanō*) that may suggest taking someone to one's side: "take to oneself"—suggesting intimate presence. We are disciples of His in waiting, and being with Him is what we are waiting for.

What Paul said in 1 Thessalonians 4:16 is matched by what he said in 2 Thessalonians 2:1: "Now, brethren, concerning the coming of our Lord Jesus Christ and our gathering together to Him. . . . " The word *gathering* (Greek *episunagōgē*) carries the idea of an assembling or meeting together—and this won't be a Zoom meeting!

This idea of Jesus' coming to gather His own to Himself appears, at least in passing, in other references to the Second Coming. Sometimes Jesus represented what will transpire at the end of the age in the terms of a harvest. John the Baptist used this same metaphor in Matthew 3:12, saying that the One coming after him would "gather His wheat into the barn," words Jesus echoed in His parable of the wheat and tares when the owner of the field said to his reapers, "First gather together the tares and bind them in bundles to burn them, but gather the wheat into my barn" (Matthew 13:30). In both of these the wheat symbolically represents the followers of Jesus. In Matthew 24:30–31 (and Mark 13:26–27) Jesus speaks more directly in reference to His second coming, saying that He will be seen "coming on the clouds of heaven with power and great glory" and "will send His angels with a great sound of a trumpet, and they will gather together His elect from the four winds, from one end of heaven to the other."

What could possibly be more encouraging and exciting than to know that Jesus is coming back to this earth to gather to Himself, for eternal fellowship with Him, all of us who follow Him in faith! We can only imagine what that will be like, but we don't have to imagine that it will be glorious.

2. *Jesus is coming to raise the dead in Christ.* The quotation from 1 Thessalonians 4:16 has already promised this: "The Lord Himself will descend from heaven with a shout. . . . And the dead in Christ will rise first." This passage apparently represents believers who have already died as accompanying Jesus from the heavens on His voyage to earth, their risen bodies reunited with their spirits to meet Him in the air. This is what Paul elsewhere calls "the redemption of our body" (Romans 8:23), having just promised (verse 11) that the Holy Spirit, "who raised Christ from the dead will also give life to your mortal bodies." In 1 Corinthians 15 Paul represents this resurrection as a change from mortality to immortality, at a time when "Death is swallowed up in victory" (verses 53–54).

Furthermore, this victorious remaking is not experienced by the dead in Christ only. At the same time they are restored to life, living believers are likewise transformed. In 1 Thessalonians 4:17 Paul is content to signal this by saying only that we will be caught up with them to meet the Lord. But in 1 Corinthians 15 he provides more detail: "We shall not all sleep, but we shall

all be changed—in a moment, in the twinkling of an eye, at the last trumpet. For the trumpet will sound, and the dead will be raised incorruptible, and we shall be changed" (verses 51–52). All His followers, at His return, will experience the same transformation to immortality in final and eternal victory. We will be redeemed in body and spirit, forever without weakness, death, or sin.

I must add that the saints are not the only ones who will be raised from the dead; but passages like these in Thessalonians, Romans, and Corinthians are speaking specifically about the resurrection (or transformation) of *believers*. Other passages reveal that there will be a resurrection of both the wicked and the righteous: in Acts 24:15, for example, when Paul affirms before Felix that "there will be a resurrection of the dead, both of the just and the unjust." Whether the resurrection (and judgment) of the lost will occur at the same time as that of the saved is subject to differences of opinion; I will touch on this matter in other chapters.

For now, it is enough to say that a passage like 1 Thessalonians 4:13–18 speaks only of the resurrection of saints in connection with the Second Coming. If Jesus will reign on earth after His second coming, that fact will apparently rule out the resurrection of the wicked immediately at His coming. That, too, is a question for another chapter. Meanwhile, regrettably, the Second Coming is not something the wicked look forward to.

What matters to all believers, then, is that when Jesus returns to earth He will raise all believers who have previously died and transform all believers living at the time—a final victory over death for the faithful. That is the "blessed hope" we have, and of which Paul speaks in Titus 2:11–13, affirming that the grace of God is "teaching us that, denying ungodliness and worldly lusts, we should live soberly, righteously, and godly in the present age, looking for the blessed hope and glorious appearing of our great God and Savior Jesus Christ."

3. *Jesus is coming to reign.* Whether the reign of Jesus will be a millennial reign on this earth or take some other form—a question we will return to in Chapter 4—the fact remains that Jesus comes to earth as King, and kings reign in one way or another. Thus, in Matthew 25:31 Jesus introduces a pas-

sage by saying, "When the Son of Man comes in His glory and all the holy angels with Him, then He will sit on the throne of His glory" (ESV: "on his glorious throne"). In 1 Corinthians 15:25, in an important eschatological passage (which I will analyze in detail later), Paul promises, "For He must reign till He has put all enemies under His feet."

It seems very likely that this reigning is grounded in the fact that Jesus is the Davidic Messiah, the ultimate fulfillment of the Davidic covenant in which God promised that there would forever be a descendant of David's to reign. I will return to a fuller discussion of the reign of Christ in Chapter 4. Regardless whether Jesus reigns for a millennium or not, His reign will be *eternal.* Once He has taken the throne, He will not relinquish it; all claimants to the throne will be permanently vanquished. In the end, He "delivers the kingdom to God the Father," to be co-regent with Him forever, having put "an end to all rule and all authority and power" (1 Corinthians 15:24).

Chapter 4 will deal with the reign of Jesus and important biblical material in more detail; I will give attention also to Revelation 20. Meanwhile, every Christian should rejoice in the expectation of the reign of Jesus when He returns. There may well be a present, "spiritual" reign of Jesus in the hearts of those who know Him, but that seems to fall well short of His destiny to inherit the throne of David over the kingdoms of this world.

4. *Jesus is coming to reward the righteous and punish the wicked*—in much the same way (and with the same basic question of timing) as His raising both righteous and wicked from the dead. Another way to say this is that He is coming to *judge.* This is the sense of Matthew 16:27: "For the Son of Man will come in the glory of His Father with His angels, and then He will reward each according to his works."

Just as there are passages that speak only of the resurrection of the righteous dead, connected with the return of Christ, likewise there are passages that speak only of the reward of the righteous at that time. An example is 2 Timothy 4:8: "Finally, there is laid up for me the crown of righteousness, which the Lord, the righteous Judge, will give to me on that Day, and not to me only but also to all who have loved His appearing."

As with the previous point, that Jesus is coming to reign, this one is also important enough to develop in more detail in a chapter to follow. In that chapter I will mention some of the differences of opinion that exist among Bible interpreters about such things as whether there is more than one time of judgment. But the impact of this truth is not affected by such differences. It is enough to know that "we shall all stand before the judgment seat of Christ" and "each of us shall give account of himself to God" (Romans 14:10, 12)—another passage speaking specifically about those serving Christ. We can anticipate reward for faithful service, at the same time being uncomfortably aware of missed opportunities. This two-sided truth is something Paul addresses in 1 Corinthians 4:1–5 and connects to the Second Coming in his closing admonition: "Therefore judge nothing before the time, until the Lord comes, who will both bring to light the hidden things of darkness and reveal the counsels of the hearts. Then each one's praise will come from God" (verse 5). This passage, too, is addressed to those serving the Lord.

I will not engage, here, in discussion of differences in reward (or punishment). It may be that, for believers, what Paul says in the passage just quoted is enough: namely, that each will have, from God, the praise he or she ought to receive.

The Nature of Jesus' Coming

Without attempting to say everything possible, I will emphasize a selected number of things that are important to know about the return of Christ.

Jesus' Return as Bodily

Surely Jesus will return in the body He received at His resurrection on the third day following His crucifixion. Probably no one who believes in the Second Coming would question this. The angel who instructed the disciples at Jesus' ascension said, "This same Jesus … will so come in like manner as you saw Him go" (Acts 1:11).

We know far less than we would like about His resurrection body. Apparently He was able to appear, suddenly, in a room without opening the door (John 20:19) and to disappear unexpectedly (Luke 24:31). Yet He was able to eat (Luke 24:42–43). Beyond that we can only speculate, and that is not important for our purpose in this discussion. According to Paul, in 1 Corinthians 15, there is such a thing as a "spiritual body" (verse 44), and that is probably the kind of body Jesus had after His resurrection. More important, it also seems clear that when we are raised from the dead—or transformed if alive when He returns—our bodies will be like His (verse 49); see also 1 John 3:2: "Beloved, now we are children of God; and it has not yet been revealed what we shall be, but we know that when He is revealed, we shall be like Him, for we shall see Him as He is."

Jesus' Return as Visible

The "so" (*thus, in this way*) in Acts 1:11 is important; it links to "in like manner." His promised descent will be, in important ways, like His ascent, something similarly glorious, enveloped in a cloud. Jesus had already revealed this when He said to the high priest at His trial, "You will see the Son of Man … coming on the clouds of heaven" (Matthew 26:64; Mark 14:62). Revelation 1:7 echoes this: "Behold, He is coming with clouds, and every eye will see Him"—which marks yet another way His return will be like His departure: visible to the eyes of human beings present at the time and place He appears.

The "every eye" in this last verse has inescapable implications: Jesus' return on the clouds will be visible to all. This raises the question whether the Second Coming should be viewed as having two phases, one known only to the saved and the other public. I find no convincing reason to think this will be the case, but I reserve discussion of this issue for Chapter 11. Even if there will be two phases in Jesus' return—the first only "in the air" and the second to the earth—it is clear that the latter is the primary event of eschatology and His coming will be witnessed by all.

Jesus' Return As Glorious

The imagery of the Lord riding on the clouds is rooted in the Old Testament. Psalm 104:3 reports, in typical poetic fashion, that Yahweh "makes the clouds His chariot" and "walks on the wings of the wind." Indeed, the passage that Jesus was apparently referring to in Matthew 26:64 said, "Behold, *One* like the Son of Man, coming with the clouds of heaven! ... to Him was given dominion and glory and a kingdom, that all peoples, nations, and languages should serve Him" (Daniel 7:13–14).

Jesus' return in such majestic fashion, riding on the clouds and visible to all, is at least part of the reason the Scriptures assert that He will return "in glory." In Matthew 16:27, Jesus said as much: "The Son of Man will come in the glory of His Father with His angels" (see also Mark 8:38, Luke 9:26). Paul spoke of the Second Coming as the "glorious appearing of our great God and Savior Jesus Christ" (Titus 2:13). There's an exciting promise attached to this idea: "When Christ who is our life appears, then you also will appear with Him in glory" (Colossians 3:4).

Peter understood the Second Coming glory to be the very glory he and James and John had witnessed at the Transfiguration: "We did not follow cunningly devised fables when we made known to you the power and coming of our Lord Jesus Christ, but were eyewitnesses of His majesty. For He received from God the Father honor and glory when such a voice came to Him from the Excellent Glory: 'This is My beloved Son, in whom I am well pleased'" (2 Peter 1:16–17; compare Matthew 17:1–5).

The Scriptures also teach that one aspect of the glorious appearing of Christ on earth is that He will be accompanied by a heavenly entourage. Matthew 16:27, already cited, and its parallels in Mark 8:38 and Luke 9:26 promise that He will return "with His angels."[3] This representation is also apparently rooted in the Old Testament: "The LORD my God will come, and all the saints with You" (Zechariah 14:5). This passage, in turn, may reflect the picture Moses gives of Yahweh's coming to Sinai: "The LORD came from Sinai ... and He came with ten thousands of saints" (Deuteronomy 33:2). Jude 14 appears to borrow this language: "Behold, the Lord comes with ten thousands of His saints." In the New Testament, 1 Thessalonians 3:13, in a prayer for the readers to be established in holiness, refers to "the coming (Greek *parousia*) of our Lord Jesus Christ with all His saints." Finally, there is a beautiful and moving portrait of Jesus' coming in Revelation 19, depicting Him—in the imagery common to that book—as descending from Heaven on a white horse ready for a judicial confrontation. Following Him are "the armies in heaven, clothed in fine linen, white and clean," also riding on white horses (verse 14). (Even if the imagery is not taken literally, the picture is powerful. See further discussion of this passage later in this work.)

Are these who march with Jesus at His triumphal return to earth *angels* or (human) *saints*? This may be one of those questions for which yes is the answer: probably both. The word *saints* means "*holy* ones," after all. Some of the passages I have cited actually say *angels*; First Thessalonians 4:14 proves that the dead in Christ are included: "God will bring with Him those who sleep in Jesus."

Clearly, then, the Bible means us to look to the Second Coming as an overwhelmingly glorious event: publicly visible, leading a host of others, riding the clouds in shining, stunning beauty—as on the Mount of Transfiguration. Not all will be well for the world, as we will see, but for the people of God this is triumphant joy.

Jesus' Return as Hope Realized

The Second Coming, according to Paul, is our "blessed hope" (Titus 2:13), which he identifies as the "glorious appearing of our great God and Savior Jesus Christ." In the New Testament, *hope* is not mere wishful thinking, as when we say something like "I *hope* I'll live to see my children grown." Biblical hope is, in short, a *confident expectation of final salvation*. Nor is this expectation merely confident, it is equally a source of joy. This final salvation is exactly what becomes ours forever when Jesus comes back. The confidence we have is confidence which the Word of God, by the Spirit of God, works within us. Romans 5:1–5 informs us that we "rejoice in hope of the glory of God," a hope that "does not disappoint" (KJV: "maketh not ashamed"). The return of Christ brings this confident expectation to full fruition.

The inspired writer of Hebrews focuses attention on the importance of this hope in 10:23–25, urging us, "Let us hold fast the confession of our hope ....And let us consider one another in order to stir up love and good works, not forsaking the assembling of ourselves together ... but exhorting one another, and so much the more as you see the Day approaching." By "the Day" he means the day of the Lord Jesus, His glorious return to earth. The context makes this connection clear, reaching its peak in verses 36–37: "You have need of endurance, so that … you may receive the promise: 'For yet a little while, and He who is coming will come and will not tarry.'" The promise of Jesus' coming is a hope that we are to nourish in ourselves and in one another. The nearer that time approaches, the more earnestly we must actively promote this.

Probably this isn't very far from what Peter meant: "Gird up the loins of your mind … and rest your hope fully upon the grace that is to be brought to you at the revelation of Jesus Christ" (1 Peter 1:13).

The apostle John also had something to say along these lines: "It has not yet been revealed what we shall be, but we know that when He is revealed, we shall be like Him, for we shall see Him as He is. And everyone who has this hope in Him purifies himself, just as He is pure" (1 John 3:2–3). Paul promises, in Philippians 3:21, that the Lord Jesus "will transform our lowly body that it may be conformed to His glorious body." This hope includes the fact that we will be like Him, which, in turn, motivates us to make it our business *now* to be like Him in purity of mind, spirit, and body.

A well-grounded hope, then, is a confident expectation that we will enjoy eternal salvation with Jesus Himself at His return. Such a hope will serve us well as "an anchor of the soul" (Hebrews 6:19), an anchor that will hold us firm and confident regardless of the storms that mean to toss us about.

Jesus' Return as Central to Christian Faith

Christian faith and teaching have at their core the doctrine that Jesus will return. The Second Coming will be "the main event" at the end of this age. This is so essential to what Christians believe, and what makes them "tick," that without it they would not be Christians at all. One indication of this connection is found in 1 Thessalonians 1:9–10, in what was likely the very first of Paul's thirteen epistles, written about AD 50, within twenty years of Jesus' death and resurrection and ascension to His Father's house.

In this passage Paul is looking back on his second-journey visit to Thessalonica (Thessaloniki in modern Greece), when he preached the gospel there for the first time and planted a church. The letter was probably written a few months later on the same evangelistic tour. The powerful working of the Holy Spirit among Jews and Gentiles in the city was fresh to Paul's mind (1:5). They had received the gospel he preached with joy and became followers of Paul and of Jesus (1:6), and in doing this they set an example for others in faith and witness (1:7–8).

In verses 9 and 10, then, Paul summarizes what transpired when they became Christians. In doing so he encapsulates the meaning of their conversion, reducing it to its simplest essentials: "You turned to God from idols to serve the living and true God, and to wait for His Son from heaven, whom He raised from the dead, even Jesus who delivers us from the wrath to come."

Put it this way: being saved, at its heart, consisted of four things: (1) they turned to God; (2) they turned from the idols they previously worshipped; (3) they began serving/worshipping God; and (4) they began waiting for the return of Jesus. The first two indicate their repentance and faith; the last two indicate the new direction and character of their lives: serving God and waiting for Jesus to come back.

In other words, expectant waiting for the return of Jesus to this earth is an essential part of what it means to be a Christian. When Paul distilled our faith to its essence, he included this waiting as one of the four most basic elements of conversion. Clearly, when he evangelized Thessalonica, where he had no more than a few weeks to teach them (see Acts 17:1–10), he had instructed them about the Second Coming as part of their grounding in the faith.

All Christians are disciples of Jesus in waiting.

The Time of Jesus' Coming

Not much needs to be said on this subject, given that we do not know when Jesus will return to earth. Jesus Himself said, "Watch therefore, for you do not know what hour your Lord is coming" (Matthew 24:42). Even He did not know: "But of that day and hour no one knows, not even the angels in heaven, nor the Son, but only the Father" (Mark 13:32). This is a puzzling statement; I make some sense of it by considering it to be true only of Jesus as the God-man and expressing things from the perspective of His human nature. The consciousness of Jesus, who was both God and man, is something of a mystery to us; apparently His awareness as a human being was under the control of His divine nature.

All attempts to set dates for the return of Christ are worthless speculation. All such efforts in the past, some of which have been announced and received with widespread excitement and alarm, have been exposed as false; they might even have contributed to the disbelief of some.

From a practical viewpoint, we are to recognize that Jesus' coming was not intended to be immediate—or even soon, as we might define "soon." From a human perspective, the possibility of thinking His coming to be delayed has always existed, but we must not read the passing of time as "delay" with God. Peter reminds us that God's timing is not ours, that anything that seems like delay has its purpose in God's program and perfect timing (2 Peter 3:8–9). In the same passage Peter warns about those who scoff at the preaching that Jesus will return, ridiculing the idea with their skeptical question, "Where is the promise of His coming [His promised coming]? For since the fathers fell asleep, all things continue as they were from the beginning of creation" (2 Peter 3:4).

The lesson is that we must be ready at all times, lest His coming catch us unprepared like the coming of a thief in the night. He has given us work to do, and we must be found busy at that work when He comes. I will discuss these matters in the following chapter.

Meanwhile, we need not spend a lot of time focusing on so-called "signs" of His coming. The general tenor of Jesus' instructions about His coming suggests, instead, that His coming will be unannounced and unexpected when it occurs. Still, Paul said "You, brethren, are not in darkness, so that this Day should overtake you as a thief" (1 Thessalonians 5:4). Subsequent chapters in this work will consider conditions attendant to the coming of Jesus, as well as the fact that there are "signs of the times" that do *not* point to an immediate return; instead, they characterize the age and may well grow in intensity toward the end of the age.

Endnotes

[3] Not all manuscripts in all three Gospels include "holy," but that is the meaning.

Chapter 2

How Should We Then Live?

When we are watching and ready for Jesus to come back to earth, how will that show up in the way we live? What does the New Testament teach in this matter? Second Peter 3:11 expresses this question in a context affirming the Second Coming: "Since all these things will be dissolved, what manner of persons ought you to be in holy conduct and godliness?" Indeed, the New Testament mentions many expectations of us, defining how the knowledge that Jesus is coming again should affect us. I have said that we are disciples-in-waiting. How, then, shall we wait? How do we live with an eye to the clouds?

On Being Ready

Perhaps the very first thing Jesus would say to us on this matter is that we must *be ready* for His return. When He had the most to say about His coming, in the Olivet Discourse, He followed it immediately with "Therefore you also be ready, for the Son of Man is coming at an hour you do not expect" (Matthew 24:44). As this admonition makes clear, we do not know just when He will come again, and that makes it of highest importance that we keep ourselves ready at all times.

He followed this with two parables that illustrate what He meant. I will expound these parables in more detail later. Meanwhile, one (Matthew 24:45–51) narrates a story about a servant whose master went away and left him in charge of meals for the family and other servants. Two possibilities emerged: he could be faithful in his duties and please his master regardless when the master returned; or he could tell himself that his master wasn't coming for a while and begin to indulge himself and neglect his duties. In the latter case, the master's return would catch him unexpecting and unprepared, and he would be severely punished.

The other parable (Matthew 25:1–13) tells about ten virgins-in-waiting who were selected to meet a bridegroom and accompany him to the wedding celebration. Not knowing just when to expect the groom, five of the virgins took extra oil for the lamps they would use in the evening activities; the other five—described as *foolish* in the story—assumed the groom would come soon enough that they needed no special preparation. They took no extra oil. Only the first five were wise and ready when the groom came, later than he might have; the foolish five lost their opportunity to be an honored part of the festivities.

I will mention these again when discussing the need to "occupy" until Jesus returns. The point in both parables is that people were not ready because they did not deal rightly with the fact that they could not know when to expect the crucial arrival. The timing was not the most important thing on their minds. Perhaps the servant in the first parable was unprepared because the master returned too soon, and those in the second because the groom came too late. That doesn't really matter. What matters is that they did not realize they had to be prepared for … whenever.

It's interesting that Jesus told several parables, like these two, that involve a person going away and returning at a time previously undefined. One is in Luke 12:35–38, regarding "men who wait for their master, when he will return from the wedding." Jesus says, "Blessed are those servants whom the master, when he comes, will find watching"—whether in the second watch or in the third watch of the night (verses 37–38). He closes this parable with essentially the same words as in Matthew 24:44: "Therefore you also be *ready*, for the Son of Man is coming at an hour you do not expect (Luke 12:40). The time of the Second Coming has not been and will not be revealed. It may be soon; it may be "delayed"—though not for reasons we humans associate with delay (2 Peter 3:9). Our responsibility is not to live in consciousness of a date but to be ready at all times.

Matthew 24:44 can more literally be translated something like this: "For this reason, you also be in a state of readiness, because—at what time you don't think—the Son of Man is going to come." The adjective translated *ready* (Greek *hetoimos*) can also mean *prepared*—as in Luke 14:17, when a man scheduled a banquet, invited people, and finally sent his servants to tell those invited that "all things are now *ready*." It is used for such things as Christians being "*ready* for every good work" (Titus 3:1) or to give an answer to those asking a reason for their hope (1 Peter 3:15). In Acts 21:13, Paul is *ready* to be imprisoned or even to die for Jesus' sake, if need be. On another occasion he writes that he is *ready* to go to Corinth even if that means having to exercise unpleasant discipline (2 Corinthians 10:6; 12:14). All such instances reveal that this word isn't merely making sure one has what is needed for an occasion but is mentally and emotionally prepared, eager to be part of the occasion.

Just so, Christians are—in the words of 1 Peter 1:13—to "gird up the loins of your mind, be sober, and rest your hope fully upon the grace that is to be brought to you at the revelation of Jesus Christ." That's a great way to express what it means to be ready for Jesus to come back to this earth. The rest of this section will fill this out in helpful and practical detail.

On Watching

A word that is comfortably paired with being ready is *watching*. Two Greek verbs are translated, accurately, this way. One (*agrupneō*) literally means *not sleeping*; the other (*grēgoreō*) means being *awake*. Both mean to keep awake, to be awake and alert—an important part of being ready. We see this in a literal way when Jesus tells His disciples in Gethsemane on the night before He died, "Stay here and *watch* with Me" (Matthew 26:38); He wanted them to be awake with Him and praying. Obviously when we read in Scripture that we're to be awake for the coming of Jesus, that doesn't mean we never get any sleep. Instead, we are to be spiritually awake and alert, on watchful guard against spiritual foes and threats—which include apathy and indifference to the impending return of Jesus.

This understanding leads directly into the idea of wakefulness for the purpose of *being on guard*, as seen in Luke 12:39, "Know this, that if the master of the house had known what hour the thief would come, he would have *watched* and not allowed his house to be broken into." Interestingly, Jesus borrows these very words in Revelation 3:3 as a warning to be watching and on guard when He comes—whether that passage should be interpreted of a near visit or of His second coming.

In Luke 21:34–36, immediately following Luke's version of the Olivet Discourse, Jesus emphasizes and elaborates on this:

> But take heed to yourselves, lest your hearts be weighed down with carousing, drunkenness, and cares of this life, and that Day come on you unexpectedly. For it will come as a snare on all those who dwell on the face of the whole earth. *Watch* therefore, and pray always that you may be counted worthy to escape all these things that will come to pass, and to stand before the Son of Man.

Here's what Jesus is saying. His return will be unexpected, not announced in advance. Those who are not watching—not ready, not awake and alert spiritually—will be caught off guard, like an animal trapped in an unseen snare. They will be living in selfish indulgence, occupied with the concerns of the here and now. They will not stand before Him. But true Christians, in contrast, being watchful and expectant, will confidently stand before Jesus as His.

Indeed, their watching will involve prayerful readiness, including praying that they may escape the trials that He has spoken of in the larger Olivet Discourse (Mark 13:7–33; see the treatment of this in Chapter 7). No doubt their praying will include, in the words of Revelation 22:20: "Even so, come, Lord Jesus."

For that matter, prayer is often linked to watchfulness in the New Testament, so that "Watch and pray" has become a watchword in Christian circles. In the garden experience already referred to, Jesus told the disciples to watch and pray (Luke 21:36; Matthew 26:41; Mark 14:38; the verb is *agrupneō* in Luke, *grēgoreō* in the other two, showing their interchangeability). Mark 13:33—which is apparently parallel to Matthew 24:42, at the end of the Olivet Discourse—has "Take heed, watch and pray; for you do not know when the time is." (See also Ephesians 6:18 and Colossians 4:2 for the link between prayer and watching; there the NKJV "being vigilant" is "watching" or "being alert.")

Many other passages urge us to be watching for Jesus' coming. I have already cited Luke 21:34–36, at the end of the Olivet Discourse and following the parable of the fig tree. The parallel passage in Matthew 24:42–44 reads:

> Watch therefore, for you do not know what hour your Lord is coming. But know this, that if the master of the house had known what hour the thief would come, he would have watched and not allowed his house to be broken into. Therefore you also be ready, for the Son of Man is coming at an hour you do not expect.

This passage makes clear, given the comparison between verses 42 and 44, that watching is an essential part of being ready. Verse 43 provides an excellent mini-parable, of sorts, to illustrate both the need for being awake and on guard and the unexpectedness of Jesus' return to this earth.

On Eager, Expectant Waiting

Living in light of the Second Coming goes beyond a quiet or passive readiness and watching. It should be more like an eagerness, an exciting expectancy. All of us know what it is like to wait for the arrival of a loved one whose return is near. The New Testament teaches us to look for the return of Christ with a longing for joyful fulfillment.

Start with 1 Thessalonians 1:9–10. As I've mentioned before, there Paul summarizes the conversion experience of those who made up the church in Thessalonica. He says they turned away from the idols they had previously served and turned to God. They did this with two ends in view: to serve the living God, and to *wait for* His Son from Heaven. The verb translated *wait for*

(Greek *anamenō*) is used only this once in the New Testament; it means to await or expect. The Christian life is, by definition, a life of expectant waiting for Jesus to return. Whether that describes us or not, it ought to.

The same idea, expanded on, appears in Hebrews 9:28: "Christ was offered once to bear the sins of many. To those who *eagerly wait for* Him He will appear a second time, apart from sin, for salvation." Those who *eagerly wait* for Jesus, here, are believers, all who have accepted His redemptive work in bearing their sins. This Greek verb (*apekdechomai*) is a strong compound that conveys an eager expectancy. No wonder believers wait thus eagerly for Him; when He comes He will bring their eternal salvation!

The very same verb appears in Philippians 3:20: "Our citizenship is in heaven, from which we also *eagerly wait* for the Savior, the Lord Jesus Christ." Paul goes on to explain in more detail the final salvation He will bring us when He appears: He will "transform our lowly body that it may be conformed to His glorious body" (verse 31), and that is part of His bringing all things into subjection to Himself. Who isn't eager to be transformed physically like the risen Christ?

First Corinthians 1:7 has this verb again, describing Corinthian believers as "*eagerly waiting for* the revelation of our Lord Jesus Christ." Then Paul explains (verse 8) that when He returns—in the day of our Lord Jesus Christ, that is—we will stand before Him blameless (ESV: "guiltless"). While Galatians 5:5 doesn't speak directly of the Second Coming, it does refer to it indirectly as the occasion when our hope for righteousness will be fulfilled, an occasion for which we *eagerly wait.* This is apparently the same promise as in 1 Corinthians 1:7–8.

The words in 2 Timothy 4:8 are a little different, but they appear to convey the same sense of eager expectancy. Paul says, "There is laid up for me the crown of righteousness, which the Lord, the righteous Judge, will give to me on that Day, and not to me only but also to all who have loved His appearing." Here is the same expectation of righteousness, in the figure of a crown, and "that Day" is surely the Day of Judgment associated with Jesus' return. Don't miss that Paul's expectation is not for him alone, he says, but for "all who *have loved* His appearing." This is the usual verb for *love (agapaō)*, which in the Bible is always more than mere emotion. It is a willing devotion and attachment, a deliberate choice. "Have loved" is perfect tense in Greek, which views an action as a finished or completed state, brought to its intended goal or end. Paul is looking at the Day of Judgment in the perspective of what has been found true. God has examined these believers and pronounces the verdict: they have loved the return of Jesus and in their love have lived in the light of that return. Their hearts were set on the appearance of Jesus as the fulfillment and culmination of what they lived for. God's sentence: they must be crowned with righteousness.

Surely Paul—and the Lord Himself—intends that this be so for all Christians, for each one of us. We are to *love* our Lord's coming, to *wait eagerly and expectantly* for it. The very meaning of our lives is bound up in that waiting, and our eagerness to see Him reveals our hearts.

On Conducting Ourselves Appropriately

As we've seen, we look forward eagerly to the return of Christ when we can expect to stand before Him transformed and blameless, entirely sanctified and righteous. But it would be a mistake to think that this end is the only sense in which our living in the light of His return produces righteousness. The New Testament includes many appeals to us to live righteously now because He is coming again. We are to conduct ourselves in a way that is appropriate for our expectation.

First John 3:2–3 expresses this broadly and simply and picks up on what has been expressed above about the hope of being like Him when He is revealed:

> Beloved, now we are children of God; and it has not yet been revealed what we shall be, but we know that when He is revealed, we shall be like Him, for we shall see Him as He is. And everyone who has this hope in Him purifies himself just as He is pure.

Verse 2 expresses essentially the same truth that we have already seen in the discussion of Philippians 3:20–21; namely, that when Jesus comes we will be transformed into His likeness. Then verse 3 gives it a practical and present-time twist: to have this hope for the future means we will purify our lives here and now. Living in the light of Jesus' coming means we will conduct our lives in such a way that we can stand before Him with confidence.

Other passages in the New Testament flesh this out. Titus 2:11–14 is a helpful example. Interestingly, Paul affirms that God's grace *teaches* (!) us to live a certain way in "looking for the blessed hope and glorious appearing of our great God and Savior Jesus Christ" (verse 13). The word translated "teaches" (Greek *paideuō*) isn't the usual one; this one focuses on the kind of teaching or training given in the education and development of a youngster; it can even include the idea of disciplined instruction. "Looking for" (Greek *prosdechomai*) is closely related to the word used (above) in Hebrews 9:28; Philippians 3:20; and 1 Corinthians 1:7. This one also means to wait for or expect, perhaps with the added idea of welcoming what one is awaiting. In passing, we notice that the Second Coming is called, here, the "blessed hope." One reason this hope is blessed lies in how it transforms our lives.

Paul indicates, then, just how our welcoming expectancy for Christ ought to express itself in our conduct. He does this on two sides, both negatively and positively. On the one hand, we must deny both ungodliness and worldly lusts. On the other, we must live soberly, righteously, and godly in the present age. All these descriptive words are interesting and together paint a picture of godly living in the light of Jesus' return.

Ungodliness is living life without being conscious of God and His ways; *impiety* would be a synonym. *Worldly lusts* or *passions* are the unrestrained desires that lie behind the wickedness of people whose roots are in this world order (not citizens of Heaven). There are many such passions and all lead to self-indulgence and violation of the revealed will (law) of God. God's saving grace educates us to reject such deeds.

On the positive side are three lovely graces. To live *soberly* is to live with self-control. To live *righteously* is to practice what is right. To live *godly* is the opposite of ungodliness, to live with a consciousness of God and His law. These three words are on the other side of the coin from the two negative ones. Right living is both negative, defined by what we refuse to do, and positive, defined by what we practice. What is positive is seen more clearly in the light of what is negative.

Living according to these two basic principles is the expression of genuine, saving faith. Such living is highly motivated by our awareness that Jesus is going to come back soon. We will stand before Him then, and both He and we will be very conscious of how we have lived.

Another passage that speaks clearly to how we ought to live, in light of what will transpire in connection with the Second Coming, is 2 Peter 3:11–12:

> Therefore, since all these things will be dissolved, what manner of persons ought you to be in holy conduct and godliness, looking for and hastening the coming of the day of God, because of which the heavens will be dissolved, being on fire, and the elements will melt with fervent heat?

I will analyze this passage in Chapter 11. For now, it is enough to emphasize that, once again, God's Word is speaking to us about how we ought to conduct our lives in light of what we know about the return of Jesus and the catastrophic conflagration of our world that will follow in "the day of God."

In short, here is the manner in which we ought to live: "in holy conduct and godliness." The word translated *conduct* (Greek *anastrophē*) originally refers to turnings, in this case the ordinary turns that life takes and so the ways we behave or act or conduct ourselves. *Holy* ways are ways that are set apart or consecrated to God. *Godliness* has essentially the same meaning as living godly in Titus 2, discussed above, the opposite of ungodliness.

In addition to everything else, there's a word here in 2 Peter that is somewhat startling: "*hastening* the coming of the day of God." Can we, in fact, *hasten* Jesus' *parousia*? The Greek word thus translated (*speudō*) means to hurry or hasten or speed up. The NIV renders "speed its coming." Some interpreters view this as meaning, simply, to be in a hurry for or to be eager for. Surely that much is included, but in light of the translations (NKJV, ESV, and NIV), we should probably understand that our eagerness for the Lord's coming, as manifested in our appropriate conduct, will indeed hasten the day itself.

One more verse should probably be considered under this heading: 1 John 2:28, which says: "And now, little children, abide in Him, that when He appears, we may have confidence and not be ashamed before Him at His coming." The Christian's need to *abide* (Greek *menō*) in Christ is a common theme in John's epistle and the Gospel of John; it means to continue, to remain, or to stay, and so to be constant or persevere. In this verse, the specific motivation for such "staying put" is how we will appear before the Lord when He comes back. Thus, remaining in Him includes living in such a way before Him that we can stand before Him confidently and without embarrassment.

In all these passages the words are broad and cover many specific manifestations in real life. When we realize that at the end of the age Jesus will return and our world will burn, we will be properly motivated to live in a way that demonstrates consecration to and constant consciousness of God and His prescriptions and principles for our conduct. Only that sort of living is appropriate for an ongoing awareness that Jesus is going to return and we will stand before Him.

On "Occupying" Until He Comes

This terminology comes from the King James version of Luke 19:13, in a parable (verses 12–27) very similar to one I have commented on (Matthew 25:14–30); it is not merely another version of the same story. In this parable a person of noble birth went away to receive official authority to govern. (This was common in the Roman world of Jesus' time.) When he went, he left his servants with money to put to work for him in his absence. Ten of them, in fact, received the same amount. A *pound* (KJV) or *mina* (recent versions) was a weight of silver, for example, somewhere from 425 to 600 grams, apparently equivalent to about a hundred days' wages—and so a significant amount. While he was away, he said, the servants should "occupy" or "do business" (NKJV), putting the funds to work in some way, as verse 15 indicates. He would return, although he did not know how long it would be until then, and he would require an accounting from each one whenever that would take place.

In the parable, all of that occurred. Ruling authority was granted and the man returned, and each servant reported. Some had earned well, some better than others. All were rewarded accordingly. At least one (like the servant in the similar parable) had not put the money to work at all and was harshly judged.

The point is that the nobleman was not going to return immediately; there would be an undetermined and undefined time first. But the servants had work to do, service to render, responsibilities with which to occupy themselves while their master was away. They also would have to stand before him at his return and give account as to how well they had fulfilled the assignment he gave them.

This same general idea occurs in other passages, especially in the parables following the account of the Olivet Discourse in the Synoptic Gospels. In Matthew 24:45–51, as we have seen, a parable shows the difference between a "faithful and wise servant" and an "evil servant." That master had also gone away and left the servant with household management responsibilities. The faithful and wise servant is the one of whom Jesus says, "Blessed is that servant whom his master, when he comes, will find so doing" (verse 46). The servant who will be judged harshly has done the opposite. Instead of tending to the business entrusted to him, he has gone on an orgy or bullying self-indulgence.

Perhaps the parable in Mark 13:32–37 is the same as this one, but it has some helpful wording. For one thing, it makes clear that the departing master left each servant with assigned "work" (verse 34). The warning there is against being caught "sleeping" when the master returns (verse 36), rather than being about the work assigned, and the exhortation is to "Watch . . . for you do not know when the master of the house is coming—in the evening, at midnight, at the crowing of the rooster" (verse 35).

The parable of the talents in Matthew 25, so similar to the one in Luke 19, involved the same money management responsibility entrusted to three servants. When the master returned, each gave account as to how he had handled that responsibility while the master was away.

Luke follows his account of the Olivet Discourse in a way that is different from Matthew and Mark. Instead of another parable, Jesus gives a clear warning that is directly related to how we are to be about His business until He returns. This is Luke 21:34–36, and the focus is on how we do *not* want to be found. Attached to the firm command to *watch* (cited earlier in this chapter) is this important word: "But take heed to yourselves, lest your hearts be weighed down with carousing, drunkenness, and cares of this life, and that Day come on you unexpectedly" (verse 34). This danger is as serious as, or even more serious than, the danger of being asleep just mentioned. It is similar to that of the servant (above) who abused his authority and beat his fellow servants and indulged himself to eat and drink with the drunkards.

The point, of course, is that we are to be about the Lord's business rather than living with only this world's values—or lack of values—to govern us. Carousing and drunkenness are bad enough; being burdened with the cares of this life is just as bad. In other words, as disciples-in-waiting, we are to live according to the values of the kingdom of God. We are to live with eternal values in view. Our lives are to be governed by the concerns He has left us to pursue.

What is this "work" He has left for us to be about while He is away? In short, it encompasses everything He has taught us in His Word about how to live and serve Him. For sure, some of these things are singularly spelled out. Consider Acts 1, for example, where the question about His return to inaugurate His kingdom was high on the list of questions the disciples had, during the forty days He spent time with them between His resurrection and His ascension. They asked directly, "Will You at this time restore the kingdom to Israel?" (verse 6). He responded that this was not for them to know, but what *was* for them was to be baptized with the Holy Spirit in power and then to be about the business of being witnesses to Him from Jerusalem to the end of the earth (verses 7–8). Primary among the responsibilities He has assigned us, in His absence, then, is the evangelization of the peoples of the earth. Blessed is that servant who, when His Lord comes, will find so doing.

The reason for the apparent delay in His return is the work He has assigned us. While that includes evangelizing the world as primary, there are other things. One of these is to build and nourish the Church, the Church which He identifies as His bride who awaits His coming and the wedding feast (Revelation 19:7–8).

Consider also what Paul says about the observance of the Lord's Supper in 1 Corinthians 11:26: "For as often as you eat this bread and drink this cup, you proclaim the Lord's death till He comes." In other words, maintaining the life and worship of the Church is part of what we do with a view to the coming of the Groom to claim His Bride. In Ephesians 5:25–30, Paul speaks pointedly to this concern, appealing to husbands to love their wives as Christ loved the Church and gave Himself for it, "that He might sanctify and cleanse her with the washing of water by the word, that He might present her to Himself a glorious church, not having spot or wrinkle or any such thing, but that she should be holy and without blemish" (verses 26–27). We are to be about the business of preparing the Church for her eternal union with her Lord.

Many other things could be mentioned; I cite just one more: we are to be about the business of building our own lives to be blameless and holy before Him when He comes. In other words, we are to grow in sanctification. Such a concern is not only for the Church collectively, but also for each of us individually, as belonging to God. Here's where a passage like 1 Thessalonians 3:13 comes in. Paul is praying for his readers (verse 12) with this goal in mind: "so that He [the Lord] may establish your hearts blameless in holiness before our God and Father at the coming of our Lord Jesus Christ with all His saints."

This represents something important in Paul's theology of the Second Coming. Believers who stand before Jesus then as saints, holy and blameless, are what he, and we, work for: both for others and for ourselves. At the end of chapter 2 of this same letter, Paul expresses with obvious emotion his love and concern for the Thessalonian believers. They are his "hope, or joy, or crown of rejoicing ... in the presence of our Lord Jesus Christ at His coming" (verses 19–20). For Paul, a mature believer was something like a trophy to present to Jesus when He comes, and this was what he labored for: "that we may present every man perfect [whole, complete, a finished work] in Christ Jesus. To this end I also labor" (Colossians 1:28b-29a). Again, he viewed this precisely in the light of the return of Christ, as seen in 1 Corinthians 1:8: "that you may be blameless in the day of our Lord Jesus Christ." His great prayer for all those he ministered to must surely have been the same as for the Thessalonians: "Now may the God of peace Himself sanctify you completely; and may your whole spirit, soul, and body be preserved blameless at the coming of our Lord Jesus Christ" (1 Thessalonians 5:23).

Jesus' coming is the purest motivation for our labors in sanctification. This is what we must be doing until and when He comes back.

On Enduring to the End

Finally, living in the light of Jesus' return requires enduring or persevering. In a sense, the time between now and then serves as a test of our faith, and it is only as we persevere in faith until His coming that our faith achieves its goal.

Hebrews 10:35–38 indicates this connection between enduring and the Second Coming.

> Therefore do not cast away your confidence, which has great reward. For you have need of endurance, so that after you have done the will of God, you may receive the promise: "For yet a little while and He who is coming will come and will not tarry. Now the just shall live by faith; but if anyone draws back, My soul has no pleasure in him."

Hebrews includes several warning passages like this one, urging endurance. At least on the surface, the implication seems to be that a regenerated person can turn away from God to his or her eternal loss; but it is beyond my purpose here to argue for this possibility. Whether the truly regenerate can apostatize or not, both Hebrews and other Scriptures urge regenerated readers not to be complacent but to make it a point to persevere to the end: that is, to the full and final consummation that is the goal of the Christian experience.

The word translated *endurance* (Greek *hupomonē*) can accurately be expressed by words like endurance, perseverance, steadfastness, constancy, or even (especially in the KJV) patience. It literally means something like "staying under" or "bearing up under" various tests or trials. Here in Hebrews it appears to mean a determined commitment to stay true to what one has believed—to faith, in other words. The writer of Hebrews is appealing to his readers to realize that they will be tested, by the passing of time if nothing else, and that there is a promise awaiting their successful completion of the course. All this is in light of what he quotes from Habakkuk 2:3, applying it directly to the coming One. "Stay true to Jesus," he seems to be saying, "He is coming soon."

James 1:12 offers a similar appeal, though speaking indirectly rather than directly of the coming of Christ: "Blessed is the man who endures temptation; for when he has been approved, he will receive the crown of life which the Lord has promised to those who love Him." Here *endures* is the verb form of the noun in Hebrews 10, and the "temptation" can be any sort of trial. Enduring through such testing leads to approval, and that will be manifested, precisely, in receiving the crown of (eternal) life, which the Lord has promised to give, when He returns, to those who love Him.

Indeed, James comes back to this in 5:7–8:

> Therefore be patient, brethren, until the coming of the Lord. See how the farmer waits for the precious fruit of the earth, waiting patiently for it until it receives the early and latter rain. You also be patient. Establish your hearts, for the coming of the Lord is at hand.

Here the verb translated "be patient" (verses 7 and 8) and "waiting patiently" (verse 7) is a different one (Greek *makrothumeō*), which conveys the idea of keeping one's passions at a distance and thus under control. Consequently the emphasis is more on patience than on endurance, although the two ideas are closely related. James uses an example as an illustration: a farmer remains calm, waiting expectantly and unruffled, for the fruit of his labors. He knows how things work, and under normal circumstances, if he sows and cultivates, the seasonal rains will come and the fruit can be expected in time.

Waiting for the coming of Jesus is somewhat like that. There will be a period of waiting, but the Lord has promised to come. Meanwhile, it is our responsibility to pursue the work He has commissioned us to busy ourselves with. We have His promise. With that assurance we can establish our hearts and wait expectantly and patiently for our Lord.

It seems likely that Jude 20–21 adds a touch to this need to persevere in light of the coming of Christ:

> But you, beloved, building yourselves up on your most holy faith, praying in the Holy Spirit, keep yourselves in the love of God, looking for the mercy of our Lord Jesus Christ unto eternal life.

The ultimate motivation here, expressed as "looking for the mercy of our Lord Jesus Christ unto eternal life," seems clearly to refer to the Second Coming. "Looking for" is the same word as the one used in Titus 2:13. We are looking expectantly for the final culmination of His mercy when we enter eternal life. In order to arrive at this goal, we are enjoined to "keep [our]selves in the love of God." That is perseverance or endurance, too.

Jude provides, in verse 20, two means toward keeping ourselves in living union with the love of God. First, we need to build ourselves up in the "most holy faith" by which we are saved. This is to strengthen our faith, to grow in it, and it is like erecting a building strong enough to withstand a storm. We thus strengthen our faith deliberately, pursuing the truth and practice that provide fertile soil for faith to thrive.

Second, we are to be praying—praying in the Holy Spirit, that is. Already we have seen the need for prayer in watching for Christ's coming. Praying in accord with the Spirit's promptings and understanding of the will of God will contribute mightily to our enduring to the end, to persevering until the return of Jesus to this earth.

Enduring to the end shows itself, and is enabled by, a steady gaze on the coming of Jesus as a goal toward which we are pressing. Two passages come to mind in this regard; one is in Philippians 3 where Paul describes his own intense pursuit of what was to be his at the consummation. There Paul represents himself as an athlete determined to finish the race. His consuming desire is to "attain to the resurrection from the dead" (verse 11), which occurs when Jesus returns. He knows he has not already laid hold of the prize, but he presses on in order to do so (verse 12). Forgetting past achievements, he stretches out eagerly for what lies ahead (verse 13). There is a prize awaiting, and that is his goal; he pushes hard toward it—like a runner stretching his chest to break the tape at the finish line. If he succeeds, he will be called up to the judge's stand (verse 14). This call is, indeed, the call of God in Jesus Christ, and it comes to all who press on to the end of the race.

Though not in the same imagery, 1 Peter 1:13 expresses the same intense pursuit: "Gird up the loins of your mind, be sober, and rest your hope fully upon the grace that is to be brought to you at the revelation of Jesus Christ." In Peter's day, people "girded their loins" by pulling up the long train of their robe and tying it around the waist. They did that to be able to move about freely in work or to run. Only here Peter represents this as a settled determination; the verbs (*gird up* and *hope*) are aorist tense in Greek, viewing the action as finished, done with. This is the disposition of one with a settled commitment to a course of action.

The motivation, of course, is "the grace that is to be brought to you at the revelation of Jesus Christ." Have we already received God's grace? Absolutely! But there is yet another stage, a final stage of grace to be experienced when Jesus returns. A settled commitment, a determined resolution to make that grace ours will contribute mightily toward our enduring for the *parousia* of our Lord.

Chapter 3

Other Conditions Associated With the Coming of Jesus

I have referred earlier to the possibility of "signs" preceding or portending the second coming of Jesus to this earth. On the one hand, the tendency of Jesus' teaching on the subject of His return, as we have seen, is toward uncertainty; people, including believers, do not know when to expect Him to appear. Indeed, one biblical picture of the situation of His coming reveals that people are going about "business as usual." Even believers should be doing their duty, which includes both being ready for His return and carrying on the mission He has assigned them.

There are "signs of the times," of course, things to expect that characterize the entire age between His ascension to Heaven and His return to earth. The first part of the Olivet Discourse (Matthew 24:4–44; Mark 13:5–37; Luke 21:8–36) responds to the disciples' question about timing by describing such things as wars, pestilences, and natural disasters. While these may intensify as the present age wears on, they are not signs of His coming as such; "The end is not yet," said Jesus. These difficulties signify only "the beginning of sorrows" (Matthew 24:6–8 and parallels); Luke 21:9: "the end will not come immediately." I will deal with the Olivet Discourse in Chapter 7 tracing the eschatology of the Gospels and the teaching of Jesus.

On the other hand, there are some indications that certain circumstances will attend the Second Coming in a way that leads up to the dramatic appearance of Christ, coming on the clouds of His glory, setting foot on mother earth in public view. Perhaps we should say that "the day of the Lord," which certainly centers in Jesus' return, actually begins a little earlier. My purpose in this chapter is to provide some discussion of conditions that accompany the Second Coming shortly before the main event.

The Judicial Wrath of God

There are many indications in Scripture that the day of the Lord involves a defined expression of the wrath of God in judgment on the wicked. This theme is anchored in the Old Testament and carries over into the New Testament, and it is not limited to the book of Revelation.

The phrase, "the day of the Lord," can be used, generally, of any occasion when God intervenes in human affairs to effect His own purposes, a time to take a hand in things and set them right. While this may be broad enough to result in blessing for the godly, it usually indicates judicial action against those who are disobedient to God and contrary to His will.

Consequently, "the day of the Lord" can easily be used of dramatic events that have nothing to do with the great Day of God Almighty in the future—other than their foreshadowing the eschatological Day. Thus the prophet Joel, for example, who uses the phrase often, apparently sees a soon-coming plague of locusts as "the day of the LORD" that is "at hand" (Joel 1:15). Likewise, Isaiah 13:9–13, in context, speaks of the coming destruction of Babylon in the same terms: "Behold, the day of the LORD comes, cruel, with both wrath and fierce anger" (verse 9); "Therefore I will shake the heavens, and the earth will move out of her place, in the wrath of the LORD of hosts and in the day of His fierce anger." Indeed, Isaiah appears to frame the near destruction of Babylon in terms that anticipate the great, eschatological day of the Lord in His wrathful judgment of the sins of those who have refused His lordship.

Even so, "the day of the Lord" is a common expression for what will transpire at the end of the age, including especially the second coming of Christ—which accounts for the fact that in the New Testament that Day is sometimes spoken of as the Day of Christ, and "the day of the Lord" is understood to mean the day of the Lord Jesus.

Whether in the Old or New Testament, then, "the day of the Lord" is—as much as anything else—a time when God acts judicially with wrath on the wicked. It is true that the Old Testament prophets, for the most part, speak of the day of the Lord and of His wrath in terms of more immediate judgment on Israel or Judah or even on other nations like Assyria or Babylon. Even so, they sometimes look beyond the immediate to the end of the age and frame their picture in terms that foreshadow the final, eschatological display of God's wrath on the nations that resist God's rule. I've suggested that such may be the case in Isaiah 13:9, 13. Jeremiah provides a good example of this, speaking broadly of the very character of God—in contrast to false gods—in Jeremiah 10:10: "But the LORD is the true God; He is the living God and the everlasting King. At His wrath the earth will tremble, and the nations will not be able to endure His indignation."

Most important for our purposes in this discussion are references to the coming wrath of God in the New Testament. They establish, at least, that the wrath of God will come on the wicked and that deliverance from that wrath is only in our Redeemer, Jesus Christ. Let 1 Thessalonians 1:9–10 serve as a prime example, indicating that one becomes a Christian to "wait for His Son from heaven … even Jesus who delivers us from the wrath to come." Both of these elements are confirmed in this passage: that there is wrath coming, and that Jesus is our deliverer from that wrath. See also Romans 5:9: "We shall be saved from wrath through Him"; and Colossians 3:6: "The wrath of God is coming upon the sons of disobedience." (Here "sons of disobedience" is a Hebraistic expression that means persons characterized by disobedience.)

Paul's treatment of "the righteous judgment of God" in Romans 2 is pertinent to this discussion. Having introduced this topic in 1:32, he warns those—including Jews—who have hard and unrepentant hearts that they are "treasuring up for [themselves] wrath in the day of wrath and revelation of the righteous judgment of God" (2:5). He adds that for them there will be "indignation and wrath, tribulation and anguish, on every soul of man who does evil," whether Jew or Gentile (2:8–9).

The question, here, is whether this coming wrath refers *only* to eternal punishment in Hell or includes an outpouring of judgment here on earth leading up to the Second Coming. God is always angry with sin and He often initiates judicial action as a consequence. To be sure, the *coming* wrath will represent God's *final* and ultimate judgment against the wicked, and it is associated with the return of Jesus to this world. Yet it seems likely that this outpouring of wrath in the day of the Lord will include an increasing amount of suffering inflicted on the wicked here on earth, leading up to the Second Coming. Passages cited above, especially 1 Thessalonians 1:9–10 and Romans 2, may contain hints of this.

An important reason for thinking that there will be a time of suffering on earth, at the behest of the just wrath of God, appears in the book of Revelation. Adding a measure of weight to this are some apparent connections between Revelation and the teaching of Paul in 2 Thessalonians. Since I will be dealing with "Eschatology in Revelation" in Chapters 12–15, I will only outline this evidence briefly here.

One important question about Revelation is whether the main body of that work speaks of the future. The central vision of Revelation is chapters 4–11, carrying a single motif: namely, the opening of a scroll with seven seals. Revelation is apocalyptic and filled with symbols, but what does this opening of the seven-sealed book symbolize? Some think the primary reference is to the past (preterists), or to early church history (historicists), or to any time (idealists), or to the future (futurists).

I believe the best way to determine the symbolism of this main vision, and of its temporal reference, is to analyze what is said when the last of those seals is opened. When that seventh seal is broken, seven trumpets sound; then, at the blowing of the seventh trumpet is this word from "loud voices in heaven": (literally) "The kingdoms of this world have become [the kingdoms] of our Lord and of His Christ, and He shall reign forever and ever" (Revelation 11:15). In other words, what is depicted by the opening of the seven-sealed book, by the Lamb slain but standing alive, is what brings that Lamb to the throne of His Lordship. In that case, it seems likely that the main vision of chapters 4–11 is not entirely future but depicts the entire present age. Even so, this vision *brings history to the second coming and the reign of Jesus*. Then, in chapters 12 through 20:10, there follow several visions that revisit and provide more detail for the more critical times of that long period depicted in the main vision. That way, the text brings us again to the Second Coming—and to whatever may follow the second coming of Jesus in His triumphant taking of his rightful place as King of Kings.

I will deal with this more extensively in subsequent chapters devoted specifically to reading Revelation. For now, if the brief summary just given is correct, then whatever is symbolized in the strange—not to say weird, in some cases—visions of Revelation applies to all the present age, including (but not limited to) the future, before the Lord returns. The parts of those visions that apply most to the critical days immediately preceding the Second Coming have much to say about an outpouring of the wrath of God on the earth. As I've said, the Lord is *always* angry about sin and displays, in various ways, His holy wrath against those who reject His rule and attempt, themselves, to rule. But that wrath intensifies all the more as the end of the age and the coming of Christ draw near. Thus Revelation speaks at least a dozen times about God's wrath—and we should note that "the wrath of God" itself is not a symbol of something else. Here are some of the most telling passages.

Revelation 6:16–17—When the sixth seal is broken, frightening disturbances cause the wicked to hide themselves "from the wrath of the Lamb," saying "the great day of His wrath has come, and who is able to stand?" Perhaps Jesus made passing reference to this when mourning women accompanied Him, bearing His cross, on the way to Golgotha; see Luke 23:28–30. However, if He was instead predicting the coming destruction of Jerusalem, perhaps the "tribulation" of that judgment in AD 70 was itself a pointer to the tribulation to come shortly before Jesus returns to earth at the end of the age.

Revelation 11:18—After the voices following the sounding of the seventh trumpet, mentioned above, twenty-four elders say, "Your wrath has come, and the time of the dead, that they should be judged."

Revelation 14:8, 10—The announcement that "Babylon is fallen" includes that she "has made all nations drink of the wine of the wrath of her fornication": that is, the wrath of God brought on her because of her spiritual fornication. There is a warning against allegiance to "the beast" lest one "drink of the wine of the wrath of God, which is poured out full strength into the cup of His indignation."

Revelation 15:1; 16:1—The seven last plagues (the "bowl judgments") are represented as symbolizing the pouring out of "the wrath of God" on the earth.

Revelation 16:19—"Babylon," in her fall, is "remembered before God, to give her the cup of the wine of the fierceness of His wrath."

Revelation 19:15—Jesus, returning in glory, "treads the winepress of the fierceness and wrath of Almighty God."

I will devote more attention to Revelation in Chapters 12–15. For now, this conclusion seems justified: Near the end of the age and the coming of Jesus the wrath of God will intensify and be demonstrated in a number of different ways that have global effects and cause a great trial of suffering (or tribulation). The final period before Jesus comes will include an outpouring of God's judicial wrath, called, in Revelation 7:14, "the great tribulation." I am not sure that this will be seven (or half seven) years, given that numbers in Revelation are not necessarily literal. (More about this, too, in a subsequent chapter.)

If anyone should find it surprising that there will be worldwide judgment at the end of this age, perhaps remembering the Genesis flood will mitigate that surprise.

The Man of Sin (Antichrist?)

I mentioned, above, that there is an apparent connection between some of the visions in Revelation and Paul's treatment of the Second Coming in 2 Thessalonians. It is time, now, to turn to that passage for more careful analysis.

In his earlier letter to the Thessalonian believers, Paul spoke directly about the return of Christ to this earth (4:13–5:11). At that point he was responding to the concerns of some who appear to have been troubled by the fact that believing loved ones had died before the Lord's return. Consequently, he emphasized the fact that when Jesus returns the dead in Christ will suffer no disadvantage. They will rise from the dead and be caught up to meet Christ along with living believers (4:13–18). He also emphasized that his readers, who "walk in the light" and not in spiritual darkness, could and should be watching and ready when that time comes (5:1–11).

After that letter had been sent, there arose another misunderstanding among the Thessalonian Christians, perhaps caused or contributed to by a letter that was falsely represented as being from Paul. That letter contained misleading information; we know nothing more about that, other than what Paul seems to be correcting in 2 Thessalonians.

First (1:3–10), Paul expressed empathetic concern for the troubles his readers were experiencing at the hands of hostile unbelievers. His readers should know that their trials were to be expected and that the Lord Jesus, "when [He] is revealed from heaven with His mighty angels" (1:7), will recompense both the persecutors and the persecuted. To the former He will pay tribulation of their own, and to the latter He will give rest with Jesus and His followers (1:6–7).

Then Paul expands on this with further description for both sides. He promises that Jesus will, "in flaming fire," take vengeance on all who do not know God and who do not obey the gospel. That punishment will take the form of "everlasting destruction from the presence of the Lord" (1:8–9). But to those who know the Lord Paul promises that "in that Day," when He comes, Jesus will "be glorified in His saints" and "be admired among all those who believe" (1:10).

This much of 2 Thessalonians adds little, if anything, to what I have already said about the Second Coming. Indeed, it raises the same question as the passage in Matthew 25:31–46: namely, whether these two sides of judgment will occur at the same time or at different times. I repeat what I have said in discussing that passage, that the blessing of the saved occurs immediately on His return; but if there is any continuing history on earth, such as a Messianic reign of Christ, following the Second Coming, the assignment of the lost to eternal punishment will take place later.

Then, in 2:1–12, Paul moves on to provide additional information that speaks directly to circumstances leading up to the arrival of Jesus on earth. There was apparently a wrong notion being circulated at Thessalonica, to the effect that "the day of the Lord"—"the day of Christ" in a number of manuscripts; the meaning is the same—had already come and gone. Given what the Thessalonians knew from Paul's first letter, this falsehood would mean to them that Jesus had already come and they had missed out. This was a deeply troubling idea, of course; they were shaken, disturbed (2:2). So Paul proceeds to correct that error (2:3–12), and what he says, though brief, is important for our picture of circumstances leading up to the Second Coming.

Before "that Day" comes, he says, there are some things that must take place first. He mentions two things that are apparently very closely related: (1) "the falling away" and (2) the revealing of "the man of sin"—also called "the son of perdition." Whatever one's view of the Second Coming, this passage requires that these two things occur before Jesus stands on the earth. The question, however, is what these two mean. Paul is apparently speaking in a more or less straightforward way and not symbolically.

The first of these, "the falling away," seems to mean a specific turning away from the Lord. The Greek word is *apostasia*, our "apostasy"—although any specific doctrine about apostasy should not be read into this passage. The ESV translates "the rebellion." Nothing more is said about this to enable us to define it better. Typically, the word applies to people who have had at least some knowledge of God but have willfully turned away from Him. As the compound Greek word seems to imply, they have stood (*stasis*) away (*apo*) from God; they may well be in open rebellion. Whether this is a broad turning away from truth within the professing church, at the time, or within the common culture, is not said. Either may be possible, or both; many interpreters are inclined to think of this as within the professing church. It is possible that this turning away from God provides the context for the great outpouring of God's wrath that I have described above.

The "man of sin"—"man of lawlessness" in a number of manuscripts—is easier to define but not necessarily to identify. He is a person characterized by sinful wickedness, by violation of the law of God. That he is also called "son of perdition"—a Hebraistic expression like "sons of disobedience" in Colossians 3:6, above—means that he is a person characterized by, and so destined for, eternal perdition or damnation. Paul is saying, apparently, that such a person will appear before the coming of Jesus.

The rest of this passage, verses 4–12, is introduced by a relative pronoun, *who*, that begins a lengthy description of this "lawless one" (as he is also called in verse 8). It is important to analyze this description carefully. Paul makes the following points.

(1) He usurps the place of God for himself (verse 4). In opposition to God, he presents himself as God and occupies the place of God publicly: "he sits as God in the temple of God." (Even though some manuscripts do not have "as God," the meaning is the same.) Obviously he seeks and receives such worship as would ordinarily be directed to the true God.

(2) He is presently (at least in Paul's time) being restrained or hindered from full manifestation (verses 6–7). The identity of this restrainer, or restraining influence, is difficult. Paul, having instructed the readers along these lines in person earlier (verse 5), does not say enough to make this clear. In verse 6, "what is restraining" is grammatically neuter and so may be a force or influence; but in verse 7, "the one restraining" (literally) is masculine and thus apparently personal. Some interpreters think of this restraint as something like the presence of law and order in the world; others think of it as the presence of the Church; yet others think of it as God Himself—the active Holy Spirit, usually. We have no way of resolving this, but it is clear that, one way or another, God has a leash on the lawless one's full manifestation and will not permit it until it fits His timing and He lifts the restraint ("taken out of the way").

(3) He is also identified as, or at least as a manifestation of, "the mystery of lawlessness" that "is already at work" (verse 7). Thus, even in Paul's time, long past to us, there was a power at work in the world that will ultimately come to a head in the "lawless one." That this is "mystery" simply means that it is something God must reveal for man to recognize. This expression is neuter and seems clearly to represent a force that is at work to undergird all wickedness in the world and so to undermine all that is godly. The lawless

one will simply allow that power to dominate him and he will personify it in his activities. This may imply that he will exercise the power of government.

(4) He will certainly be revealed when God allows (verse 8a). As always, *revealed* means to have the veil removed, to be visibly active. One implication may well be that God's people will recognize him for what he is.

(5) He will be destroyed by the Lord Jesus at His coming (verse 8b). Both the lawless one and the Lord Jesus will be *revealed*, but Jesus will "consume" (ESV: "kill") the lawless one "with the breath of His mouth" and "destroy" (ESV: "bring to nothing") him with "the brightness of His coming" (Greek: the *epiphaneia* of His *parousia*: ESV: "the appearance of his coming"). Jesus, at His return, will put down this false claimant to God's throne and occupy it Himself, thus bringing the work of this impostor to nothing.

(6) While he is active, he will do supernatural works by the power of Satan (verse 9). The phrase "power, signs, and lying wonders" seems intentionally parallel to similar phrases in Acts that describe the mighty works of the apostles performed in the power of God. No doubt this lawless one, being empowered by Satan rather than by God, uses these to validate his claim to be God. The word *lying* practically describes all three nouns in the phrase; these supernatural works lie, they deceive. When Jesus puts an end to him, these works will be exposed for what they are.

(7) Before this exposure, however, his supernatural works succeed in deceiving the people who will perish (verse 10a). Paul calls this "unrighteous deception" because it falls on unrighteous people and serves to advance the cause of unrighteousness in the world.

(8) His successful, unrighteous deception of those who are perishing is a token of the righteous judgment of God (verses 10b-12). That God "sends" this deception means that it is His deliberate decision to allow this Satanic work.

It is often true in Scripture, as here, that the lies people believe are in fact signs of God's judgment for their own error. That this is the case here is made clear in verse 10b: this deception comes upon them "because they did not receive the love of the truth, that they might be saved." God provided saving truth, they rejected it, and God judicially decided to expose them to the deception of Satan himself. Verse 11 simply restates this, and verse 12 repeats that this condemnation is theirs because they "did not believe the truth but had pleasure in unrighteousness."

This indication of God's own purpose in sending such deception, by the hands of those hostile to Him (including Satan himself behind the lawless one), matches what has been said above about God's removing the restraint that presently holds back the full manifestation in the world of the man of sin.

Comparing Revelation 13

Although I am reserving most attention to Revelation for later chapters (12–15), it seems appropriate to explain, now, what I meant when I said that there is an apparent connection between this passage in 2 Thessalonians (about things leading up to the Second Coming) and one of the visions or scenes in Revelation. That vision is in Revelation 13.

At this point, then, I will do this briefly, expecting to say more in the chapters on Revelation. Chapter 13 of Revelation comes within that series of visions (chapters 12–20:10) that complement and add detail to the central vision of chapters 4–11. One of the things these chapters do is to introduce the chief characters of the period leading up to the Second Coming, and so to characterize not just the waning years of that period but all of the present age. Chapter 13 does this exactly.

John sees two strange "beasts" coming up from the sea or the earth, the first in verses 1–10 and the second in verses 11–18. Our attention here is focused primarily on the first and less specifically on the second (who "exercises all the authority of the first beast in his presence," verse 12). I will list the chief elements of the description that compare well with Paul's description outlined above.

(1) He has "seven heads and ten horns," the same description that was attributed to Satan himself (as a "dragon") in chapter 12:3, 9 (verse 1).

(2) He operates as one to whom "the dragon [Satan] gave him his power, his throne, and great authority" (verse 2); compare item (6) above.

(3) He receives worship as though he is God (verse 4); compare item (1) in the analysis of 2 Thessalonians 2 above.

(4) He is allowed (by God) to be active for a limited time (represented by "forty-two months," verse 5) and "it was granted to him" (by God) to pursue his hostilities against people (verse 7). Compare items (2), (4), and (8) in the analysis of 2 Thessalonians 2.

(5) People whose names are not written in the Lamb's Book of Life—that is, those who have not obeyed the gospel and are perishing—will be deceived into submitting to him (verses 7–8); compare item (7) in the analysis of 2 Thessalonians 2.

(6) The second "beast" who serves him performs miraculous works by his power, and these works serve to deceive those who "dwell on the earth" (verses 7–8); compare item (7) above.

A reading of 2 Thessalonians 2 and Revelation 13 side by side will serve, I think, to convince the reader that there is even more to compare than I have listed here. On the surface, at least, it seems likely that the two inspired writers are describing the same force or person.

Is This the "Antichrist"?

One can hardly avoid asking this question: Is Paul or John, or both, describing that figure we have come to know as Antichrist? The name itself simply suggests one who is against or opposed to (Jesus) the Messiah, perhaps even one who attempts to take His place. But that doesn't help us much with the question whether it represents a single person or a power or force less personal.

The word is biblical, of course, although 1 and 2 John are the only books in the Bible where it appears—five times. It seems appropriate to print out those references as we begin this part of the discussion.

> 1 John 2:18: Little children, it is the last hour; and as you have heard that (the) *Antichrist* is coming, even now many *antichrists* have come, by which we know that it is the last hour.

1 John 2:22: Who is a liar but he who denies that Jesus is the Christ? He is *antichrist* who denies the Father and the Son.

1 John 4:3: And every spirit that does not confess that Jesus Christ has come in the flesh is not of God. And this is the spirit of the *Antichrist*, which you have heard was coming, and is now already in the world.

2 John 7: For many deceivers have gone out into the world who do not confess Jesus Christ as coming in the flesh. This is a deceiver and an *antichrist*.

Here are the things we learn about Antichrist from these references.

(1) Antichrist was understood to be manifested near the end of the age ("the last hour").

(2) A person who teaches falsehood about Jesus as both God and man is an antichrist.

(3) There can be many who are, at least in spirit, antichrists.

(4) Antichrist can be seen as a "spirit" that prompts falsehood about Jesus from the person who is an antichrist.

(5) Even in John's time, there were already antichrists abroad, marked by their false doctrine of Jesus.

This material teaches us that *antichrist* has broad scope. Antichrist was already active in John's day, and many are antichrists. At the same time, there is a true teaching, apparently apostolic, that antichrist will come at the last hour (or time). We should gather, then, that *antichrist* is not limited to eschatology, that there is a spirit of falsehood, especially about who Jesus rightfully is, that is always with us and is antichrist. By the same token, it comes as no surprise that, near the end of the age, leading up to the coming of Jesus, this spirit will be even more fully manifested. It seems likely, then, that this spirit will "head up" in a person such as Paul describes in 2 Thessalonians 2.

What I am suggesting is that "Antichrist" is not simply a wicked person in authority not long before Jesus returns. Antichrist has been with us ever since Jesus was here the first time. When Antichrist is finally destroyed "with the brightness of [Jesus'] coming" (2 Thessalonians 2:8)—perhaps as depicted in Revelation 19:19–20, being captured and cast into the lake of fire—that will mean the final defeat of the wickedness that challenges the identity and reign of Jesus. Thus Christians of any age can see, in this scene, the ultimate defeat of whatever forces represent the hostility of Satan against them. Those of John's day who were persecuted and killed by Domitian recognized antichrist in that wicked emperor and his office, and they knew he would be slain by the word, "the sword which proceeded from the mouth" of Jesus (Revelation 19:21; compare 2 Thessalonians 2:8), and they could take heart in that knowledge. So can martyrs or persecuted believers in any age. So can we now, when facing antichrist in whatever form the opposition to the truth may take. Finally, if Antichrist is ultimately expressed in a person or office or governmental institution near the end of the age, the Lord Jesus will be standing in the wings, ready to come and take the Antichrist's uneasy throne for Himself, for good.

Hostile Conflict Between the People of God and the Powers of Wickedness

Conflict between the forces of good and evil is nothing new. Such a battle has raged since the beginning of time, a spiritual conflict breaking out in various ways throughout the ages. Paul provided an excellent overview of it in Ephesians 6:10–18. As he said there, "We do not wrestle against flesh and blood, but against principalities, against powers, against the rulers of the darkness of this age, against spiritual hosts of wickedness in the heavenly places": that is, in the realm of spiritual realities.

Even now we are at war. Paul urged his younger companion Timothy to "endure hardship as a good soldier of Jesus Christ," reminding him that he was "engaged in warfare" (2 Timothy 2:3–4). That observation fits all who serve God. Our enemy targets us like a lion on the prowl, "seeking whom he may devour" (1 Peter 5:8). Not by accident, the Church's songbook memorializes this theme in its hymnody, exhorting us to "fight the good fight" (as Paul expressed it in 2 Timothy 4:7): "Onward Christian soldiers, marching as to war!"; "If you're in the battle for the Lord and right, keep on the firing line!"

We may expect this conflict to intensify as the age wears on and the coming of Jesus draws near. The world, as represented by earthly powers and influence, will do its best to suppress truth and righteousness. That this will intensify into systematic hostility seems already implied by what has been said about the lawless one—Antichrist—and the igniting of God's wrathful judgment on the world by the wickedness that tries to crush any semblance of the worship of God.

Another of the visions of Revelation, recorded in 12:7–17, unveils the chief characters of this conflict of the ages as it takes a more defined form shortly before Jesus returns. In that passage there is, first, a war in heaven between Michael, with his angels, and the Dragon—"the Devil and Satan"—with his angels, a war in which Satan cannot prevail (verses 7ff). Resulting from this, Satan, being "cast to the earth" (verses 12–13), "went to make war with the rest of [the woman's] offspring, who keep the commandments of God and have the testimony of Jesus Christ" (verse 17). These are believers, and Satan is already targeting believers. The nearer the end, the more furious and fierce he and his agents become. We think we already see indications of intensifying hostility.

No doubt the great "turning away" or "rebellion" against God plays a role in the eschatological manifestation of this conflict. So does the unveiling of "the man of sin" we call Antichrist. He exercises his authority under the sway of Satan himself, and followers of Jesus cannot expect to escape his fury. As I have said, all of this is already the case. It becomes ever more the reality as the end of the age approaches when the wrath of both Satan and God is intensely aroused.

I would add that, even though all this is expressed in the language of warfare and battle, the conflict need not be viewed as purely physical. Persecution and hostility can take many forms, including a warfare of ideologies, a conflict between truth and error. I will have more to say about this in analyzing the visions in the book of Revelation in Chapters 13–15.

Signs in the Skies

The Scripture also mentions one final condition that seems sure to accompany the eschatological coming of Jesus. Perhaps the best place to start is with Peter's quotation from the Old Testament prophet Joel on the Day of Pentecost. The Holy Spirit "baptized" those first 120 disciples and gave them the supernatural gift of speaking in human languages they didn't already know (Acts 2:4), following the sound of rushing wind and tongues of flame (verses 2–3). A crowd gathered and asked the meaning of these astonishing phenomena. Peter, prompted by the Holy Spirit, explained.

In that explanation he said that what was happening was the fulfillment of what Joel said, and he proceeded to quote Joel 2:28–32. In that prophecy, the Lord had said He would pour out His Spirit on all flesh (Acts 2:17). What was happening that day was a fulfillment of that promise. But Joel went on to say more, and Peter quoted this also:

> I will show wonders in heaven above
> And signs in the earth beneath:
> Blood and fire and vapor of smoke.
> The sun shall be turned into darkness,
> And the moon into blood,
> Before the coming of the great and awesome day of the LORD (verses 19–20).

Joel had spoken of things that would happen immediately "in the last days" (verse 17) and of things that would happen "before the coming of the great and awesome day of the LORD." The pouring out of God's Spirit took place at Pentecost; the "wonders and signs" of verses 19–20 will occur shortly before the return of Christ to earth. Joel's prophecy, in a manner similar to some other biblical prophecies, is fulfilled partly at Pentecost and partly at Jesus' return.

Interestingly, in that portion of the Olivet Discourse (see Chapter 7 for more detail), in the section where Jesus speaks of the "signs of the times" (rather than signs of His soon coming), Luke adds a sentence that the other two Gospels do not have: namely, "And there will be fearful sights and great signs from heaven" (Luke 21:11). Apparently Luke (or Jesus), with these words, anticipates what will apply to the Second Coming itself, to be referred to later in the discourse. Even so, the next words revert back to the subject at hand: "But before all these things, they will lay their hands on you" (verse 12). Subsequently, in Luke 21:25–27, he returns to this: "And there will be signs in the sun, in the moon, and in the stars; and on the earth distress of nations, with perplexity, the sea and the waves roaring; men's hearts failing them from fear and the expectation of those things which are coming on the earth, for the powers of the heavens will be shaken"; immediately following, Jesus says (verse 27), "Then they will see the Son of Man coming in a cloud with power and great glory." The other two Gospels provide the same information; see Mark 13:24–27 and Matthew 24:29–30.

Revelation promises the same kind of phenomena, coming late in the vision of the opening of the scroll with seven seals. When the sixth of the seven seals is opened, John sees a great earthquake, the sun as black as sackcloth, the moon like blood, the stars falling, and the sky receding (Revelation 6:12–14). In response, the people of earth, presumably the wicked, respond by fleeing to hide in caves and mountains, calling for the mountains and rocks to fall on them and hide them "from the face of Him who sits on the throne and from the wrath of the Lamb, For the great day of His wrath has come" (Revelation 6:16–17).

These passages are tantalizing; we could wish for more information. At the least, it appears that there will be unusual portents in the heavens that will be terrifying, signaling the outpouring of God's wrath and the soon coming of Jesus.

Conclusion

Preceding the Second Coming, there will be conditions on earth such as have been mentioned here, circumstances that represent the fullest expression of hostility to God and to those who serve Him, circumstances that trigger His judicial wrath in a way the world has not experienced before, and some signals of warning in the natural order. The two main conditions will be what are traditionally called the Tribulation and the Antichrist, though perhaps without some of the trappings that often accompany discussion of those realities.

I would not attempt, for example, to define the amount of time this tribulation or trouble will last, nor the length of time during which a final antichrist will wield influence in the world. I say this because the measures of time in Revelation appear to be symbolic rather than literal—a matter to be discussed later. Dispensationalists typically refer to the 1,260 days, which equals 42 months or three and a half years (perhaps also a "time and times and half a time") as the last half of a seven-year tribulation. They also tend to say that the Antichrist is revealed and exercises his power during that last half. While this reading is possible, it seems more likely that the numbers simply indicate a measurable but not lengthy time. Regardless, there will be serious trouble on earth, resulting from the eruption of God's judicial wrath. There will be conflict between the forces of evil and the forces of God; this conflict will involve Antichrist as leader of the conflict against Christ and God.

Important note: one does not have to be a dispensational premillennialist, or a premillennialist at all, to hold that there will be a time of focused troubling of the world and an antichrist leading up to the coming of Jesus. I have no desire to pursue this, but I will observe that Louis Berkhof, a highly respected Reformed theologian, and an amillennialist, in his "Doctrine of the Last Things," in the section entitled "Great Events Preceding the Parousia," lists "The Great Apostasy and the Great Tribulation," as well as "The Coming Revelation of Antichrist" as among those events. Of the first he says, "Paul clearly represents the great falling away as preceding the second coming, II Thess. 2:3, and reminds Timothy of the fact that grievous times will come in the last days, I Tim. 4:1, 2; II Tim. 3:1–5."[4] Of the second, after tracing the idea of hostility toward God through various biblical descriptions of "the anti-Christian power," he observes "that probably this power will finally be concentrated in a single individual, the embodiment of all wickedness"; and he connects this to Paul's "man of sin" in 2 Thessalonians 2.[5]

The passage in 2 Thessalonians 2, as analyzed earlier in this chapter, is the key to understanding that there will be defined circumstances in play shortly before the return of Jesus to this earth. Even if we did not have the book of Revelation, that passage would make necessary the most important parts of what I have said in this chapter.

Endnotes

[4] Louis Berkhof, *Systematic Theology* (Grand Rapids: Eerdmans. 1949), 700.

[5] Berkhof, 702.

Chapter 4

Jesus Is Coming to Reign

Jesus is coming back to earth to reign. Whether we think of this reign as being on earth—for a thousand years?—or as more cosmic and eternal than that, one thing seems sure: the Scriptures teach that He is destined to rule and they associate His return with that destiny. No doubt the Lord reigns now, whether Father or Son; this is the "already" aspect of the kingdom of God. But in order to speak biblically, we should also think of the "not yet," of a coming revelation of Jesus Christ as King of kings and Lord of lords to take His rightful place of authority and reign.

God Already Reigns Eternally

To begin with, the Bible exalts eternal God—without necessarily distinguishing Father, Son, and Spirit—as the King who reigns eternally, regardless of the time or place. The Psalms, for example, are filled with this affirmation:

Psalm 47:2, 8—"The Lord Most High ... is a great King over all the earth.... God reigns over the nations; God sits on His holy throne."

Psalm 93:1—"The Lord reigns, He is clothed with majesty."

Psalm 96:10—"Say among the nations, 'The Lord reigns.'"

Psalm 99:1—"The Lord reigns; let the peoples tremble!"

Psalm 103:19—"The Lord has established His throne in heaven,
And His kingdom rules over all."

The Davidic Covenant Promises a Reigning Messiah

Then there are "Messianic" psalms that speak of the coming Messiah as one who will reign. Psalm 110:1–2 is one of these: "The Lord (*Yahweh*) said to my Lord (*Adonai*), 'Sit at My right hand, till I make Your enemies Your footstool.' The LORD shall send the rod of Your strength out of Zion. Rule in the midst of Your enemies!"

This Messianic destiny for the incarnate God-man is inextricably tied to His identity as Son of David, with whom Yahweh made a permanent covenant, as originally recorded in 2 Samuel 7. David thought to build a "house" (temple) for Yahweh (verse 5), but Yahweh sent to tell him that He would build David a "house" (in the sense of a dynasty of descendants, verse 11). What that meant, specifically, was that there would always be a lineal descendant—a son—of David to sit on the throne of Israel. In that way, "Your house and your kingdom shall be established forever before you. Your throne shall be established forever" (verse 16).

With respect to any specific descendant of David—like Solomon, the first—this covenant included conditional features, depending on whether a given descendant was faithful to Yahweh. But God's ultimate intention for this covenant was *not* conditional. There would be a Savior-Messiah, descended from David, who would fulfill the promises of the covenant perfectly and permanently. That person, of course, was Jesus Christ. So the New Testament introduces Jesus to us as "the Son of David" (Matthew 1:1).

The Old Testament already painted this picture in realistic prophecy. Hear Isaiah 9:6–7:

> For unto us a Child is born,
> Unto us a Son is given;
> And the government will be upon His shoulder ...
> Of the increase of His government and peace
> There will be no end,
> Upon the throne of David and over His kingdom,
> To order it and establish it with judgment and justice
> From that time forward, even forever.

Or consider Jeremiah 23:5–6:

> "Behold, the days are coming," says the LORD,
> "That I will raise to David a Branch of righteousness;

A King shall reign and prosper,
And execute judgment and righteousness in the earth.
In His days Judah will be saved,
And Israel will dwell safely;
Now this is His name by which He will be called:
THE LORD OUR RIGHTEOUSNESS."

Almost the same words occur again in Jeremiah 33:15–16, to which is added this (verse 17): "For thus says the LORD: 'David shall never lack a man to sit on the throne of the house of Israel.'"

Psalm 89 celebrates the Davidic covenant, saying such things as:

I have made a covenant with My chosen,
I have sworn to My servant David:
"Your seed I will establish forever,
And build up your throne in all generations" (verses 3–4).

I will set his hand over the sea,
And his right hand over the rivers (verse 25).

Also I will make him My firstborn,
The highest of the kings of the earth (verse 27).

His [David's] seed also I will make to endure forever,
And his throne as the days of heaven (verse 29).

His seed shall endure forever,
And his throne as the sun before Me;
It shall be established forever like the moon,
Even like the faithful witness in the sky (verses 36–37).

The New Testament Connects His Reign to the Second Coming

What is clear, so far, is that Jesus Christ, as the Son of David, was predestined to reign. The New Testament makes clear that this destiny will reach its fullest realization when He returns in glory to this earth. Several passages either teach or assume this connection.

First Corinthians 15:23–25 (to be dealt with in Chapter 11) provides an order for future resurrections (the subject in the context): (1) first the resurrection of Jesus Christ Himself, (2) then the resurrection of those who are His *at His coming*, (3) finally, at the end of His reign (note "He must reign till …"), "the end." That "end" comes when He has put all enemies under His feet, and at that time He will have put down all rule and authority and power and will deliver the kingdom to the Father—and, no doubt, will share an eternal reign with the Father.

The Revelation makes the connection between Jesus' return to earth and His reign even clearer, especially in two passages. The first is at the end of the vision of the opening of the scroll with seven seals—in a passage that seems surely to solve the riddle of the symbolism of this scroll and its opening. When the seventh seal is broken and the scroll is fully open, loud voices break out in heaven, saying, "The kingdoms of this world have become the kingdoms of our Lord and of His Christ, and He shall reign forever and ever!" (11:15).[6] This triumphant announcement is followed by the song of the twenty-four elders around the throne (verses 17–18), in which they exclaim that the Lord has taken His great power and reigned, and that this follows the pouring out of His wrath in judgment on the wicked and rewarding of His servants who fear His name.

This is obviously linked, then, to the return of Jesus to assume the full fruits of His redemptive work. Coming in glory He takes the throne to put down all rule but His own. In the final scenes of Revelation the same connection is made again in a series of closely connected scenes stretching from 19:11 through 20:10: Jesus comes on a white horse, prepared to rule and judge (19:11–16); He captures the Beast and False Prophet and consigns them to the lake of fire (19:17–21); Satan is bound in the abyss for "a thousand years" (20:1–3); Jesus, together with His followers, reigns for the same period (20:4–6); finally, Satan is released to foment a final rebellion but is defeated and cast into the lake of fire where the Beast and False Prophet already are (20:7–10).

This series of connected events is followed by the Great White Throne Judgment and the eternal state (20:11ff). The connections are stated in the text itself; for more detail, see the treatment of Revelation later. When Jesus returns to earth, He will reign on earth.

In conclusion, it seems completely understandable that Jesus will reign on earth, regardless how long. Old Testament promises of the reign of David's son, the greater David and Messiah, are most naturally taken to refer to a reign on earth. Jesus did not take a throne and reign when He came the first time. An earthly reign when He comes again will bring His messianic office to full completion.

The Coming and Reign of Jesus and the Kingdom of God

Closely connected to Jesus' reign are biblical references to "the kingdom of God." We have seen that Jesus both reigns forever and has a defined reign on earth in the age to come. What the Bible says about the kingdom of God—or, sometimes, especially in Matthew, the kingdom of heaven,—is somewhat similar. As many biblical interpreters agree, there is both an "already" and a "not yet" aspect to the kingdom of God. In this section, I am more interested in the "not yet" aspects, but I will spend some time first on the former.

It seems clear enough that sometimes, in the New Testament, the kingdom of God refers to present experience and is not specifically eschatological. Consider, for example, the exchange between Jesus and Nicodemus in John 3. At first glance, at least, when Jesus says that one must be born again in order to "see" or "enter" the kingdom of God (verses 3, 5), that appears to mean that when people are born again they are born into the presently existing kingdom of God. It may be possible that Jesus meant that one must be born again now in order to experience the kingdom of God later, but that does not seem the likely meaning in the context of His discussion with Nicodemus.

Then consider Mark 10, where the kingdom of God is mentioned several times. First, in verses 14–15, Jesus refers to the little children brought to Him: "Of such is the kingdom of God," He said, and anyone who "does not receive the kingdom of God as a little child will by no means enter it." Again the question: Does one "enter" the kingdom of God when receiving it, or subsequently? Later in the same chapter (Mark 10:23–24) Jesus observes that it is difficult for the rich to "enter" the kingdom of God. The question still is, Does He mean enter it at death or eschatologically, or does He mean enter it in the present? The disciples appear to take it in the latter sense when they ask, "Who then can be saved?" But even those words might refer either to the present or the eschatological future.

In other words, there is often a measure of ambiguity when the Bible speaks of *entering the kingdom of God*. The primary point of reference might be either now, in this life; or when one dies; or at the end of the age when Jesus comes to earth to reign. When I look carefully at any New Testament verse that speaks of the kingdom of God, I often find it difficult to decide whether it means entering the kingdom now or later.

Some instances appear likely to have present-time reference. On one occasion Jesus seemed to say that even in His day some people were pressing forcefully into the kingdom; for this see Matthew 11:12, where the precise meaning is debated by interpreters. But Jesus did "preach the kingdom of God" and emphasized that it was "at hand," which would seem to mean that one could at that time enter it (see Matthew 3:2; 4:17, 23; 10:7; and Luke 4:43; etc.).

In Mark 12:34 Jesus says to an inquisitor, "You are not far from the kingdom of God." Luke 10:9, 11 also mention occasions when the kingdom of God was near. In Luke 11:20 Jesus affirms that His casting out of demons means that "the kingdom of God has come upon you." In Luke 13:18–21, in two similar parables, Jesus certainly appears to speak of the present reality of the kingdom of God. This is probably along the same lines as Luke 17:20–21, when Jesus says that the kingdom of God "does not come with observation" and "is within you."

In Romans 14:17 Paul observes that "the kingdom of God is not eating and drinking, but righteousness and peace and joy in the Holy Spirit." It does not seem possible to interpret him to be making an eschatological reference.

The same is true for Colossians 1:13: "He has delivered us from the power of darkness and conveyed us into the kingdom of the Son of His love."

A thorough or technical study of all such passages is beyond the scope of this work and does not contribute to building one's eschatology.[7] Let it be enough to say, at this point, that there is much in the New Testament to support the idea that a person can become a part of the kingdom of God—or enter it—in this life by becoming a follower of Jesus by faith. If some passages speak of entering the kingdom of God at death, they do not contribute to our study of eschatology—although they speak to what we may call "personal eschatology."

What is important for this study, then, is that the kingdom of God can also refer to the reign of Christ that begins with His return to earth; and to enter that kingdom is an eschatological matter. A number of biblical passages refer to this aspect of the kingdom of God. In Matthew 5:20–22, for example, Jesus says "Unless your righteousness exceeds the righteousness of the scribes and Pharisees, you will by no means enter the kingdom of heaven." While that *could* refer to entering the kingdom now, the contrast in the context is between this and being in danger of judgment or hell fire. Consequently, Jesus is very probably warning about a future failure to enter the kingdom of God.

For that matter, "entering the kingdom of God" may sometimes refer to what transpires at death—to "*personal* eschatology," in other words. Acts 14:22 may be one of these, although ambiguity is possible. But Mark 9:43–48 seems clear enough; Jesus three times recommends self-maiming, if necessary, to avoid an offense that would doom a person to hell fire. Better, He says, to "enter into life" maimed or lame or half blind (verses 43, 45, 47). Equal to "enter life," in verses 43 and 45 is "enter the kingdom of God" in verse 47, which makes sense as an expression for the transition from earthly life to life after death as a person of faith. On more than one occasion Paul warns that the unrighteous "will not inherit the kingdom of God" (1 Corinthians 6:9–10; Galatians 5:21); in such passages there may be a reference to what transpires at death.

However, entering the kingdom may be primarily and consciously eschatological. This probability is clear in Matthew 8:11: "Many will come from east and west, and sit down with Abraham, Isaac, and Jacob in the kingdom of heaven." This expresses the kingdom situation in terms of a formal dinner and is clearly eschatological; see also Luke 22:30, where Jesus promises His disciples a kingdom and says they will "eat and drink at My table in My kingdom, and sit on thrones judging the twelve tribes of Israel."

Hebrews 12:28 promises that "we are receiving a kingdom which cannot be shaken." In context, the present-tense participle "receiving"—as often in the New Testament—is probably futuristic: "we are going to receive." Second Peter 1:11 also seems clearly to speak of the future, eschatological kingdom of the Lord Jesus, promising—to those who "make [their] call and election sure" by developing spiritually (as verses 5–10 teach)—that "an entrance will be supplied to you abundantly into the everlasting kingdom of our Lord and Savior Jesus Christ."

Matthew 20:21–23 is interesting in this regard. The mother of James and John asked Jesus to seat her sons on His right and left "in Your kingdom," a request He deflected by saying that such a thing would be His Father's to award. The point is that at least she and her sons considered that Jesus had a coming kingdom and her sons would have a part in it; and He did not correct her. Matthew 26:29 is similar; Jesus tells His disciples, while eating with them and instituting the Lord's Supper, that He will not again drink of this fruit of the vine "until that day when I drink it new with you in My Father's kingdom." In the parallel passage, Luke 22:18, He says He will not drink it again "until the kingdom of God comes." He is again reflecting the banquet image mentioned above. This, too, is obviously eschatological.

What Jesus said immediately before His transfiguration seems significant in this regard: "There are some standing here who will not taste death till they see the kingdom of God present with power" (Mark 9:1; Matthew 16:28—"till they see the Son of Man coming in His kingdom"; Luke 9:27—"till they see the kingdom of God"). That Jesus meant this to be fulfilled (in a proleptic way) in the transfiguration that followed seems highly likely; but Peter himself, one of the three disciples witnessing this event, would subsequently link Jesus' transfiguration glory to His second coming: "We made known to you the power and coming (*parousia*) of our Lord Jesus Christ" (2 Peter 1:16). He insists that he witnessed the glory of that coming on the Mount of Transfiguration.

This incomplete survey of "the kingdom of God" in the New Testament leads me to say, first, that the phrase means, in its simplest and broadest sense, *the domain where God rules.* In that sense, God is always King, and even the wicked live in His domain, under His dominion. But the phrase applies in a special sense to those who submit to His dominion or rule, and in that sense, it is always possible—as provided by His grace—for people to be in His kingdom. They *enter* the kingdom of God, we may say biblically, when they make that submission to Him by faith and are transferred from the domain of spiritual darkness to the kingdom or dominion of God's dear Son (Colossians 1:13). All of this is within the "already" aspects of the kingdom of God, always present.

The "not yet" aspects come to the front when we speak of God's kingdom as future, as the Bible often does. Even here, there are two different senses possible. In the more general sense, a person of faith *enters* the kingdom of God at death, which can be equated to saying that the person "enters into (eternal) life." God's dominion over the realm of the blessed dead is unique and special. This is eschatology in the broadest sense; as I've indicated it is sometimes called "personal eschatology"—which includes death, eternal life, resurrection, judgment, and rewards.

But the most specific use of "the kingdom" in eschatology is the reign of Jesus on earth for "a thousand years"—whether that number is taken to be exact or a way of representing an indefinitely long period of time. In this sense, people *enter* the kingdom when Jesus returns and takes His throne. They enter it with Him, and this includes the righteous dead who are raised at the time as well as living believers whose bodies are changed from corruption to incorruption.

In other words, this discussion of "the kingdom of God"—insofar as it relates to eschatology—is a subset of the discussion, above, that Jesus is coming to reign. His eschatological kingdom is synonymous with His reign.

Conclusion

The idea of a future reign of Jesus on earth, inaugurated at His return, is strongly supported by the section of Revelation that begins in 19:11 and extends, with close connections, to 20:10. But even without that passage the biblical narrative seems to point to a reign of Jesus on earth. If that is the case, then we may say that the "not yet" aspects of "the kingdom of God" begin when He returns and sits on the "throne of His glory" (Matthew 25:31).

This reign seems especially appropriate, even required, for the biblical theme of the Davidic Messiah and His destiny.

Endnotes

[6] The majority of the manuscripts, including the oldest ones, have singular *kingdom* instead of plural; the meaning is the same either way.

[7] There are many good books devoted to the study of the kingdom of God. Anyone interested in the subject will do well to consult them.

Chapter 5

JESUS IS COMING TO JUDGE

This chapter is a necessary extension of the previous one; the fact that Jesus will reign, in its essential definition, includes that He will judge. *Judging*, in the fullest sense of the word, is one of the chief functions of a king, almost synonymous with *ruling*. Thus, when Jesus promises that His disciples "will also sit on twelve thrones, judging the twelve tribes of Israel" (Matthew 19:28), whatever else that may mean, it means they will be ruling with Him.

In the Old Testament, that connection was always taken for granted and often stated. Thus, during the period of the judges, for example, it was understood that they, in *judging* Israel, were giving it authoritative leadership, especially but not exclusively military leadership. In Judges 2:18, this idea is introduced in summarizing the role of the judges: "When the Lord raised up judges for them, the Lord was with the judge and delivered them out of the hand of their enemies all the days of the judge." As a result, using language like that used of kings, the book of Judges often indicates how long a particular judge served; Jair, for example, "judged Israel twenty-two years" (Judges 10:3). Ruth 1:1 refers to the period as "the days when the judges ruled."

Unsurprisingly, then, when Israel decided in favor of a monarchy, the kings were, by definition, the judges. Consequently, when the Lord graciously offered King Solomon the opportunity to make a request, he said, "Give to Your servant an understanding heart to judge Your people, that I may discern between good and evil. For who is able to judge this great people of Yours?" (1 Kings 3:9). In 2 Kings 15:5 (2 Chronicles 26:21), when King Amaziah/Uzziah became leprous, his son Jotham "was over the royal house, judging the people of the land."

This "judging" that was the function of a king was broader than the office of our judicial officers who preside at trials and determine guilt and punishment. Where the United States has three different branches of government—legislative, executive, and judicial—the Israelite monarchy had just the one. The king made the laws, enforced them, and held offenders accountable—and much more, no doubt with the help of many others.

Just so, Jesus as King is Jesus as Judge. When He comes and takes His throne, He will prescribe the rules and enforce them with swift and perfect justice. But that kind of "judging" is broader than the judgment that is the subject of this chapter—which also is an aspect of his reign as King.

What we are concerned with here, primarily, is the narrower sense of "judgment" that we refer to in phrases like "stand before Him in judgment." This is the kind of judgment which Hebrews 9:27 refers to in promising "it is appointed for men to die once, but after this the judgment." We will all stand before Him to give account and receive a verdict. Such judgment is a matter of "personal eschatology," from one perspective; but since it comes at a tribunal (or tribunals), it has implications for public eschatological events.

An examination of the various New Testament passages that speak of this judgment leads to a number of observations.

General, Undefined Expressions

Many passages speak in a general and relatively undefined way of "the judgment," thus making the point that all will face judgment but not defining the time or circumstances of that judgment. Some of these may even speak of the "day of judgment" but offer no additional information as to how that "day" relates to any other eschatological events. If we had only passages that refer in this way to a time of judgment in general, we might even think that each person's day of judgment would be individually determined, perhaps at death, although that is not the case. Yet many references to judgment are about *what* transpires and not about *when*. Among these are the following.

Matthew 5:21–22—some "will be in danger of the judgment."

Matthew 10:15 (also 11:22, 24)—"it will be more tolerable" for some "in the day of judgment"; compare Luke 10:14.

Matthew 12:36—men will give account of "every idle word . . . in the day of judgment."

Acts 24:25—Paul reasoned with Felix about "the judgment to come."

1 Timothy 5:24—the sins of some are "preceding them to judgment."

There are many more passages like these, where eschatological judgment is left general and otherwise undefined, not connected with any other specific eschatological events.

Indications That Judgment Has Been Committed to Jesus

A number of passages make clear—and this begins to have definite eschatological implications—that judgment has been committed to Jesus. He is the Judge.

John 5:22—"The Father ... has committed all judgment to the Son." (See also 5:27.) John 3:35 might already have anticipated this when Jesus said, "The Father loves the Son, and has given all things into His hand," and immediately spoke of the destiny of those who believe in Him as compared to the destiny of those who do not.

Acts 10:42—Peter testifies that "it is He [the risen Jesus] who was ordained by God to be Judge of the living and the dead."

Acts 17:31—Paul (on Mars Hill), a little less directly but no less clearly, proclaims that God "has appointed a day on which He will judge the world in righteousness by the Man whom He has ordained."

Romans 2:16—similarly, refers to "the day when God will judge the secrets of men by Jesus Christ."

2 Timothy 4:1—"The Lord Jesus Christ ... will judge the living and the dead at His appearing and His kingdom." As will be noted again, this verse clearly connects the eschatological judgment of Jesus with His second coming and kingdom reign.

Believers Will Participate With Him in Judgment

Some passages indicate that transformed (including resurrected) believers will participate with Jesus in His role as judge.

Matthew 12:27—Jesus rebukes those who said He was casting out demons by the authority or Beelzebul. He reminds them that some of their "sons" were also, with Him, casting out demons, and He warns: "They shall be your judges." (In verses 41–42, also Luke 11:31–32, He speaks of some examples of this; some Old Testament characters will "rise up in the judgment" and condemn His hearers.)

Matthew 19:28—Jesus tells His disciples, "In the regeneration (ESV: new world), when the Son of Man sits on the throne of His glory, you who have followed Me will also sit on twelve thrones, judging the twelve tribes of Israel." Luke 22:29–30 repeats and confirms that this "judging" has the broader sense of "ruling."

1 Corinthians 6:2–3—Paul asks, with stinging rebuke, "Do you not know that the saints will judge the world? … that we shall judge angels?"

This participation by saints with Jesus in His reign as King and Judge is obviously what Revelation refers to as "ruling" with Him; see Revelation 3:21, for example, where Jesus promises that the one who overcomes will "sit with Me on My throne," and 20:4, where the text describes some who "lived and reigned with Christ for a (or "the") thousand years." Indeed, Revelation 22:5b appears to mean that all the saved will "reign forever and ever"; this reigning of the redeemed has the same dual aspects that the reign of Jesus Himself has: namely, reigning for "a thousand years" (whatever that means) and reigning forever.

Jesus Will Judge His Followers

Christ's judgment at His coming includes a session when He judges His servant-followers in regard to their lives and service to Him. Several passages refer to this sobering reality.

Romans 14:10–12 comes in a context discussing different convictions among Christian brothers and sisters. Some eat meat, some only vegetables. The latter judge or condemn the former, and the former are indifferent to the latter's scruples, to the point of causing them spiritual harm. Paul urges that there is no need to "judge" one's brother since "We shall all stand before the judgment seat of Christ" (verse 10), and "Each of us shall give account of himself [not of anyone else!] to God" (verse 12).

Second Corinthians 5:10 uses the very same phraseology in a somewhat different context, urging readers to strive to be found pleasing: "We must all appear before the judgment seat of Christ, that each one may receive the things done in the body, according to what he has done, whether good or bad." Since this is connected with the time when we, in new bodies (verses 1–5), will be present with the Lord, this refers to judgment at the return of Christ and the end of the age, rather than to judgment at death. (If there is individual "judgment" at death, not much is said about it in the Bible.)

First Corinthians 3:8–17, as a passage, provides one definitive picture of what may be the nature of this judgment. Paul compares different ministers (like himself and Apollos) to "builders" who will be judged for how they have built, measuring the endurance of their contributions. "The Day" will reveal this by "fire" and will "test each one's work, of what sort it is." Some will be found to have contributed wood, hay, and stubble, while others' works will be like gold, silver, or precious stones. Though the ministers in both categories will "be saved" (verse 15b) yet the works of some will be consumed in the fire of judgment and they will forfeit any reward that might have resulted had their works survived the testing.

First Corinthians 4:2–5 offers a picture that compares well with this one, summing up in verse 5—"Therefore judge nothing before the time, until the Lord comes, who will both bring to light the hidden things of darkness and reveal the counsels of the hearts. Then each one's praise will come from God." Human judgment doesn't count, only the judgment made by the Lord Himself, at His coming.

The Judgment of Believers Involves Reward

Immediately connected with this judgment of believers is the biblical teaching about rewards for those who are saved. A number of passages refer to this concept, including some of those just cited.

First Corinthians 3:8–17 and 4:2–5, just discussed, make clear that this judgment of life and service leads to reward. The Lord's judgment at His coming will bring to light what might otherwise be hidden and will reveal the "counsels of the hearts"—and so our motives and intentions. Then "each one's praise will come from God" (4:5). This simple observation *could* serve as the whole explanation for the teaching of rewards. When each is praised as deserved, no other reward may be needed. In 3:14, using the imagery of building materials that burn up versus those that endure, Paul says: "If anyone's work which he has built on it endures, he will receive a reward." That reward could be the appropriate praise from God; it is possible, of course, that something more, undefined, will be in the reward.

Second Timothy 4:8 *might* serve to add to this discussion. Paul says, "There is laid up for me the crown of righteousness, which the Lord, the righteous Judge, will give to me on that Day, and not to me only but also to all who have loved His appearing." This *could* mean that "the crown of righteousness" is a reward only for some, defined as those "who have loved [Jesus'] appearing." That would lead, of course, to a discussion of what it means to do this in a way that others do not. More likely, this is a "crown" for all believers, who by remaining faithful to Jesus choose to live in light of His coming. (Some Bible teachers, especially dispensationalists, make heavy use of references to different crowns in the New Testament and regard them as different rewards for different believers. This understanding does not seem justified in the context here or in other places where crowns are mentioned.)

James 3:1, however, reminds us that there may well be levels of judgment: "My brethren, let not many of you become teachers, knowing that we shall receive a stricter judgment." Christians have probably always understood that the greater one's responsibility, the more serious the judgment. We who teach others—and I am sobered by this verse—have more to give account for.

First John 4:17 gives me some basis for encouragement even as I am sobered by the preceding passage: "Love has been perfected among us in this: that we may have boldness in the day of judgment; because as He is, so are we in this world." When our hearts have come to experience the love of our Savior in its fullest perfection, we know we can stand with confidence before Him to give account, regardless what form the adjudication and rewards may take.

Jesus as Judge of the Wicked

Not only will Jesus judge His faithful followers in that Day, He will also judge those who have rejected Him, and that is a fearful future to contemplate. Two matters will occupy most attention in this section: (1) the fact that He will judge the wicked; and (2) the question whether that judgment will be at the same time as the judgment of the righteous.

The Promised Judgment of the Wicked

A number of passages make this fact clear and inform us about the dire consequences of this judgment.

Luke 12:8–9 warns that "whoever confesses Me before men, him the Son of Man also will confess before the angels of God. But he who denies Me before men will be denied before the angels of God." This apparently refers to eschatological judgment.

Romans 2:5–12 is along the same lines, emphasizing that the Lord "will render to each one according to his deeds": eternal life to those who persevere in righteousness, but indignation and wrath to those who persist in being self-seeking and disobedient to the truth (verses 6–8). In regard to the latter, Paul warns those who are hard and impenitent in heart that they are "treasuring up" for themselves "wrath in the day of wrath and revelation of the righteous judgment of God" (verse 5)—an obvious eschatological reference. He adds, reversing the order, that "tribulation and anguish" will befall each person who performs evil, but "glory, honor, and peace" will be the experience of each who performs what is good (verses 9–10).

Jude 14–15 may provide added support for a judgment of the wicked in connection with the Second Coming: "Behold, the Lord comes with ten thousands of His saints, to execute judgment on all, to convict all who are ungodly among them."

Matthew 25:31–46 is also connected directly to the Second Coming; "when the Son of Man comes in His glory, and all the holy angels with Him, then He will sit on the throne of His glory" (verse 31), and he will judge "all the nations" (verse 32). He will separate them into two groups like a shepherd who separates a flock of sheep from a herd of goats. To those to His right (like the sheep) He will say, "Come, you blessed of My Father, inherit the kingdom prepared for you from the foundation of the world" (verse 34). To those at his left (like the goats) He will say, "Depart from Me, you cursed, into the everlasting fire prepared for the devil and his angels" (verse 41).

The Question When the Righteous and Wicked Will Be Judged

The question is whether the judgment of the wicked will occur at the same time as the judgment of believers. Will both occur immediately at the Second Coming? A number of passages, like Matthew 25:31–46 just referenced, speak of the two sides of the judgment together, and they do so in a way that, at least on the surface, would seem to place the judgment of both righteous and wicked at the same time and at His return. At the same time, if we understand Scripture to teach that there will be a reign of Christ on earth over people still living natural lives, the view that both wicked and righteous will be judged at the same time will not "work."

Those who believe there will be one and only one general judgment, at the time of Christ's return, cannot at the same time believe there will be a reign of Christ on earth, over people living natural lives, following His second coming. I say this for a fairly obvious reason: namely, if there should be a final judgment of the entire population of the earth—righteous and wicked—at the Second Coming, a judgment that issues in consignment to Heaven or Hell for eternity, then there would be no one alive to populate the earth with people in their natural lives. That presents a problem, and it seems to me that there are three possibilities open to us.

(1) We may believe that there is but one general judgment of both righteous and wicked at Jesus' coming, and that this is what is depicted as "the Great White Throne Judgment" in Revelation 20. In that case, then, Jesus will not reign on this earth over people living natural lives, people who may submit to Him or resist His lordship. In that case, furthermore, one must decide that Jesus' present reign, combined with His eternal reign in glory, is the full measure of His destined reign as the Davidic Messiah. In addition, one who holds this view will need to satisfy himself or herself as to how to interpret the book of Revelation in a way that accounts, especially, for the passage 19:11–20:10. (See the subsequent chapters on Revelation for discussion of this.)

(2) We may understand that, even though Jesus speaks of judgment of the righteous and of the wicked "in the same breath," He does that to make sure we know that both will be judged, even though they will not be judged at the same time. This way, we can separate the judgment of believers—both resurrected dead and transformed living ones, who meet Jesus "in the air" (1 Thessalonians 4:16–17)—from the judgment of the wicked, and of believers converted during Jesus' reign, at the end of His reign. This will be "the Great White Throne Judgment" depicted in Revelation 20.

(3) Yet another possibility is that the believers raised from the dead and transformed living believers at the time of Jesus' coming, will not experience *final* judgment immediately at His coming but will be judged at the end of Jesus' reign. This way, there will be one and only one general judgment at the end of His reign on earth, as depicted in Revelation 20. The close association of the judgment with the triumphant return of Jesus may make this possibility unlikely, but regardless of the timing it is the victorious, returning Jesus who takes His throne as King and judges—in the broader and narrower sense of *judging* discussed above.

When considering these possibilities—or any others that may exist—one will want to weigh the passages that speak of both judgments as though they take place at the same time, passages that tend to support the first of the three possibilities just listed. I have already commented on some of these but will revisit them and others briefly here.

Matthew 25:31–46, analyzed in detail in another chapter of this book, is one of the more obvious passages. The key points are these: (1) Jesus sets the time: "When the Son of Man comes in His glory, and all the [holy] angels with Him, then He will sit on the throne of His glory" (verse 31)—which sounds like everything that follows will be on that specific occasion. (2) Exercising judgment, He will gather and separate "all the nations" into two groups, the righteous at His right and the wicked at His left. (3) To the righteous He will give inheritance in His kingdom for eternal life, while the wicked He will consign to everlasting fire for everlasting punishment.

Romans 2:5–12 gives essentially the same impression. (1) Paul speaks of "the day of wrath and revelation of the righteous judgment of God," as though the rest of what he says occurs on this Day when God will "render to each one according to his deeds." (2) In the very same sentence, grammatically, he defines this as bringing eternal life to those who continue "in doing good," but bringing "indignation and wrath, tribulation and anguish" to those who do evil and obey unrighteousness instead of the truth. This, too, at least on the surface, appears to represent the judgment as a separating function that deals with the righteous and the wicked at the same time. Although the Second Coming is not specifically mentioned, that appears to be the intended occasion for this judgment.

Other passages that also point in the same direction include 2 Thessalonians 1:3–10, where again (as in Romans 2) Paul speaks of "the righteous judgment of God" (verse 5) and refers to "tribulation" for hostile unbelievers and "rest" for the persecuted believers, seemingly at the time "when He comes, in that Day, to be glorified in His saints" (verses 9–10). Jude 14–15 does not deal with the judgment of the righteous, but it appears to connect the judgment of the wicked with the second coming of Jesus.

There is also John 5:24–30, where Jesus, after emphasizing that He has received authority to judge and to give life (verses 26–27), promises that the time is coming when "all who are in the graves" will hear His voice and come to life in response: "those who have done good, to the resurrection of life, and those who have done evil, to the resurrection of condemnation" (verse 29).

The passage seems to locate both resurrections (and the implied judgments) at the same time, apparently at Jesus' second coming. However, the phrasing "the resurrection of life" and "the resurrection of condemnation" certainly is open to the understanding that while both are the work of the returning Lord, they may be separated in time.

What, then, are the reasons for considering that the judgment of the wicked, at least, will not occur until the end of the reign of Christ on earth *after* His second coming? Perhaps the very first reason is that some New Testament passages appear to teach that there *will* be a reign of Jesus on earth following His return. Apparently, during this reign the basic population of earth will be people living their natural lives. In this view, there will be some saints, raised from the dead or transformed to immortality at Jesus' coming (1 Thessalonians 4:13–18; 1 Corinthians 15:51–52). There will be some wicked already destroyed at His coming, including "the man of sin" (2 Thessalonians 1:8; 2:3, 8). But a large population on earth will remain to continue their natural lives as the reign of Christ begins. I have already mentioned the teaching of Revelation 19–20 that undergirds this view. I will deal with this more substantively in Chapters 12–15 on eschatology in Revelation. For now I will simply observe that if there were no people living naturally during the reign of Jesus, there would be none to rebel, with Satan, at the end of His reign (Revelation 20:7–10).

Meanwhile, tentatively accepting that such a reign will occur, I can suggest a way of reading the passages above that will cohere with that view. That way is to understand that a general reference to Jesus' judgment when He returns can easily blend together two aspects of that judgment that will occur at separate times. Jesus will judge both the righteous and the wicked from His throne when He reigns, yes, but not at the same time. The righteous who have died, with those who are alive and transformed at His coming, He will judge at His coming. The wicked of all time, together with those converted during His reign, He will judge at the end of His reign, at what is described as the Great White Throne Judgment depicted in Revelation 20.

Or, as an alternative to this which I have suggested in the third possibility listed above, perhaps those caught up to meet Jesus in the air will not have their works judged until the end of Jesus' reign. If someone should object to this on the grounds that their eternal destiny has already been settled, I would respond that the eternal destiny of those whom "Death and Hades" give up for the Great White Throne Judgment (Revelation 20:13) has also already been settled. I see no conclusive objection to thinking that those caught up to meet the Lord in the air (both resurrected dead and transformed living) will not have their works finally judged until the Great White Throne Judgment at the end of the reign of Jesus. Nothing would need to be determined about them when He arrives, beyond their salvation, except what is required for the assignment of their roles in reigning with Him.

At the same time, I see no conclusive objection to the view that those resurrected and transformed to meet the Lord in the air, at His coming to earth, will face their full judgment at that time. Other reasons for being open to this separation of the two judgments in time include the fact that a number of passages speak *only* of the judgment of the righteous or of the judgment of the wicked; and that 1 Corinthians 15:23–26 speaks clearly about an "order" of resurrection (and judgment, by implication) that separates the resurrection of the righteous from the time when Jesus will reign until He has put all enemies—including death as the last enemy—under His feet.

I find myself, then, leaning toward the view I have listed above as a second possibility: namely, that those who meet Jesus in the air at His coming will be fully judged immediately. But I would not entirely discard the possibility of the third view: namely, that the final judgment of these will not come until the Great White Throne Judgment (Revelation 20) when all others, including both wicked and righteous, are judged. The study of Revelation in Part Two of this work may help us form conclusions about this matter.

Part Two

ESCHATOLOGY IN THE BIBLE, A SURVEY

Anyone who has read Part One of this book will soon become aware that a lot of what was there is grounded in what is here in Part Two. I did this on purpose; I wanted to begin with, and emphasize, what is at the heart of biblical eschatology: namely, the second coming of Jesus. That's what Part One is about.

Frankly, we could probably do without all the rest. The return of Jesus to this earth is the main event, the one that the New Testament places on center stage and teaches us about. Even so, our obligation to the Scriptures, as the inspired Word of God, requires us to give serious attention to what the Bible has to say. In this part of the book, then, I am going to do almost nothing other than to go through the Scriptures, especially the New Testament, to see what they have to teach us about the theology of last things—which we call eschatology. No doubt the reader will notice that I will revisit many of the passages already referenced in order to provide a more basic analysis of those passages.

As will be obvious, my approach is to set forth what the Bible itself has to say. Some interpretation is necessary for that, but the analysis is the main thing. Anyone who chooses to interpret anything in a way that is different must at least build on the passages that I will treat in this part of the book.

I have divided this part into four major sections. First I will analyze, in four chapters, what the Bible says about eschatology in the four Gospels and the teaching of Jesus found in those Gospels. I found somewhat surprising how much time Jesus spent teaching about His return and the end of the age.

Then comes what Acts and the Epistles reveal about eschatology, in two chapters. In other words, while the first section focuses on the teaching of

Jesus, the second section focuses on the teaching of the apostles, including some epistles written by men who were not technically apostles but learned from them and passed on to us the "apostolic deposit" (as we might call it) of truth.

The third section undertakes, in three chapters, to analyze the book of Revelation and its implications for eschatology. Without doubt, this is the material where interpretation is most problematic, given the long-standing differences of opinion among sincere, Bible-believing students of Scripture regarding the way to read this mysterious Apocalypse. I did my best to approach Revelation without pre-commitment to any system of interpreting the book, and I offer, for others' consideration, a view that may be somewhat different from either of the traditional schools of thought. It will no doubt be subject to adjustments—or to be scrapped entirely!—at the hands of interpreters who focus even more attention on the book than I have.

In the fourth and final section I will offer one chapter on what the Old Testament contributes to eschatology, using only a sample—albeit an important sample—from the book of Jeremiah. While my purpose does not include analyzing the entire Old Testament, I felt it important to show what the Old Testament can contribute to the eschatological landscape. Although Jeremiah's great book does not touch on everything the Old Testament has to say about eschatology, it does serve to show what the main issues will be, especially in regard to what role ethnic Israel may play, if any, in eschatology.

Chapter 6

ESCHATOLOGY IN THE GOSPELS AND TEACHING OF JESUS I: OVERVIEW

One of the striking characteristics of the proclamation of Jesus, as presented in the four Gospels, is its eschatological nature. To be sure, a great deal of His teaching was about how to become and be a true disciple of His. But always in view, even if sometimes more in the background, were implications for events at the end of the age. Mark, for example, introduces Jesus to his readers as one "preaching the gospel of the kingdom[8] of God, and saying, 'The time is fulfilled, and the kingdom of God is at hand. Repent, and believe in the gospel'" (Mark 1:14b–15). Matthew 4:17 introduces Jesus' public ministry in the same way, having already highlighted John the forerunner as offering the very same message (3:2). Other statements in the Gospels confirm that Jesus preached the kingdom of God (Matthew 4:23; Luke 4:43) and instructed His disciples to do so (Matthew 10:7).

As we have seen in the previous section, while "the kingdom of God," for Jesus and the Gospel writers, had its "already" aspects, there were always at least overtones of the eschatological, "not yet" kingdom in such announcements.

My purpose in this chapter is to provide an overview of the way Jesus and the Gospels dealt with eschatology. There will inevitably be some overlap with what I have said about the Second Coming in Part One, but I will endeavor to keep that overlap to a minimum and treat those things more briefly. In Chapters 6–9 I will analyze in more detail the key passages in the Gospels where eschatology is the subject of discussion and not merely of passing mention.

The Messianic Hope and Coming Reign of Messiah

As early as in Gabriel's announcement to the young virgin Mary, this element was emphasized in the predictions about the Child to be born: "He will be great, and will be called the Son of the Highest; and the Lord God will give Him the throne of His father David" (Luke 1:32).

Throughout Jesus' time on earth many were hoping that Jesus was the Davidic Messiah and would rule. Indeed, He encountered a number of pious Jews who were "waiting for the kingdom of God," and on their encounter with Him they understood that He would fulfill that hope. Take Simeon of Jerusalem, for example, who encountered the baby Jesus on circumcision day; he is described as "waiting for the Consolation of Israel," and the Holy Spirit had revealed to him that he would live to see "the Lord's Christ (Messiah)." He took the babe in his arms and prophesied that he would be a "light" for both Gentiles and Israel (Luke 2:25–32). The saintly old Anna, who came up right after Simeon, must also have been one of the ones waiting (Luke 2:36–38). So, too, was Joseph of Arimathea "waiting for the kingdom of God" (Mark 15:43; Luke 23:51), and one trusts he entombed Jesus with that hope still alive.

Indeed, Jesus taught His disciples to pray, "Your kingdom come. Your will be done on earth as it is in heaven (Matthew 6:10; Luke 11:2). One telling illustration of this expectation is the request of James and John. In Mark's account (10:35–40) the brothers approached Jesus, saying, "Grant us that we may sit, one on Your right hand and the other on Your left, in Your glory." Matthew 20:21 has the mother asking these seats for them in His kingdom, showing that the glory mentioned is the glory of a king on a throne. This speaks to anticipation that the Messiah would reign, and the brothers and their mother obviously expected it soon.

Saying the same thing was the crowd accompanying Jesus' triumphal entry into Jerusalem on that first "Palm Sunday": "Blessed is the kingdom of our father David that comes in the name of the Lord!" (Mark 11:10; compare Luke

19:38). Matthew 21:4–5 links with this the words of Zechariah 9:9—"Behold, your King is coming to you, lowly, and sitting on a donkey, a colt, the foal of a donkey"—with its obviously messianic implications. So does John 12:13 and 15, where their words were very explicit: "Blessed is He who comes in the name of the Lord!' The King of Israel!"

This exuberant expectation lay behind an earlier enthusiasm to force Jesus' hand: "When Jesus perceived that they were about to come and take Him by force to make Him king, He departed again to the mountain by Himself alone" (John 6:15). Even as late as after Jesus' resurrection, there was still in the minds of the disciples the possibility that the messianic reign would begin soon: "Lord, will You at this time restore the kingdom to Israel?" (Acts 1:6).

Indeed, any number of incidents recorded in the Gospels speak to the expectation that Jesus was the Davidic Messiah and would have a kingdom on this earth. Jesus, although He did not deny that there would eventually be such a kingdom, consistently deflected questions about His role as Messiah and king. At the same time, He spoke of His coming and His throne, and the messianic expectation was inevitably implied in such statements. In reference to His transfiguration, for example, He said, "For the Son of Man will come in the glory of His Father with His angels, and then He will reward each according to his works. Assuredly, I say to you, there are some standing here who shall not taste death till they see the Son of Man coming in His kingdom" (Matthew 16:27–28; compare Mark 9:1; Luke 9:27).

More than once Jesus referred to a time "when the Son of Man sits on the throne of His glory" (Matthew 19:28). At His trial He said essentially the same thing to the Jewish high priest (Matthew 26:64; Mark 14:62). With the same messianic kingdom implications He indicated that He would sit down with them and eat and drink with them in banquet celebration in that kingdom: "I will no longer drink of the fruit of the vine until that day when I drink it new in the kingdom of God" (Mark 14:25; compare Luke 22:18; Matthew 26:29). Luke 13:28–29 paints an appealing picture of this, when Abraham, Isaac, and Jacob, plus all the prophets and people who come from the east, west, north, and south, will "sit down in the kingdom of God"—where "sit down" is, literally, "recline at table" (ESV).

In Mark 12:35–36 Jesus answered a question, "How is it that the scribes say that the Christ (Messiah) is the Son of David?" That He quoted the messianic Psalm 110 as applying to Himself shows His own awareness of what the future held for Him.

Much more could be said on this point. Clearly, an important part of the eschatology of the Gospels and of Jesus Himself was that He was the Davidic Messiah, destined to take the throne of a messianic kingdom. This is part of what gave His entire ministry an eschatological coloring. To repeat, while that kingdom had "already" aspects, it also looked forward to a time "not yet," beyond His original ministry on earth.

A Triumphant Return to This Earth

The messianic destiny just described, which was not fulfilled during Jesus' first visit to earth, required a second coming, a return to the scene. Where His first coming led to a humiliating crucifixion, He would come back for the glorification. To be sure, He was raised from the dead and ascended to His Father, but that much was witnessed only by a few. Only a public, triumphant return would finally fulfill the expectation—and promise—that He would yet reign as David-Messiah, a king. This, too, is an important part of the eschatology of Jesus and the Gospels.

Part One of this work has treated the Second Coming in greater detail. My purpose here is only to show how this fits into an overview of the eschatology of the Gospels and of the message of Jesus Himself.

Jesus spoke often of His coming when it was obvious that He was looking to the undefined future. When His "hour" came He informed the disciples of His impending departure, and they were in distress. He said to them, "Let not your heart be troubled … I will come again and receive you to Myself" (John 14:1, 3). Even to the hostile priest-judge, presiding over the Jewish high court and determined to get Him executed, Jesus said, "Hereafter you will see the

Son of Man sitting at the right hand of the Power, and coming on the clouds of heaven" (Matthew 26:64; Mark 14:62; compare Luke 22:69).

He did not, however, save such glimpses into the future for His final hours. Even in contexts where His return was not the primary subject-matter, He made passing references to that coming, as in Mark 8:38 where He was referring to the requirements of discipleship and said, "For whoever is ashamed of Me and My words in this adulterous and sinful generation, of him the Son of Man also will be ashamed when He comes in the glory of His Father with the holy angels" (compare Luke 9:26; Matthew 16:27). Another of these passing references is in Luke 18:8, where He was speaking of the fact that God will "avenge" His own speedily; Jesus adds, "Nevertheless, when the Son of Man comes, will He really find faith on the earth?"

Consider also the conversation Jesus had with Peter after His resurrection, at the end of a unique fishing experience. When Peter raised a question about John, Jesus said, "If I will that he remain till I come, what is that to you?" (John 21:22).

More important than these references are larger passages in the Gospels where Jesus speaks at some length about His coming. These include the Olivet Discourse and several parables and will provide the subject-matter of the following chapters. They require closer analysis and will add to the realization that the eschatology of Jesus and the Gospels emphasized His second coming and related events.

A Separating Judgment With Eternal Implications

Connected with the expectation of a messianic kingdom and a returning king, but important enough to treat on its own, the eschatology of Jesus and the Gospels included a significant measure of attention to His coming judgment that would entail eternal blessedness or punishment. Jesus spoke of this often.

Even before Jesus began His public ministry, forerunner John the Baptist indicated that the One coming after him would ultimately effect judgment: "I indeed baptize you with water unto repentance, but He who is coming after me is mightier than I. … His winnowing fan is in His hand, and He will thoroughly clean out His threshing floor, and gather His wheat into the barn; but He will burn up the chaff with unquenchable fire" (Matthew 3:11–12; compare Luke 3:16–17). Already this looks forward to the role of Jesus-Messiah as judge, to separate the wheat from the chaff, "gather" the former and "burn with fire" the latter. One wonders whether John was able to sort out the difference between his cousin's first and second coming in saying this; perhaps not, but he certainly understood that He would judge in this way.

These very themes reoccur often. In Matthew 19:28–29, for example, Jesus refers to those who would qualify as "wheat" in John the Baptist's parabolic reference: "When the Son of Man sits on the throne of His glory … everyone who has left [loved ones] for My name's sake, shall receive a hundredfold, and inherit eternal life." On the other side, in Matthew 23 Jesus effectively anticipates His judgment on the "chaff"; He warns that the scribes and Pharisees, in making a proselyte, make him "twice as much a son of hell as yourselves" (verse 15). He denounces them as "serpents" and rhetorically asks in biting terms, "How can you escape the condemnation of hell?" (verse 33). On both sides, such thoughts assume eschatological judgment that issues either in eternal life or in an eternal, fiery Hell.

The same is true of the passing reference to judgment and the possibility of "hell fire" in Matthew 5:20–22. While Matthew 7:21–23 does not speak specifically of fire, it does indicate a judgment conducted by Jesus, "in that day," that will involve entering the kingdom of Heaven for some and departing (eternally) from Him for others after He denies ever knowing them.

So does the passage in Mark 9:43–48, which advises maiming oneself so as to "enter into life" rather than, without cutting away the offending member, to "go to hell, into the fire that shall never be quenched" (verse 43; verse 47 makes "enter the kingdom of God" parallel to "enter into life"; compare Matthew 5:29–30). Jesus is looking ahead to the judgment, with its eternal consequences on both sides—eternal life versus eternal fire. He Himself will adjudicate this.

Sometimes Jesus indicates different degrees in rewards or punishment at judgment, especially for the latter. In Luke 10:13–15, for example, He chastises various cities for their rejection of the light He offered; it will be "more tolerable for Tyre and Sidon at the judgment" than for Chorazin and Bethsaida, while Capernaum "will be brought down to Hades."

There is no reason to doubt that Jesus was referring to His ultimate role as judge in passages like Luke 12:8–9—"I say to you, whoever confesses Me before men, him the Son of Man also will confess before the angels of God. But he who denies Me before men will be denied before the angels of God" (compare Matthew 10:32–33, where "before My Father" replaces "before the angels"). That this will be before the angels or the Father situates it at the judgment, and again Jesus refers both to the righteous and to the wicked.

Perhaps the best example of the particular eschatological consciousness being described here is the picture of judgment in Matthew 25:31–46—a passage already discussed and to be analyzed in more detail in a chapter to follow. Jesus foretells specifically that He will return and sit on a judgment throne. He will separate the "sheep" from the "goats," reward the sheep with eternal life, and assign the goats to everlasting punishment (verse 46).

This is therefore one of the key elements of Jesus' eschatology. At His return He will take His seat on a throne and will judge all nations (Matthew 25:32). The result will have eternal consequences: cursing for the wicked, blessing for the righteous. In an earlier chapter I have discussed the question whether the judgment of the righteous and of the wicked will occur at the same time. My inclination is to two different occasions, but one and only one "general judgment" is possible. See the discussion there.

Resurrection

Essential to that judgment is the resurrection of the dead by Jesus, likewise linked to His second coming.

It is obvious that Jesus believed in "the resurrection of the dead"—as general and undefined as that expression is. In His day, the Sadducees did not share that belief, and His confrontation with them on this point of doctrine was powerful; see Mark 12:18–27; Matthew 22:23–32; and Luke 20:27–38. They thought to defeat Him with their tale of seven brothers who married the same woman (according to the Mosaic law of levirate marriage), pressing on Him the question, "Whose wife will she be in the judgment?" Jesus, recognizing that they were ridiculing the idea of "the resurrection of the dead" and an afterlife, cited the Old Testament assertion made by God to Moses at the burning bush, that He is the God of Abraham, Isaac, and Jacob. Since God said this long after all three had died, it demonstrated that God is not the God of the dead but of the living. So the patriarchs still live. Jesus also spoke, in the same exchange, of "those who are counted worthy to attain that age, and the resurrection from the dead" (Luke 20:35), thus linking this with a time beyond the present age.

For the most part, Jesus assumed the fact of the resurrection. In Luke 14:14, for example, He undergirded His admonition, to be generous with those who cannot repay, with a promise: "You shall be repaid at the resurrection of the just."

Especially in the Gospel of John, Jesus emphasized that He is the one who will provide resurrection from death. John 5:25–30 is especially fundamental to this truth.

> [25] Most assuredly, I say to you, the hour is coming, and now is, when the dead will hear the voice of the Son of God; and those who hear will live. [26] For as the Father has life in Himself, so He has granted the Son to have life in Himself, [27] and has given Him authority to execute judgment also, because He is the Son of Man. [28] Do not marvel at this; for the hour is coming in which all who are in the graves will hear His voice [29] and come forth—those who have done good, to the resurrection of life, and those who have done evil, to the resurrection of condemnation. [30] I can of Myself do nothing. As I hear, I judge; and My judgment is righteous, because I do not seek My own will but the will of the Father who sent Me.

I have reproduced the entire passage because of the importance of the details for the purpose of this discussion. Jesus is aware He has received authority from God the Father, both to raise people from the dead and to judge them (verses 26–27). It will be His voice that calls them forth from the grave (verses 25, 28), just as His voice called Lazarus from the tomb outside Bethany (John 11:43). Carrying out His mission, He will raise all the dead (verse 28). Some of them will be restored to life to receive life, while others will be raised to receive condemnation (verse 29). Thus will be the consequence of His righteous judgment (verse 30).

We can add this passage to those discussed under the previous heading, which tend to speak of the judgment—and now also of the resurrection—of both the wicked and the righteous in the very same sentence, as though they occur at the same time. See also the discussion above about judgment.

I have just mentioned the resurrection of Lazarus in John 11. While it does not add to what is defined here, it does confirm. Jesus affirmed that *He* is "the resurrection and the life" (verse 25). When He assured Martha, "Your brother will rise again" (verse 23), it is reasonably obvious that He was speaking of Lazarus' resurrection *then*, but also of his resurrection *at the last day*—as Martha expressed the eschatological resurrection (verse 24).

Like Martha, Jesus Himself had used the expression "at the last day" as the context for the resurrection. See John 6:39–40; there Jesus explained that it is the Father's will that He, the Son, raise, at the last day, what the Father has given Him, and indeed that this brings to everyone believing in Him the gift of eternal life. It is interesting that both here and in John 11 Jesus speaks specifically about the righteous. Even so, the passage above—John 5—has made clear that the wicked are also raised by Him for judgment and its eternal consequence.

It cannot be overemphasized that for the righteous who are raised from the dead, the consequence is everlasting/eternal life. Whenever this expression occurs, there is the implication of their having been raised from the dead; see, for a few of many examples, John 4:14; 5:24; 6:47, 51, 54, 58, 68; 10:28;

and 12:50. By obvious implication, such references are eschatological, both from a personal perspective and as a reality coming at the end of the age.

Equally certain is the resurrection and consequent judgment of those who have rejected Christ, as the passages cited above make clear. Whether the resurrection of the righteous and of the wicked occur at the same time, or at two different times, is a matter of difference of opinion among interpreters. In an earlier chapter I have discussed this at some length, as it applies to judgment; the same observations will apply to the resurrection.

Clearly, the eschatology of Jesus and the Gospels includes the resurrection of the dead, both saints and sinners, as required for His judgment, for eternal life or death. The four elements of this eschatology discussed in this overview chapter only begin to cover the subject. The next chapters will continue to draw out the eschatology of Jesus and the Gospels by analyzing some specific texts.

Endnotes

[8] Although "of the kingdom" is not in all manuscripts here, the direct quotation to follow shows it to be meant.

Chapter 7

ESCHATOLOGY IN THE GOSPELS AND TEACHING OF JESUS II: THE OLIVET DISCOURSE

At this point, our attention turns to the analysis of primary passages in the Gospels that treat the Second Coming. Three chapters will cover this material, and where else should we start than with the teaching of Jesus Himself, as found in what is called "the Olivet Discourse," reported in all three Synoptic Gospels—in Mark 13, Matthew 24, and Luke 21.

I will provide the text of the entire discourse in a tabular form that makes direct comparison of them straightforward. I will also provide this material in sections, treating (1) the part that was *not* eschatological but characterizes the whole present age (not "signs" of His coming, but "signs of the times"); (2) the part that dealt with the destruction of Jerusalem—which was in the near future; (3) the part that looked farther ahead, specifically, to the return of Jesus Christ to earth; and (4) the part that served as a conclusion, divided into (4–a), a parable, and (4–b), the lesson.

As will be clear, all three Gospels present this discourse according to this same outline. At the end of each table I will provide, in attached notes, brief observations.

Part One:
Things That Are NOT Eschatological but Characterize the Present Age

Mark 13:5–13	Matthew 24:4–14	Luke 21:8–19
5“Take heed that no one deceives you. 6For many will come in My name, saying, ‘I am He,’ and will deceive many.	4“Take heed that no one deceives you. 5For many will come in My name, saying, ‘I am the Christ,’ and will deceive many.	8“Take heed that you not be deceived. For many will come in My name, saying, ‘I am He,’ and, ‘The time has drawn near.’ Therefore do not go after them.
7But when you hear of wars and rumors of wars, do not be troubled; for such things must happen, but the end is not yet.	6And you will hear of wars and rumors of wars. See that you are not troubled; for all these things must come to pass, but the end is not yet.	9But when you her of wars and commotions, do not be terrified; for these things must come to pass first, but the end will not come immediately.”
8For nation will rise against nation, and kingdom against kingdom. And there will be earthquakes in various places, and there will be famines and troubles. These are the beginnings of sorrows.	7For nation will rise against nation, and kingdom against kingdom. And there will be famines, pestilences, and earthquakes in various places. 8All these are the beginning of sorrows.	10Then He said to them, “Nation will rise against nation, and kingdom against kingdom. 11And there will be great earthquakes in various places, and famines and pestilences; and there will be fearful sights and great signs from heaven.
9But watch out for yourselves, for they will deliver you up to councils, and you will be beaten in the synagogues. You will be brought before rulers and kings for My sake, for a testimony to them.	9Then they will deliver you up to tribulation and kill you, and you will be hated by all nations for My name’s sake.	12But before all these things, they will lay their hands on you and persecute you, delivering you up to the synagogues and prisons. You will be brought before kings and rulers for My name’s sake. 13But it will turn out for you as an occasion for testimony.
11But when they arrest you and deliver you up, do not worry beforehand, or premeditate what you will speak. But whatever is given you in that hour, speak that; for it is not you who speak, but the Holy Spirit.	11Then many false prophets will rise up and deceive many. 12And because lawlessness will abound, the love of many will grow cold.	14Therefore settle it in your hearts not to meditate beforehand on what you will answer; 15for I will give you a mouth and wisdom which all your adversaries will not be able to contradict or resist.
12Now brother will betray brother to death, and a father his child; and children will rise up against parents and cause them to be put to death.	10And then many will be offended, will betray one another, and will hate one another.	16You will be betrayed even by parents and brothers, relatives and friends; and they will put some of you to death.
13And you will be hated by all for My name’s sake. But he who endures to the end shall be saved.	13But he who endures to the end shall be saved.	17And you will be hated by all for My name’s sake.
10And the gospel must first be preached to all the nations.”	14And this gospel of the kingdom will be preached in all the world as a witness to all the nations, and then the end will come.”	18But not a hair of your head shall be lost. 19By your patience possess your souls.”

Observations:

- In this section Jesus warns of what to expect that *might* be interpreted as signs of the end and so trouble the disciples' minds, assuring them that these are but "signs of the times." These include false christs, wars, natural disasters, etc. An unstated implication may be that such things will intensify before the end of the age. Disciples can expect persecution, but their job is to be proclaiming the good news of salvation in the kingdom of God.
- Matthew adds (verses 10–12) some details not included by Mark or Luke, but does not include the expanded description of Mark (verses 11–13) and Luke (verses 12–17) on how Jesus' disciples can expect to be mistreated, including the promise of the Spirit's guidance when they must answer before tribunals.
- Luke slips in (verses 11b, 12a) a glimpse into eschatology with a reference to fearful sights and great signs in the heavens; but he immediately (by his "before all these things") returns to the present-age treatment of Jesus' witnesses. This could, but may not, come from the reference to "the beginning of sorrows" in Mark and Matthew, implying that the natural disasters will be followed, in the end times, by much more fearsome portents.
- Luke also (verses 18–19) gives more information about enduring to the end. The verb *endure* (Greek *hupomenō*) and noun *patience* (Greek *hupomonē*) have the same root.

Part Two:
The Destruction of Jerusalem in the Near Future

Mark 13:14–23	Matthew 24:15–28	Luke 21:20–24
[14]"So when you see the 'abomination of desolation,' spoken of by Daniel the prophet, standing where it ought not "(let the reader understand)," then let those who are in Judea flee to the mountains.	[15]"Therefore when you see the 'abomination of desolation' spoken of by Daniel the prophet, standing in the holy place" (whoever reads, let him understand), [16]"then let those who are in Judea flee to the mountains.	[20]"But when you see Jerusalem surrounded by armies, then know that its desolation is near.
[15]Let him who is on the housetop not go down into the house, nor enter to take anything out of his house. [16]And let him who is in the field not go back to get his clothes.	[17]Let him who is on the housetop not go down to take anything out of his house. [18]And let him who is in the field not go back to get his clothes.	[21]Then let those who are in Judea flee to the mountains, let those who are in the midst of her depart, and let not those who are in the country enter her. [22]For these are the days of vengeance, that all things which are written may be fulfilled.
[17]But woe to those who are pregnant and to those who are nursing babies in those days. [18]And pray that your flight may not be in winter.	[19]But woe to those who are pregnant and to those who are nursing babies in those days! [20]And pray that your flight may not be in winter or on the Sabbath.	[23]But woe to those who are pregnant and to those who are nursing babies in those days! For there will be great distress in the land and wrath upon this people.
[19]For in those days there will be tribulation, such as has not been since the beginning of the creation which God created until this time nor ever shall be. [20]And unless the Lord had shortened those days, no flesh would be saved; but for the elect's sake, whom He chose, He shortened the days.	[21]For then there will be great tribulation, such as has not been since the beginning of the world until this time, no, nor ever shall be. [22]And unless those days were shortened, no flesh would be saved; but for the elect's sake those days will be shortened.	[24]And they will fall by the edge of the sword and be led away captive into all nations. And Jerusalem will be trampled by Gentiles until the times of the Gentiles are fulfilled."
[21]Then if anyone says to you, 'Look, here is the Christ!' or, 'Look, He is there!' do not believe it. [22]For false christs and false prophets will rise and show signs and wonders to deceive, if possible, even the elect. [23]But take heed; see, I have told you all things beforehand."	[23]Then if anyone says to you, 'Look, here is the Christ!' or 'There!' do not believe it. [24]For false christs and false prophets will rise and show great signs and wonders to deceive, if possible, even the elect. [25]See, I have told you beforehand. [26]Therefore if they say to you, 'Look, He is in the desert!' do not go out; or 'Look, He is in the inner rooms!' do not believe it. [27]For as the lightning comes from the east and flashes to the west, so also will the coming of the Son of Man be." [28]For wherever the carcass is, there the eagles will be gathered together."	

Observations:

- In this section Jesus warns of something else that will *not* be a sign of His coming; it will be the special distress of the Jews experienced in the destruction of Jerusalem—which took place in AD 70 under the Roman general Titus. Matthew's addition at the end (verses 26–28) confirms that Jesus has *not* yet spoken about His coming—which, as surely as lightning or vultures flocking to a carcass, will be obvious and public.
- Mark (verse 14) and Matthew (verse 15) identify this with the "abomination of desolation" of Daniel 9:27, whether intended as *the* fulfillment of it or as another instance of the same kind of thing at work.
- Only Luke (verse 24) represents this as marking the beginning of "the times of the Gentiles."
- Mark (verse 19) and Matthew (verse 21) represent this as a time of "tribulation" (Greek *thlipsis*) or "great tribulation" (Greek *thlipsis megalē)*—neither with a "the" to make it definite. Luke (verses 22–23) apparently speaks of "vengeance" (Greek *ekdikēsis*), "great distress" (Greek *anagkē megalē*), and "wrath" (Greek *orgē*), instead, especially the "great distress." He makes clear this is an outpouring of God's wrath on "this people," the Jews. But in Mark (verse 19) and Matthew (verse 21); the promise that there will never again be such tribulation would appear to rule out another eschatological "great tribulation"—*unless* elements of this passage are intended to have a dual fulfillment (once in AD 70 and another in the end times), in which case this section could be taken to speak, by a later fulfillment, of the last days. Regardless, the *primary* fulfillment was in the impending destruction of Jerusalem by the Romans.

Part Three:
The Second Coming of Jesus

Mark 13:24–27	Matthew 24:29–31	Luke 21:25–28
24"But in those days, after that tribulation, the sun will be darkened, and the moon will not give its light; 25the stars of heaven will fall, and the powers in the heavens will be shaken.	29"Immediately after the tribulation of those days the sun will be darkened and the moon will not give its light; the stars will fall from heaven, and the powers of the heavens will be shaken.	25"And there will be signs in the sun, in the moon, and in the stars; and on the earth distress of nations, with perplexity, the sea and the waves roaring; 26men's hearts failing them from fear and the expectation of those things which are coming on the earth, for the powers of the heavens will be shaken.
26Then they will see the Son of Man coming in the clouds with great power and glory.	30Then the sign of the Son of Man will appear in heaven, and then all the tribes of the earth will mourn, and they will see the Son of Man coming on the clouds of heaven with power and great glory.	27Then they will see the Son of Man coming in a cloud with power and great glory.
27And then He will send His angels, and gather together His elect from the four winds, from the farthest part of the earth to the farthest part of the heaven."	31And He will send His angels with a great sound of a trumpet, and they will gather together His elect from the four winds, from one end of heaven to the other."	28Now when these things begin to happen, look up and lift up your heads, because your redemption draws near."

Observations:

- In this section Jesus speaks clearly of His return in glory.
- At the Second Coming, there will be great and fearful portents in the skies, which Luke refers to as "signs."
- Jesus' coming, as predicted here, will be visible and glorious.
- The gathering of the elect to Jesus will be part of the manifestation, perhaps referring to what Paul describes as our being caught up to meet Him in the air (1 Thessalonians 4:13–18).
- Does Luke mean, by our "redemption," the same thing as the gathering of the elect? Or is this an additional observation as to when we may look up in expectation of Jesus' arrival and our final redemption? The latter seems more likely; see the notes with the following section for more on the emphasis of Luke.

Part Four-A:
A Parable

Mark 13:28–31	Matthew 24:32–35	Luke 21:29–33
[28]"Now learn this parable from the fig tree: When its branch has already become tender, and puts forth leaves, you know that summer is near.	[32]"Now learn this parable from the fig tree: When its branch has already become tender and puts forth leaves, you know that summer is near.	[29]"Look at the fig tree, and all the trees. [30]When they are already budding, you see and know for yourselves that summer is now near.
[29]So you also, when you see these things happening, know that it is near—at the doors!	[33]So you also, when you see all these things, know that it is near—at the doors!	[31]So you also, when you see these things happening, know that the kingdom of God is near.
[30]Assuredly, I say to you, this generation will by no means pass away till all these things take place. [31]Heaven and earth will pass away, but My words will by no means pass away."	[34]Assuredly, I say to you, this generation will by no means pass away till all these things take place. [35]Heaven and earth will pass away, but My words will by no means pass away."	[32]Assuredly, I say to you, this generation will by no means pass away till all things take place. [33]Heaven and earth will pass away, but My words will by no means pass away."

Observations:

- The point of the parable is that when the disciples see things Jesus has spoken of, they will know that the attendant events are near. After all, as in both Mark (verse 23) and Matthew (verse 25) Jesus has told them these things beforehand. But He has described *two* groups of events: the destruction of Jerusalem and the Second Coming; which of those is the focus here? The lesson of the parable can apply to either. The disciples living then could actually experience only the first.
- In Mark (verse 29) and Matthew (verse 33), "these things" (Greek *tauta*) appear to stand in contrast to "that day and hour" in section Four-B, below. Luke, however, does not proceed to "that day and hour." Indeed, Luke's treatment is clearly different in a number of ways, perhaps reflecting the same basic teaching given at another time with a little different emphasis. Unlike Mark and Matthew, Luke says "the kingdom of God" is near (Mark 13:29; Matthew 24:33; Luke 21:31), and the final lesson drawn in Luke 21:34–36 is quite different in its point from that drawn in Mark and Matthew (Section Four-B below). What seems likely is that the focus in Mark and Matthew in section Four-A is on recognizing the impending destruction of Jerusalem ("these things" in

contrast to “that day”), while Luke focuses almost exclusively on the Second Coming with little if any attention to the destruction of Jerusalem. He has in view the effects on the whole earth.

- In Mark and Matthew, then, section Four-A focuses primarily on the destruction of Jerusalem. In that regard, it was literally true that all of the “present generation” at the time of the discourse might not have passed before that event. That will not work for Luke, however, if what I have just said is correct, that in his account the focus is on the Second Coming. If that is right, it can be said that the generation only lived to see the destruction of Jerusalem as something of a *type* of the Second Coming.

Part Four-B:
The Lesson: Be Watching for the Lord’s Return

Mark 13:32–37	Matthew 24:36–44	Luke 21:34–36
32 “But of that day and hour no one knows, not even the angels in heaven, nor the Son, but only the Father.	36 “But of that day and hour no one knows, not even the angels of heaven, but My Father only. 37 But as the days of Noah were, so also will the coming of the Son of Man be. 38 For as in the days before the flood, they were eating and drinking, marrying and giving in marriage, until the day that Noah entered the ark,	
33 Take heed, watch and pray; for you do not know when the time is. 34 It is like a man going to a far country, who left his house and gave authority to his servants, and to each his work, and commanded the doorkeeper to watch. 35 Watch therefore, for you do not know when the master of the house is coming—in the evening, at midnight, at the crowing of the rooster, or in the morning— 36 lest, coming suddenly, he find you sleeping. 37 And what I say to you, I say to all: Watch!”	39 and did not know until the flood came and took them all away, so also will the coming of the Son of Man be. 40 Then two men will be in the field: one will be taken and the other left. 41 Two women will be grinding at the mill: one will be taken and the other left. 42 Watch therefore, for you do not know what hour your Lord is coming. 43 But know this, that if the master of the house had known what hour the thief would come, he would have watched and not allowed his house to be broken into. 44 Therefore you also be ready, for the Son of Man is coming at an hour you do not expect.”	34 “But take heed to yourselves, lest your hearts be weighed down with carousing, drunkenness, and cares of this life, and that Day come on you unexpectedly. 35 For it will come as a snare on all those who dwell on the face of the whole earth. 36 Watch therefore, and pray always that you may be counted worthy to escape all these things that will come to pass, and to stand before the Son of Man.”

Observations:

- All three accounts end with the need to be watchful for the second coming of Jesus, observing that no one will know when that event will occur, Mark and Matthew say this directly, Luke says only that the Day may come unexpectedly. The point of all three is that those who are watching and ready will not be caught unprepared. But all three are different enough that they may reflect different applications that Jesus Himself made at different times.
- Mark and Matthew have the same basic point of view, here, while Luke (as noted above) has a somewhat different one, focusing on how the Second Coming may catch "the whole earth" off guard and prove to be a "snare."
- Mark and Matthew use different parabolic illustrations to underscore the need for watchfulness in light of the fact that the time remains unknown. Mark's parable (verses 34–35) concerns a householder who goes away and leaves servants in charge without their knowing just when he will return. Matthew, in more direct comparison, uses a parable (verse 43) about a householder who, himself, does not know when a thief may break in. Only Matthew cites the biblical example of the flood (verses 37–39) or speaks about two women or men who are separated by an unexpected visitor (verses 40–41). In this last example it is not clear just how or why one is taken and the other left; either could be for good/escape/blessing or ill/judgment/punishment, and since Jesus does not explain, speculation is probably fruitless. The point, after all, is that life will be going on as usual without the time of crisis being announced and known.
- Only Matthew follows this with three more parables teaching the need for watchfulness and preparation, and only Matthew adds to these a fourth segment picturing judgment at His coming—usually called "the judgment of nations":

  (1) 24:45–51—parable contrasting the servant whose master's return finds him faithful with one whom that same return finds guilty of evil deeds in his absence;

(2) 25:1–13—parable contrasting wise and foolish virgins waiting for the arrival of a bridegroom;

(3) 25:14–30—parable concerning a man who went abroad and left various servants with various "talents" to invest in his absence;

(4) 25:31–40—segment concerning the judgment of nations at Jesus' return.

All of these will be dealt with in the following chapter.

Chapter 8

ESCHATOLOGY IN THE GOSPELS AND TEACHING OF JESUS III: PARABLES AND TEACHING IN MATTHEW 24–25

As noted in the preceding chapter on the Olivet Discourse, all three Synoptic Gospels use a parable of a fig tree to emphasize one of the practical implications of the Discourse: namely, the importance of being prepared for Jesus' return to earth in spite of the fact that "of that day and hour no one knows, not even the angels of heaven, but My Father only" (Matthew 24:36). Matthew is unique in following that warning with three parables and an additional segment that focus attention on the second coming of Jesus. In this chapter I will provide an analysis of these four passages and what they teach us about the return of Jesus.

The Parable of the Servant Ruling in His Master's Absence (24:45–51)

This parable follows immediately after Jesus observes, "Therefore you also be ready, for the Son of Man is coming at an hour you do not expect" (verse 44). We are safe in assuming that the parable will illustrate something about being ready for the return of Jesus.

In the parable the master of a household goes away and leaves in charge one of his servants, to provide for the feeding of the whole family (which would include other servants), as regularly scheduled. Clearly implied is that the time of the master's return has not been made known. Two possibilities are considered.

First, if the servant-in-charge is faithful, the master, when he returns at a time unannounced, will find the servant busy, doing what he was instructed to do. In that case, the master will promote the servant to a place of responsibility over all his goods; the servant, being judged faithful, will be thus blessed.

The other possibility is that the servant-in-charge will not be faithful. Since this takes up the greater part of the parable, perhaps we are intended to learn most from it, from what ought *not* to be true of us. This servant's experience can be analyzed as follows:

(1) Most basic, apparently, is that the servant tells himself ("says in his heart"), "My master is delaying his coming." Obviously, this conclusion leads to the behavior indicated next.

(2) The servant, instead of making proper provisions for his fellow servants, "begins to beat" them.

(3) He also, in self-indulgence, spends time eating and drinking (perhaps carousing) with drunkards.

(4) The master returns unannounced, at a time when the servant is not expecting ("looking for") him and has not thought he would come back ("is not aware of"). By clear implication, the master finds the unfaithful servant in the midst of his indifference and misconduct.

(5) As a consequence, the master will "cut him in two" and assign him a "portion with the hypocrites," leading to "weeping and gnashing of teeth."

Parables are meant to teach lessons. What are we expected to learn from this one?

First, the parable is obviously intended to support the idea that the time of the Second Coming is not announced beforehand. The very last thing said before the parable begins is: "Therefore you also be ready, for the Son of Man is coming at an hour you do not expect" (verse 44). This is something said often in the New Testament and in various wordings. Perhaps the most familiar way is that He will come "as a thief in the night" (1 Thessalonians 5:2; see the treatment of that passage in another chapter).

Second, we are charged to "be ready," which indicates that we do not have to be caught by surprise—by the Second Coming, that is—as people usually are by the coming of a thief (1 Thessalonians 5:4—"But you, brethren, are not in darkness, so that this Day should overtake you as a thief."). We will not be ready and watching by knowing when He is coming; we will be ready and watching by looking for Him at all times.

Third, being ready will include, as with the faithful and wise servant in the parable, being about the service He has called us to. For all of us, that will involve living in obedience to Him; we are called to such a lifestyle. If He has given us specific "ministries" (in the broadest sense of that word), we will be actively and faithfully engaged therein. In fact, He has given us all a ministry of one sort or another.

Fourth, there will be appropriate reward or punishment, accordingly. In the case of the one punished, here, it is clear that Jesus views the wicked servant as scheduled for execution and sharing the eternal destiny of pretenders. At this point the more direct meaning lurking behind the parable breaks through to be visible; our eternal destiny is at stake in being ready for Jesus to return.

The Parable of the Wise and Foolish Virgins Waiting for the Bridegroom (25:1–13)

This parable immediately follows, which probably justifies us in assuming it has similar lessons to teach us. The narrative is set in the context of a first-century Palestinian marriage ceremony. Without getting enmeshed in the detailed customs of the time, we can assume the circumstances. The bridegroom was going to leave his home, go to the bride's house to fetch her, and take her to where they would live. The virgins were young, unmarried women who would accompany them in celebration, to take place after the darkness had fallen: thus the need for lamps to light the way.

There were ten of them, and we are told up front that five were wise and five not-so-wise. Probably all ten expected the bridegroom soon after dusk, but five took along extra oil for their lamps, just in case; the other five did not. The unexpected thing happened: an unanticipated delay. As they waited and waited, they napped, perhaps thinking they needed to rest in order to be fresh when the big moment arrived.

The delay lasted until midnight—who would have thought such a thing! The word came. The groom was on his way. They all arose and prepared for his coming, trimming their lamps. After such a delay, the oil that was already in the lamps was running low, and the ones who didn't have extra oil asked the ones who did if they could have some of theirs. No, they said, we may need all we have; you'll have to go buy some. But when they went to buy, the groom came by and only the five who had prepared for a possible delay were able to go on with him and into the wedding festivity. The five foolish virgins came late, knocked, but were denied access. The groom said he didn't know them.

Although that's the end of the parable, Jesus attaches a lesson: "Watch therefore, for you know neither the day nor the hour in which the Son of Man is coming" (verse 13)—the same point as in 24:44, quoted above. If we seek the lesson of this parable, then, that's really the main one. We don't know when He will return, and so we must be ready at all times.

I tend to think that we can tweak this basic lesson and draw out a closely related implication: namely, be prepared for a delay. The possibility of delay runs like a sub-theme through a lot of the teaching of the New Testament about the Second Coming. In the parable analyzed above (24:45–51), the wicked servant said to himself, "My master is delaying his coming." But then he missed what that meant and allowed himself to be distracted from his duties. Sometimes people are excited when the revival is fresh in their minds, and they might be "ready" if they met the Master right then. But we aren't tested by our sense of commitment to God right after we've made it. Instead, we're tested by the long haul and how we persevere in living and serving as He has called us to. So we need to make a meaningful commitment, one that will hold up for whatever time we have to wait.

The Parable of the Servants Who Were Given Money to Invest While Their Master Was Abroad (25:14–30)

Immediately following came another parable, part of the same context introduced by 24:44, at the end of the Olivet Discourse: "Therefore you also be ready, for the Son of Man is coming at an hour you do not expect." In this parable, however, the point is no longer about watching lest one be caught by surprise and unprepared at the return of Jesus, but about the accounting—the judgment, in other words—that attaches to His return.

In the parable, a man of some means prepares to be abroad for a while and decides to entrust to his servants the management of some of his wealth. One must not think of these *talents* as abilities; they are money to use in trade, to invest (see verse 27, where "money" is the Greek *arguria*, "silver coins"). It is nigh impossible to express the actual value in our day, since (for one thing) a talent (a measure of weight) of gold, for example, would be worth more than a talent of silver. Regardless, the value of a talent of silver would be large, probably the equivalent of nearly two years' wages for a day laborer.[9]

Judging his three servants to have different levels of ability, the lord of the servants gave five talents to one, two to another, and one to yet another. Jesus does not tell the instructions he gave them, but the parable makes clear they were to put the money to work for the purpose of growing it. The servants with five talents or two talents doubled theirs, but the servant with one hid the money to keep it safe.

That the lord came back "after a long time" (verse 19) has some significance and relates to what I have said, above, about the theme of delay. While catching the servants by surprise is not suggested, the fact that they were to be about the business he had charged them with until he returned is clear, and that was going to be a while. Also significant is the fact that they had to make an accounting (verse 19b), which no doubt they knew all along.

When the two servants who had doubled the original investment reported, they were highly commended for their faithfulness and given increased responsibility (verses 20–23). "Ruler over many things," in both cases, doesn't mean one with authority to govern others; instead, the idea is, more simply, that they were "over little/few things" and now will be placed "over much/ many things." In other words, this is what they were responsible for.

But when the servant who hid the money entrusted to him came, the result was very different; given the length of this section (verses 24–30), it may be that there is the most to learn here. His report is three-fold: (1) he took into account his perception of the master as stern and demanding; (2) he was afraid; (3) he therefore hid the money to keep it safe and now returns it to his master with neither loss nor gain.

The master's response was equally different: (1) the servant is wicked and lazy; (2) he should at least have put the money with moneylenders to draw interest; (3) the talent he had must be taken from him and given to the one who had doubled five talents into ten. Here the real-world meaning of the parable gets so close to the surface (as noted above and as often the case with parables or analogies) that the permanent lesson breaks through the veneer of the story. The principle, which Jesus states in verse 29, is that the person who has been busy and earned more will receive even more, but the person who has wickedly and lazily earned nothing will be stripped of everything. Worse still, this servant who has been of no use to his master is to be cast "into the outer darkness" (verse 30). This outcome is intended to be read, no doubt, the same way as that of the evil servant in the first of the three parables; see Matthew 24:51. The same "weeping and gnashing of teeth" accompanies it.

The lessons here seem reasonably obvious. While Jesus is away He has entrusted to us responsibilities in the way of living for and serving Him. These differ from one of His servants to another, but each "adds value" to the cause of the gospel and the kingdom of God. All His followers are expected to make their contributions to this program, and each will give account, accordingly, when Jesus returns. Anyone who makes no effort is, by definition, wicked and will wind up with nothing in the kingdom of God, to be consigned to eternal darkness. The very attitude of such a person reveals that he or she does not truly know the Lord.

Concluding Observations About the Three Parables

These parables do not teach much, directly, about the Second Coming, at least not about when or how. They assume that Jesus will return to earth. What they teach us, primarily, is that at His return there will be an "accounting": judgment, in other words. That judgment will revolve around what we have been and done while we are waiting for Him: namely, whether we have been faithful in fulfilling the responsibilities He has entrusted to us. These include all aspects of Christian living and serving: as He said just before He went away, "teaching them to observe all things that I have commanded you" (Matthew 28:20).

At the same time, they teach us that there will be time for His followers to put this obligation into practice. We are to be expectant and eagerly waiting for Him, but we are also to be prepared for the passing of time before that happens. Not lulling ourselves into indifference by thinking, "Oh, He's not coming any time soon! We can take our time and choose our own course." Yet not, on the other hand, getting so excited by the prospects of His return that we put on clean clothes and sit and wait. I said previously that we are disciples-in-waiting. We are also disciples about His business, living and serving, while we wait.

The Segment Concerning the Judgment of Nations (25:31–40)

Although this section is not a parable, it has some elements that are comparable to parables, especially in comparing Jesus as king and judge to a shepherd who separates his sheep from goats. Even so, the scene that Jesus sets before His disciples is relatively straightforward, focusing on a judgment that separates the "righteous" (verse 37) from the "cursed" (verse 41) and indicating their respective eternal destinies and the reasons for the separation.

One notes, to begin with, that Jesus Himself links this judgment to His return to earth: "When the Son of Man comes in His glory, and all the holy angels with Him, then He will sit on the throne of His glory" (verse 31). (I will say more about the timing of this event below.) This fits precisely with what I have already said about His coming—in glory and accompanied by angels and/or saints—and His role as king-judge at that time.

This judging takes the primary form of separating into two groups, the righteous—the blessed—and the wicked—the cursed (verses 32–33). Because the whole number thus separated are identified as "all the nations," some interpreters think of this scene as depicting a judgment of nation-groups *as nations*, rather than of individuals as such. In that case, the issue becomes how various nations have treated the Jewish people. But this representation reflects a highly dispensational view of biblical history and does not seem justified by a straightforward reading of the text itself.

At any rate, following the analogy of a shepherd separating sheep from goats, Jesus says He will place the sheep—the righteous—on His right hand and the goats—the cursed—on His left. Then He will address those in each group, in turn, and describe the nature of their respective judgments.

For the righteous, Jesus judges that they gave Him food when He was hungry and something to drink when He was thirsty, hosted and provided for Him when He was a visiting stranger, gave Him clothing when He did not have enough, and came to [minister to] Him when He was sick or in prison (verses 35–36). In the same vein, He judges that the wicked did not do those very things for Him (verses 42–43).

Those in each group raise the question *when* they did, or did not, do such things for Him (verses 37–39, 44). In both cases, Jesus answers that this occurred when they did or did not do such things for "the least of these My brethren" (verses 40, 45). As noted, some (dispensational) interpreters take this to mean the Jewish people, but that does not seem to be justified by the text. It is not clear that Jesus ever referred to the Jewish people as His brothers, but it is clear that He referred to His followers by that term; see Matthew 12:48–49. As He often did, Jesus is identifying Himself with His disciples in this passage, and in His judgment He will identify those who have acted on behalf of His believing followers, at any time in history, and have in that way acted in His behalf and thereby demonstrated their faith in Him. He is separating those who have done this from those who have not.

Benevolence toward other believers, of course, will not be the *only* thing to be revealed or rewarded at the judgment seat of Christ. But such treatment will be one mark of those whose faith is genuine. No doubt Jesus could have named many other evidences of the righteousness that is by faith, other expressions of faith that by their presence or absence would distinguish between the saved and the lost. Even so, this particular evidence was on His mind at the time.

Perhaps the most important element of this passage lies in the destinies of those in the two groups. Separated in judgment by their deeds, they will be separated forever in life or death. Both at the beginning of the treatment of each group and again at the end of the passage, Jesus testifies to their final disposition. To those on His right hand, Jesus will say, "Come, you blessed of My Father, inherit the kingdom prepared for you from the foundation of the world" (verse 34), summarized as "eternal life" (verse 46). To those on the left He will say, "Depart from Me, you cursed, into the everlasting fire prepared for the devil and his angels" (verse 41), summarized as "everlasting punishment" (verse 46). This leaves no doubt that the issue is final salvation versus eternal death. One notes that entering God's "kingdom" is used, here, in its specific, eschatological sense of the eternal domain under God's dominion—as discussed previously. One also notes that for the lost it is the *punishment* that is eternal, not just the fire.

Question: When Does This Judgment Occur?

In the main, there are three possible answers to this question, as I have already indicated in discussing this question at the end of Chapter 5.

1. One possibility is that this event will take place in immediate connection with Jesus' return. In favor of this is the way the passage *sounds*: namely, that the judgment described beginning in verse 32 coincides with "when the Son of Man comes." If that "straightforward" reading is the correct reading, then it means that this is not only the end of the present age but that the eternal state will immediately follow. In that case, for Jesus to "sit on the throne of His glory" is, specifically, to sit there in this final and universal judgment of all nations and (as seen above) to assign their respective, eternal destinies.

2. Some other possibility will be required *if there is any reign of Jesus on earth following His return.* I say this in light of the fact that this judgment, if for the entire population of earth, would leave no one alive on earth to enter, as living natural lives, into such an earthly kingdom. How must we read the passage if this proves to be the case? There are two possibilities, and the first is that the judgment of the wicked, though a function of Jesus' reign (summarized in verse 31), does not occur immediately upon His return to earth but will occur at the end of His reign on earth. It will also include, at least, all who have been converted during that reign. Even though there are two judgments, both are functions of the reign of Jesus.

3. The other possibility is that no persons receive final judgment until the end of the reign of Jesus. It is true, of course, that the righteous dead are raised when He returns, and the living righteous are transformed. Their eternal destiny is already settled, a fact that proves to be no argument at all in the matter; the eternal destiny of all who have died has already been settled before judgment. If this possibility is adopted, there will be one and only one general judgment at the end of Jesus' reign on earth.

One of the issues to be discussed in this work, then, is whether other passages of Scripture require us to hold that Jesus will reign on earth following His return. That will be discussed in subsequent chapters; for now, it is enough to say that the very idea of His coming back to earth, and His role as the Davidic Messiah, as discussed already, seems to mean that Jesus will reign as King on earth. If so, His subjects will include a large population still naturally alive and capable of choosing for or against Him. Subsequent discussion of Revelation is needed before making a final decision on this matter. Either way, whether a reign on earth follows Jesus' return and ends in the final judgment, or His return leads immediately to final judgment and the eternal state, King Jesus is coming back to this earth to reign and judge.

Endnotes

[9] Craig Keener indicates, commenting on this passage, that a talent was quivalent to 600 days wages.

Chapter 9

ESCHATOLOGY IN THE GOSPELS AND TEACHING OF JESUS IV: OTHER PASSAGES

The previous three chapters have covered the most significant elements of the eschatology of Jesus and the Gospels. It remains, now, to survey, briefly, a half dozen other passages that add some detail to the eschatology seen in the major passages above.

A Coming Catastrophe?

In Matthew 5:18, Jesus, while discussing the permanence of the law of God, makes a passing reference to the possible "destiny" of heaven and earth, the created order itself: "For assuredly, I say to you, till heaven and earth pass away, one jot or one tittle will by no means pass from the law till all is fulfilled." He does not expand on this, and we are left to seek for understanding in other passages of Scripture. Second Peter 3 provides the most information about this, and Revelation 20:11 refers to a circumstance when "the earth and the heaven fled away." The Apostle John, without details, reminds us that "the world is passing away" (1 John 2:17), and we must live with awareness that nothing in the present, created order will last. I will not draw out implications from this here. Instead, the matter will naturally arise as we treat the subject of eschatology in the Acts and epistles.

Two Parables in Matthew 13

This chapter in Matthew is famous for its collection of parables that Jesus used, whether all on the same occasion or on different occasions—or both. Parables are not all alike, and there are two sides to their telling. On the one hand, as illustrations from the natural world to instruct about spiritual things, they are sometimes said to be windows of light given to enable understanding. But there is another side to this, and in this chapter, Matthew issues a warning. Parables also have a way of hiding spiritual truth from the understanding of those who have no ear or heart for spiritual things. This is the reason Matthew quotes that "hard" word from Isaiah 6:9–10 (Matthew 13:14–15) about people who are hard of hearing and have shut their eyes against the light.

Most of the parables in this chapter do not speak directly about the Second Coming, but there are two that do and thus have something to say about eschatology.

The first is typically called the parable of the wheat and the tares; it is first recorded (verses 24–30) and then explained by Jesus (verses 36–43), and it directly involves—to use Jesus' words—"the end of the age" (v. 39). In summary, the parable describes a man who sowed good seed in his field, only to have an enemy sow seed for tares, at night, in the same field. When the seeds germinated, there were both wheat and weeds (*tares*—darnel or cockle). The man's servants offered to pull up the weeds, but he cautioned them to wait and separate them at harvest time. Pulling out the bad plants sooner would risk the loss of some good plants that might be pulled up at the same time.

In the interpretation, Jesus makes seven points of symbolism. (1) The field represents the world. (2) The one who sowed good seed represents Jesus Himself, "the Son of Man." (3) The one who sowed the tares represents Satan. (4) The good seed represents "the sons of the kingdom." (5) The bad seed represents "the sons of the wicked one." (6) The harvest itself is the end of the age. (7) The reapers are the angels.

Then He explains. At the end of the age, the Son of Man—when He comes, obviously—will send His angels to gather out of His kingdom those who practice disobedience to the revealed will of God (verse 41) and cast them into "the furnace of fire" (verse 42). That will leave the righteous, without mixture, to "shine forth as the sun in the kingdom of their Father" (verse 43).

The second parable is obviously similar and is called the parable of the dragnet, in verses 47–50. Here, fishermen cast a dragnet and draw it in with whatever is in it, whether good food fish or "trash fish"—or things not fish at all. Only when the net is full do the fishermen draw it to shore and separate the good from the bad, discarding the latter. Just so, says Jesus immediately interpreting—at the end of the age the angels will come and separate the wicked from the just and cast the wicked into the furnace of fire.

Both parables picture the same main event associated with the return of Christ at the end of the age, focusing on separation between the wicked and the righteous and the destiny of both: eternal fire for the wicked, eternal shining for the righteous.

In summary, the two parables teach that there will be an end of the age, obviously marked by the coming of the Lord Jesus. There will then be a separation between those who follow the Lord and those who do not, each to his own reward. This indicates a judgment that makes the separation. The wicked will be cast into the furnace of fire, a figure associated with numerous parables and assertions in the Bible.

Here are a few of numerous examples of this final consignment to fire, many of which have already been analyzed. In Matthew 3:12 (Lk. 3:17), John the Baptist also spoke of this judicial reaping when the Messiah will "gather His wheat into the barn, but He will burn up the chaff with unquenchable fire." In Matthew 25:41, where judgment is again linked to the Second Coming (verse 31), Jesus will say to those on His left, "Depart from Me, you cursed, into the everlasting fire prepared for the devil and his angels." In Mark 9:43–48, Jesus urges that removing one's hand, foot, or eye would be better than entering the realm where "the fire is not quenched." Most pointedly, Revelation refers to the final destiny of the unsaved as being cast into the lake of fire (19:20; 20:10, 14–15; 21:8). (See also Matthew 5:22; 7:19; John 15:6; and Jude 7.)

These two parables, then, make essentially the same point as some of the other passages that I have highlighted or will highlight: namely, that Jesus will come back to this earth to conduct a separating judgment that will distinguish between the righteous and the wicked and consign each, respectively, to eternal life or eternal death; I refrain from calling the destiny of the wicked "life."

Earlier discussion has raised the question whether the judgment of the righteous and the judgment of the wicked will occur at the same time or at different times. While these parables do not separate judgment into two occasions, they also do not necessarily teach that the two will be judged at the same time. That determination will depend on other aspects of one's eschatology, including especially whether there will be a reign of Jesus on the earth following His return.

The Demand of Discipleship in Matthew 16:24–27

I have mentioned Matthew 16:27 briefly a couple of times already, especially as uttered by Jesus immediately before His transfiguration, which was a foretaste of His second coming glory. But the immediate context offers a pointed truth about discipleship: namely, the requirement for following Jesus.

Verses 24–27 should be read as one unit. Jesus urges that anyone desiring to be His disciple must take up his cross and follow Him (verse 24)—as He said many times. This involves "losing one's life" for Jesus' sake, and those who do this will *truly* "find" their lives, while those who do not will truly "lose" their lives (verse 25). One who thinks to save his life for himself, even if he should gain the whole world, is a fool (verse 26). "For the Son of Man will come in the glory of His Father with His angels, and then He will reward each according to his works" (verse 27).

Again, then, we have the separating judgment of Christ at the end of the age—whether on the same specific occasion or not. Again, the consequences are eternal. When Jesus says He will "reward each," it seems likely in the context that He is speaking of both those who eternally lose their lives and those who eternally find or save theirs. In that case, "reward" can be positive or negative. While this adds little, if anything, to our understanding of the events at the end of the age, it does serve to confirm what other passages are teaching us in that regard, and it puts discipleship now into a significant relationship with the judgment that Jesus will execute when He comes back to this earth to reign and judge.

The Present and Future Kingdom, and Jesus' Unexpected Coming: Luke 17:22–37

This teaching of Jesus about His second coming comes in a context that begins in verse 20 with a question to Him from the Pharisees: "When will the kingdom of God come?" No doubt this resulted from Jesus' frequent references to God's kingdom (see the discussion about the kingdom of God above, and in an earlier chapter). Essentially, Jesus put them off by focusing attention on an important (but different) truth about the kingdom of God. That kingdom is within you, He told them (or perhaps "in your midst," as in the ESV), and it doesn't come in a way that is observable by ordinary eyesight. We can't say, "Look! Here it is!" or "There!" Probably in these words Jesus was deliberately evading their question but implying that the kingdom of God was already there among them in His own presence and work—a truth that does not rule out a "not yet" kingdom on this earth, even though Jesus does not speak of such a thing here.

Then He turned His attention to His disciples (verse 22), and He proceeded to give them additional information. To start with, they must not be misled by those who, like the Pharisees, would try to lure them into thinking the kingdom was something other than His own presence and authority (verses 22–23). When the kingdom does come in its fullest manifestation, they will know it without a doubt. Just as the lightning lights up from one part of the sky to another and everyone sees it without even trying (compare Matthew 24:27), so will the days of the Son of Man be, public and global—referring, apparently, to His second coming (verse 24). Only that will not be right away; other things, including His suffering and death, must come first (verse 25).

When the time for His arrival, and for the full appearance of His kingdom, actually comes, things will be in some ways similar to the days of Noah, says Jesus (verses 26–27). The people who were about to perish in the Flood were entirely unaware of the danger. They were going about their lives without any thoughts of the catastrophe about to overtake them, eating, drinking, and marrying—right up to the day judgment fell.

The same was true when Lot barely escaped the destruction of Sodom and Gomorrah (verses 28–29). With no awareness of impending judgment, the wicked inhabitants of those cities were eating and drinking, buying and selling, planning and building, living as they did every day, ignorant of the sudden doom that was about to come on them. In the very day that the angels brought Lot out, almost against his will, fire and brimstone fell from the sky and the people and their cities, all they lived for, perished and left no trace but ashes.

Beginning in verse 30, Jesus applies the lesson to the situation that will prevail at His return: that is, "when the Son of Man is revealed." When that happens, people will be caught in the midst of their "normal" activities but must not turn back as though to save their possessions. The man on the roof should not go down to the lower story for anything. The one working in the field must not go back to the house. Anyone who—like Lot's wife, whom they should remember—seeks to save anything, life or livelihood, will perish with the wicked. Only those who give up their claims to life and flee to Jesus will be saved (verses 30–33).

Then Jesus adds a detail, illustrating with examples how some among those who are going about life as usual when He comes back to earth will be saved and others not. Of two men in bed asleep at night, one will be saved and the other not. Of two women grinding grain, or two men working in the field, the same is true: one is saved, the other not (verses 34–36).

It is difficult, perhaps impossible, to be sure which of each pair is saved, the one "taken" or the one "left." Some interpreters think the ones taken are saved and see this as representing those who are raptured, while the wicked are left behind to face judgment. Other interpreters reverse this, suggesting that the wicked are taken for judgment and the righteous remain for the inauguration of Christ's kingdom. In fact, it isn't clear that Jesus intended anything more than to indicate that among those going about their everyday activities, when He returns, some (like the wheat in the parable of the wheat and tares) would be gathered to Him and others assigned to hell fire. That is the lesson that is important.

In the final verse of the passage (verse 37), the disciples ask a question in response to this sobering teaching: "Where, Lord?" Apparently they mean to ask where this will take place; no doubt they also wanted to know when, so that they would be able to expect it and be ready. Jesus' answer was apparently intentionally vague, saying only that wherever carrion is (a dead body, for example), there is where carrion-eating birds (like an eagle) gather (compare Matthew 24:28). You can find one by finding the other. Jesus apparently means that where His followers are gathered to Him at His return, place and time now unknown, that's where they can expect to find Him. He will be gathering His own and rejecting those who are not His.

Like other passages we have examined, this one makes clear that the coming of the Lord will be unexpected and unannounced. It will interrupt the otherwise normal flow of life, and it will separate, in judgment, those who follow Him from those who don't.

A Parable and a Question: Luke 18:1–8

Immediately following the passage just analyzed (Luke 17:22–37), Jesus gives a parable that does not seem to speak about the Second Coming. Nevertheless, at the end of the parable (verse 8), He asks, "When the Son of Man comes, will He really find faith on the earth?" This may indicate that there is something in the parable that relates directly to His return.

The parable may be identified as the parable of the unjust judge (verse 6) or the persistent widow. In the story, there is a judge who "did not fear God nor regard man" (verse 2; compare verse 4). There is also a widow who sought a ruling that would give her justice against her (unidentified) adversary. At first, the judge put her off, but later he relented, apparently because he felt she would keep after him and wear him out with her continual coming. So he saw to it that she got the justice she sought.

Jesus makes application in the form of a question: "Won't God *avenge*—the same word as *get justice for* (verse 3)—His own chosen ones who cry out to Him day and night—for justice, no doubt—even if He does not do so immediately?" "Yes, He will," Jesus answers the question He posed.

That brings us to the obvious lesson of the parable, as expressed in verse 1: people "always ought to pray and not lose heart." The widow illustrated that importunity and Jesus wanted His hearers to know that God would be even more likely than this unjust judge, in time, to answer the prayers of His people for justice. "You can receive justice if you keep on asking," Jesus is saying, in effect, "but it may not come immediately."

That's where the Second Coming is important. Again, Jesus puts it in the form of a question He poses: "When I return, will there still be faith on the earth?" In other words, the fullness of justice for God's people will not come until He comes, and the question is whether His people will still be faithfully calling out to Him until that time. The lesson in verse 1 is still the lesson: we must continue to believe that He will come and that justice will be full and final when He does. We must continue faithfully to place before Him our prayers for that justice, including "Thy kingdom come" and "Even so, come quickly Lord Jesus."

A Special Promise: John 14:1–4

The context for this favorite passage about Jesus' coming is especially tender. Jesus was about to face death, to be followed by His resurrection and departure from this earth. The disciples, who did not understand fully, grasped just enough to know that He was saying He would be leaving them and they could not go with Him now. We can imagine how His response must have become precious to them during the days and years ahead. They are likewise precious to us.

> Let not your heart be troubled; you believe in God, believe also in Me. In My Father's house are many mansions; if it were not so, I would have told you. I go to prepare a place for you. And if I go and prepare a place for you, I will come again and receive you to Myself; that where I am, there you may be also. And where I go you know, and the way you know (John 14:1–4).

While there are not many details about the Second Coming here, the fact of that coming is strong and amounts to an unconditional promise of the Lord Himself.

The promise is firm: "I will come again." Thus we have not just the word of angels (Acts 1:11) or of the apostles (1 Thessalonians 4:13–18, for example) but the word of Him whose word can never fail, the word of Him who orchestrates time and space around Him, Jesus Himself.

One detail is that He goes to prepare a place for us who know Him personally as Savior and Lord. But we know too little about the Father's "house" or the "mansions" (ESV "rooms") that are available there; are they accommodations? It is enough to know that the Father's house is *home*! We can take Jesus' word for this as surely as we take the Word of God the Father who cannot lie (Hebrews 6:18).

The main detail is that when He comes, He will receive us to Himself. The various passages that describe the Second Coming agree on this detail, including those that speak of our gathering to Him and, especially, 1 Thessalonians 4:15–17—likewise grounded in "the word of the Lord (Jesus)"—where Paul teaches that believers, both the transformed living and the resurrected dead, will be caught away to meet the Lord, "And thus we shall always be with the Lord."

In the following verses, Jesus talks about the way to where He was going. Responding to Thomas's question, He assures them that He is the way there. Knowing Him is knowing the Father and having an eternal place in residence with Him and the Father.

Chapter 10

ESCHATOLOGY IN ACTS AND THE EPISTLES I: CONFIRMATION OF THE TEACHING OF JESUS AND THE GOSPELS

The previous chapters focused on eschatology in the teaching of Jesus, as presented in the four Gospels. In Acts and the Epistles, our focus shifts to the apostles, to their ministry (Acts) and to the inspired writings they—and a few others they laid hands on and tutored—handed down to the Church of all ages. In a sense, this represents a second stage in the development of the Christian faith, including its view of the end of the age and beyond. In many ways, what we find here confirms what has already been introduced in the Gospels, but there are helpful additions and clarifications. In this chapter we give our attention, in relatively brief analysis, to things that the apostles confirmed.

The Kingdom of God

Like John the Baptist and Jesus Himself, the apostles preached the kingdom of God, and that included eschatological ("not yet") aspects of the kingdom. During the forty days between Jesus' resurrection and His ascension, He was "speaking of the things pertaining to the kingdom of God" (Acts 1:3) and something in that must have prompted the disciples to ask if He would, at that time, "restore the kingdom to Israel" (Acts 1:6), a question He was not ready to answer.

It is no surprise, then, that when they preached, they preached "the kingdom of God"; this was true for Phillip (Acts 8:12) and Paul (Acts 19:8; 20:25; 28:23, 31)—and others, no doubt. While this expression, left undefined, is obviously broad, enough is said in Acts and the epistles to make clear that some specific future aspects of that kingdom were included in what they taught. Thus, when Paul and Barnabas, toward the end of the first missionary journey, returned along the route they had followed to encourage and strengthen the young convert-disciples, one of the things they said was, "We must through many tribulations enter the kingdom of God" (Acts 14:22).

Paul wrote several times about the "not yet" aspects of the kingdom of God, speaking, for example, about being "counted worthy of the kingdom of God" (2 Thessalonians 1:5). In 2 Timothy 4:1 he charged Timothy, "before God and the Lord Jesus Christ, who will judge the living and the dead at His appearing and His kingdom," apparently linking that kingdom directly to the Second Coming. In describing the "works of the flesh," as opposite to the "fruit of the spirit," he taught that those whose lives were characterized by the former would "not inherit the kingdom of God" (Galatians 5:21; compare Ephesians 5:5).

In the other direction, James speaks positively of those who, despite being poor, have been chosen by God "to be rich in faith and heirs of the kingdom which He promised to those who love Him" (James 2:5). Peter, too, promises—to those who enrich their faith with additional Christian graces and thus make sure their calling and election—an abundant entrance "into the everlasting kingdom of our Lord and Savior Jesus Christ" (2 Peter 1:11).

A Glorious, Awaited Appearing

In the Gospels and teaching of Jesus we have learned that the return of Jesus will be public, visible, bodily, and glorious—among other things—and that we await it with eager anticipation. The preaching and writing of the apostles and their inspired associates confirms all this. From the earliest part of their ministry, immediately following the stunning ascension of their Master, they could bear witness to the promise of two angels. They had witnessed

Jesus rising into the skies with the clouds, and the angels had announced, "This same Jesus, who was taken up from you into heaven, will so come in like manner as you saw Him go into heaven" (Acts 1:11). Some of them had already seen Him in that second-coming glory at His transfiguration, and Simon Peter was quick to inform his readers that it was by virtue of that vision that as an eyewitness he could assure them of Jesus' glorious "power and coming" yet to transpire (2 Peter 1:16–17).

So the apostles easily picture their Christian readers as eagerly awaiting Jesus' return. Thus Paul represents the Corinthians as "eagerly waiting for the revelation of our Lord Jesus Christ" (1 Corinthians 1:7). Similarly, to another church he said: "For our citizenship is in heaven, from which we also eagerly wait for the Savior, the Lord Jesus Christ" (Philippians 3:20). Even the Holy Supper bears silent witness: "As often as you eat this bread and drink this cup, you proclaim the Lord's death till He comes" (1 Corinthians 11:26). What Paul said to Titus was no doubt characteristic of his teaching for all saints: "For the grace of God that brings salvation has appeared to all men, teaching us that, denying ungodliness and worldly lusts, we should live soberly, righteously, and godly in the present age, looking for the blessed hope and glorious appearing of our great God and Savior Jesus Christ" (Titus 2:11–13).

The writer of Hebrews offers insight into the difference between Jesus' first and second comings: with regard to the first, He "was offered once to bear the sins of many," but in regard to the second, "To those who eagerly wait for Him He will appear a second time, apart from sin, for salvation" (Hebrews 9:28). Peter, likewise contrasting Jesus' prior coming in humiliation to His glorification when He returns, exhorts, "Rejoice to the extent that you partake of Christ's sufferings, that when His glory is revealed, you may also be glad with exceeding joy" (1 Peter 4:13).

Resurrection

Just as the apostles' preaching and writing confirmed what Jesus taught about the kingdom of God, so too their witness confirmed His promise to raise the dead—and transform living believers—in connection with His return to this earth. Significantly, the apostle Paul, during what must have been a time of testing when he was on trial before Jewish and Roman authorities, summed up the cause of his bonds as "the hope of the resurrection." He saw that as being at the very heart of biblical faith, both for true Judaism and especially for the Christians known as followers of "the Way." See Acts 23:6, before the Sanhedrin; 24:15, before Felix; 26:6–8, before Festus and Agrippa—echoed again in 28:20 before Jewish leaders in Rome. Specifically, he affirmed "I have hope in God ... that there will be a resurrection of the dead, both of the just and the unjust" (24:15).

The most extensive apostolic teaching about the resurrection of the dead appears, of course, in 1 Corinthians 15. Since that extensive discussion provides some details not included in Jesus' teaching in the Gospels, we will examine it in closer detail in the next chapter. For our purposes here, it is enough to call attention to verses 22–23, where Paul introduces the idea of some "order" in the resurrection: "For as in Adam all die, even so in Christ all shall be made alive. But each one in his own order: Christ the firstfruits, afterward those who are Christ's at His coming." This confirms exactly what Jesus said about His coming and the resurrection of the dead, as we have seen in previous chapters.

It also matches what Paul taught in 1 Thessalonians 4:16: namely, that when the Lord Jesus descends from heaven, "the dead in Christ will rise first." Back to 1 Corinthians 15, then, where Paul also makes clear that the living believers will undergo the same transformation from corruption to incorruption, "changed in a moment, in the twinkling of an eye, at the last trumpet" (verses 51–52). Paul was so sure that the resurrection is in the eschatological future that he denounced any teaching that it has happened already as heresy; see 2 Timothy 2:17–18.

The unidentified writer of Hebrews regarded basic teaching "of resurrection of the dead, and of eternal judgment" as eschatological but foundational doctrines of the faith (Hebrews 6:1–2). Later in his work (11:35), posting his "hall of fame of faith," he extolled some who submitted to death rather than denying their faith, "that they might obtain a better resurrection."

Like Jesus, then, the apostolic preaching promised the resurrection of the dead, both saved and lost, in connection with His second coming. They saw this as essential to and at the heart of their faith.

Judgment

Furthermore, like Jesus in the Gospels, the apostolic teaching confirmed that there will be judgment—again, both of the wicked and of the righteous—when Jesus returns to earth and reigns. Thus Peter, in a straightforward presentation of the gospel to Cornelius, included the fact that God "commanded us to preach to the people, and to testify that it is [Jesus] who was ordained by God to be Judge of the living and the dead" (Acts 10:42). Similarly, Paul's message to Gentiles in Athens included, "[God] has appointed a day on which He will judge the world in righteousness by the Man whom He has ordained" (Acts 17:31).

In Romans 2, Paul discusses "the righteous judgment of God" at length; significantly, he refers to "the day when God will judge the secrets of men by Jesus Christ" (verse 16). Later he observes, pointedly, that "we shall all stand before the judgment seat of Christ" (Romans 14:10; compare 2 Corinthians 5:10). That this is in connection with Jesus' return to earth is clear in 1 Corinthians 4:1–5, where Paul discusses the requirement that those who steward the mysteries of God must be "found faithful": that is, they must be judged. He warns, "Judge nothing before the time, until the Lord comes, who will both bring to light the hidden things of darkness and reveal the counsels of the hearts" (verse 5). Again, Paul links this directly to the Second Coming: "I charge you therefore before God and the Lord Jesus Christ, who will judge the living and the dead at His appearing and His kingdom: (2 Timothy 4:1; compare verse 8).

James speaks of this in a somewhat unique way. First he urges his readers to "be patient … until the coming of the Lord"; then he repeats and urges them: "Establish your hearts, for the coming of the Lord is at hand"; then he exclaims, "Behold, the Judge is standing at the door!" (James 5:7–9). Jude, the brother of James, also stresses this with an approved quotation: "Behold, the Lord comes with ten thousands of His saints, to execute judgment on all" (verses 14–15).

Unquestionably, then, Acts and the apostles confirm that when Jesus comes back He will judge both the wicked and the righteous—whether at the same time or at two separate times. This question of timing isn't the important thing; what matters is that all of us will be thoroughly and accurately judged, and that should have a determining effect on the way we live and serve Him now.

CHAPTER 11

ESCHATOLOGY IN ACTS AND THE EPISTLES II: PASSAGES THAT ADD TO THE TEACHING IN THE GOSPELS

While eschatology in much of Acts and the New Testament epistles closely parallels what we have seen in the four Gospels and the teaching of Jesus, there are passages in Acts and the Epistles that make their own distinct contribution to eschatology. This chapter will focus on such passages, which I have selected for the additional information they provide.

Acts 2:19–20: Peter's Message at Pentecost

The context, here, is the Day of Pentecost. Jesus' disciples, in obedience to Him, have waited in Jerusalem for the promised Holy Spirit to come over them with power. That "baptism" is accompanied by phenomena that can be heard and seen. There is a "rushing mighty wind," with divided tongues of flame resting on each of them. They burst out in other languages, speaking about "the wonderful works of God." The effects are so dramatic that a crowd gathers, and many of the observers can explain what's happening only by surmising that the disciples are intoxicated. Peter stands up and begins to address them.

Peter hastens to make clear that there is no strong drink involved, only a strong imbibing of the Spirit of God. He explains the scene as fulfilling the prophecy of Joel (verse 16), and in doing so he quotes Joel 2:28–32 (verses 17–21). While the passage does not speak directly of the future coming of

Jesus, it does speak specifically of "the last days" (verse 17) and of "the coming of the great and awesome day of the LORD" (verse 20). There is an eschatological focus in the passage then, and surely the coming of the day of the Lord corresponds in significant ways with the return of Jesus to the earth.

The first part of Joel's prophecy, then, clarifies exactly what was happening on that first Christian Pentecost: "This is what was spoken by the prophet Joel," Peter said. Verses 17 and 19, therefore, were fulfilled—at least initially—that very day. In that sense, "the last days" (verse 17) were already under way; we have been in the last days since Jesus ascended to the Father.

But verses 19–20 seem clearly to look to something future, both for them and for us.

> I will show wonders in heaven above
> And signs in the earth beneath:
> Blood and fire and vapor of smoke.
> The sun shall be turned into darkness,
> And the moon into blood,
> Before the coming of the great and awesome day of the LORD.

We could well wish for more information, but no explanation appears in the passage—although Joel adds to what is said. For our purposes, it is enough to say that these portents will go beyond the ordinary course of nature. The turning of the sun into darkness and of the moon into blood will be frightening things, extraordinary signals of divine intervention and the approach of God's wrathful outpouring of judgment as immediately preceding—or introducing—"the day of the LORD" that begins, in its most proper fullness, with the revelation of Jesus Christ.

Interestingly, in the book of Revelation, when the sixth seal (of the scroll with seven seals) is broken, we read: "I looked when He opened the sixth seal, and behold, there was a great earthquake; and the sun became black as sackcloth of hair, and the moon became like blood" (Revelation 6:12). Without taking time to analyze Revelation here (see Chapters 12–15 that explore that part of the New Testament), I would suggest that Revelation and Joel were speaking of the same phenomena. For now, we should consider that the unnatural darkening of the sun and turning of the moon blood-red will take place at some point not long before, or at the beginning of, the day of the Lord and the return of Jesus.

We can say, then, that we are already in "the last days," but the last of the last days awaits, and dreadful signs in the skies and on earth may serve to signal the approach of the critical event(s).

What this passage adds to our knowledge of eschatology is that there will be signs in nature, especially the light-bearers in the day and night sky, that will arouse great fear. They will probably be almost immediately followed by the second coming of Jesus.

1 Thessalonians 4:13–18: Meeting the Coming Lord

Paul's two letters to the church at Thessalonica were probably his earliest inspired writing.[10] As a group, these two are sometimes referred to as Paul's eschatological epistles; they seem characterized, as a whole, by Paul's anticipation of the Second Coming and the end of the age. Some mentions are more or less "passing" references, as in 1 Thessalonians 2:19; 3:13; and 5:23–24. Reading these will convince one that Paul saw the coming of Jesus as the critical event for which he labored and in terms of which he measured his hope for those he ministered to.

There must have been some question (or questions) among the believers in that city as to the meaning of what Paul had taught them when he was there just months before he wrote. Both epistles show that there was some background to the key passages that add considerable information to what we have learned about eschatology from the teaching of Jesus in the Gospels. Probably in the background of 1 Thessalonians 4:13–18 was some uneasiness caused by the death of some of the believers; perhaps they wrongly thought that all believers would live to see Jesus return to earth in person. At any rate, a concern for the Christian dead drives Paul's message in this favorite passage. We may analyze the whole into a number of propositions.

(1) Jesus will descend from heaven (verse 16), accompanied by a shout of command to the dead to come forth, an archangel's cry, and the blowing of the trumpet of God (verse 16a).

(2) Deceased followers of Jesus ("the dead in Christ") will rise from the dead, in response to the signals (verse 16b). These are they who "have fallen asleep" (verse 13), who "sleep in (or through) Jesus" (verse 14), who "are asleep" (verse 15). Perhaps the point of the phrase "sleep in/by/through Jesus" is that for Christians, as a result of the work of Christ in them, death is but a sleep. Their bodies, restored to life, will be reunited with their spirits that have come with Jesus (verse 14).

(3) Living followers of Jesus ("we who are alive and remain") will be "caught up" together with those raised from the dead to "meet the Lord in the air" (verse 17). In the Latin translation, the verb "caught up" is the source of the English word *rapture*, often used to identify this event. It suggests a forceful "snatching away."

(4) From then on, Paul and those for whom he speaks ("we") will forever be with the Lord Jesus. This teaching does away with any ignorance (verse 13) about the subject of what happens to the dead in Christ in relationship to living believers. Neither will have any advantage over the other, and the passage is a source of comfort (verse 18).

Even so, while the added information is clear and helpful, many questions are left unraised and unanswered. For one thing, Paul addresses only the implications of Jesus' second coming for believers; he says nothing here about unbelievers.

For another, he gives no information indicating that the catching up of the saved to meet the Lord in the air or sky will be at a different time from His descent to the earth. Indeed, the most natural way to take verse 17 is that those caught up will go out to meet the Lord *on His way down*. The word translated *coming* (verse 15, Greek *parousia*) was often used in New Testament times for the visit of a prominent person like a government dignitary or even a member of the royal family. It was customary to arrange for official representatives to go out to meet the special visitor and accompany him into the city. There seems no good reason to divide the Second Coming into two events rather than one; I will provide more explanation in the extended note at the end of this chapter.

This passage adds to the information we have gained in the Gospels: namely, the meeting in the air and the relationship between the dead in Christ and living believers at the time. That the latter are transformed into incorruptible existence—as much so as those raised from the dead—is stated again by Paul in 1 Corinthians 15:51–52.

1 Thessalonians 5:1–11: A Thief in the Night

Immediately after the passage just discussed Paul in effect continues his treatment of the Second Coming in practical terms, emphasizing the importance of being ready for Jesus' return at all times. Here are the major points he makes.

(1) As for the "times and seasons" of the Lord's return, there is no information to be given (verses 1–2). No time has been scheduled or announced. He will come "as a thief in the night." The *thief* comparison was first used by Jesus Himself (Matthew 24:42–44), apparently picked up from Him by the apostles (see 2 Peter 3:10; compare Revelation 16:15)—always in connection with the Second Coming.

(2) Prepared believers, however, do not need to be caught off guard, and so Jesus' return to earth need not come on them "as a thief" who catches people by surprise (verses 4–6). Followers of Jesus can be prepared and ready, expecting Him. This need not mean that they can "read the signs" so as to know that His coming is immediately at hand; the emphasis is more on being spiritually aware and ready all the time (verse 8). Whether this allows for the possibility that informed Christians may be aware of some of the things that lead up to Jesus' coming, as discussed in an earlier chapter, is not clear. Even so, that possibility seems likely; even in that case, such believers will not be able to determine exactly when the Lord will return. The more important biblical truth is that we can always be ready.

This passage does not add specific information to our eschatological catalog, but it provides an important motivation for spiritual watching and waiting.

2 Thessalonians 1:3–10: Blessing and Destruction

This second letter to the church at Thessalonica was apparently written some months after the first. Questions about the Second Coming were still being asked; apparently some were saying the day of the Lord had already come and gone (2:1–2). At any rate, the believers were experiencing serious hostility and persecution at the hands of wicked Christ-rejecters. As in 1 Thessalonians, Paul devotes two passages to the matter, and this first one represents the way he encourages those being troubled because of their faith. What Paul teaches can be summarized in three main emphases.

(1) Jesus is going to come—to be revealed, that is—"with His mighty angels" (verse 7) and will be God's instrument to mete out justice both to the persecuted believers and to the hostile unbelievers persecuting them.

(2) To those being persecuted He will provide *rest* (Greek *anesis*—release, relief, refreshment; verse 7). Furthermore, Jesus will be glorified when He returns, and there is a sense in which He, as the deserving object of their marveling admiration (verse 10), will "be glorified in His saints." Paul says no more about this tantalizing promise, but it is clear in Scripture that all those who have walked with the Lord in faith will in some way participate joyfully in His glorification (see Jesus' high-priestly prayer in John 17:22–24; compare Romans 8:17–19).

(3) On the other side of the justice equation, Jesus will mete out exquisite justice: trouble or tribulation (Greek *thlipsis*) to those who have caused trouble or tribulation for believers (verse 6). Paul spends more time developing this side of things in verses 8–9. These trouble-givers are characterized as people who "do not obey the gospel of our Lord Jesus Christ": in other words, they have actively rejected the gospel. In connection with His return, Jesus will punish them with "everlasting destruction," final banishment from the presence and power of the Lord Himself. As verse 8 makes clear, matching

so many other things we have read in connection with the Lord's judgment, this punishment will be in "flaming fire." That it will be an expression of "vengeance" means that it will be God's retributive justice, punishment that fits the crime, for their rejection of God's grace and hostility toward Christ-followers.

As has been noted in Chapter 5, some of Jesus' teaching in the Gospels speaks with one voice about judgment of the wicked and of the righteous. This passage allows for that same possibility. Even so, it does not require that the rest promised to the righteous and the fire promised to the unrighteous must be assigned at the very same judgment-scene. Both will be the judgment administration of Jesus Christ when He returns as King and Judge. As I have noted, I am inclined to the view that he will judge the righteous immediately upon His return and the wicked at the end of His reign. Meanwhile, Paul wanted the Thessalonians, and us, to know that both would be part of the judgment adjudicated by the Lord who returns in glory as King. That is the most important thing to know.

2 Thessalonians 2:1–12: What Must Come First

In Chapter 3, under the heading of "The Man of Sin," I dealt with this passage in detail; the reader should review that section for its fuller treatment. I include it again here, for brief review, as one of the main apostolic passages that adds significant information to what we have learned about eschatology in the Gospels and teaching of Jesus.

In summary, then, here are the things Paul wrote in this passage.

(1) The Lord's return had not happened yet, even though there was apparently someone (more than one?) who was saying this (verses 1–2).

(2) Two things had to happen before the Lord's return: a great falling or turning away from God (ESV "rebellion"), and the revelation of "the man of sin" (verse 3)—perhaps a person manifesting the full development of "the spirit of the Antichrist" (1 John 4:3).

(3) Paul describes at length this mysterious figure (verses 4–12); see the detailed listing in Chapter 3. Though presently restrained, directly or indirectly in accord with the will of God, he will in time be fully revealed and will

be in hostile opposition to God and the Lord Jesus, attempting to usurp the very rule of God in the world. He will do supernatural things in the power of Satan himself, impressing people to worship him. This figure may well be the "beast" described in Revelation 13:1–10.

(4) At His coming, the Lord Jesus will destroy him by the power of His word ("the breath of His mouth," verse 8).

(5) The deception caused by the Antichrist, apparently during a period shortly before the return of Christ, will be a form of divine judgment on those who have already rejected the truth (verses 9–12).

This passage provides information about eschatology that adds to what Jesus Himself made known in the Gospels. Indeed, it is almost unique in the New Testament. We learn (as has been discussed in Chapter 3) that a great turning away from God and the appearance of a "man of sin" will lead up to the Second Coming. It is possible that Revelation provides information that parallels and amplifies this, as we will see in subsequent chapters.

Romans 11:22–32: "All Israel Will Be Saved"

Paul's letter to the Romans is a masterpiece of Christian teaching, sometimes difficult to expound. Chapters 9–11 pursue a special subject, of interest to Paul and to us alike, answering questions: What has happened to Israel? Why? What, if anything, does the future hold for the Jews? Has God cast them aside? For good? Has the Christian Church replaced Israel in the economy of God?

Paul answers some of these and other questions in these three chapters. He shows, for example, that God has *not* cast away His people (11:1), given that even now, when the Christian church is composed mostly of Gentiles, "there is a remnant according to the election of grace" (11:5). Indeed, God has subjected them to a stumbling block and used that to provoke Gentiles to seek His grace (11:8–11).

Already, Paul begins to hint, at least, that this may yet lead to the turning of Israel back to God. Perhaps they, in turn, will be provoked to jealousy by the salvation of the Gentiles; even now that is true for some (11:14). The discussion (touched on all too briefly here) leads him on to wonder aloud: If Israel's stumbling has led to such blessing for the Gentiles, how much more would their acceptance? (11:15). If the "branches" of the tree of God's people were broken off so that Gentiles might be "grafted" in, is it possible that those branches might yet be grafted back in? (11:19–23).

It is possible that all this speaks only of the possibility that individual Jews might become believers in Jesus and recipients of God's grace, of course. But, especially in 11:22–32, the passage begins to look more seriously at a possible future. Verse 24, for example, seems to express this as a reality: "How much more will these, who are natural branches, be grafted into their own olive tree?"

Then Paul gives some explanation. "Blindness in part has happened to Israel until the fullness of the Gentiles has come in" (11:25)—apparently implying that there will be a future for ethnic Israel after that "fullness" has been reached. Indeed, "all Israel will be saved" (11:26), and the words of the old prophet Isaiah will be fulfilled: "He will turn away ungodliness from Jacob"; He will "take away their sins" (11:26–27). Though they are in the role of "enemies" now, for the sake of the gospel and the Gentiles, yet for the sake of the fathers there is still an election of Israel that does not finally fail (11:28–29). Though the Israelites are now in disobedience, they may yet obtain God's mercy (11:30–32).

This is a tantalizing passage. By itself, perhaps, it may not settle the question whether there is an eschatological future for ethnic Israelites, as a people, among the people of God. It is possible, with many interpreters, to spiritualize "all Israel" into an "Israel of God" (Galatians 6:16) that includes the Gentile church of this age as a replacement for ancient, ethnic Israel. But it is also possible that "all Israel" refers to ethnic Israel and that their present displacement by a Gentile church will yet be turned into a blessing for them. I will have more to say about this in Chapter 16, which focuses on the Old Testament.

Meanwhile, this passage introduces us to the question, at least, whether the coming of Christ will open a new chapter in the history of Israel as God's chosen ones in the messianic kingdom. Whether yes or no, Paul does not reveal just how or if the Second Coming fits into what he is saying.

1 Corinthians 15:20–28: Each in His Own Order

The fifteenth chapter of 1 Corinthians has a special place in the Scriptures as "the resurrection chapter." Apparently some in Corinth were questioning the idea of the resurrection of the dead (verse 12), and Paul destroys that heresy with inspired and detailed instruction. In verses 20–28 he pursues a line of thought that has implications for eschatology that go well beyond the doctrine of resurrection. I suspect that this is a neglected eschatological passage; regardless, its teaching deserves close attention. Here are the key points Paul makes.

(1) All will live again, but there will be an order to it. Christ's resurrection was first and guarantees the resurrection of others (verses 20–23).

(2) The next step in the order, after the resurrection of Christ Himself, is: "afterward those who are Christ's at His coming" (verse 23). As will be noted below, this says nothing about the resurrection of the unjust at the same time.

(3) The next step in the order of things is: "Then comes the end, when He delivers the kingdom to God the Father, when He puts an end to all rule and all authority and power" (verse 24). This adds significantly to what Paul taught in 1 Thessalonians 4:13–18. It tends to imply that there will be a "kingdom" for Jesus to rule over following His return to earth and that, as one development of that rule, He will put down, for good and for eternity, all competitors who claim the authority that rightly belongs to God.

Verse 25 expands on this by stating, simply, that Jesus "must reign till He has put all enemies under His feet." Verse 26 identifies one enemy of great significance, death, which will be the last enemy destroyed. Then verse 27a brings forth a scriptural basis for this, a reference to Psalm 8:6: God has "put all things"—everything except God Himself, of course (verse 27b)—under His feet": that is, in submission to Him, under His dominion. In Psalm 8, "under his feet" means under mankind's feet, but this is especially and representatively fulfilled in the person of the Messiah. (More about this to follow.)

(4) The final step in the order coincides with "the end," as described in the preceding point: "Now when all things are made subject to Him, then the Son Himself will also be subject to Him who put all things under Him, that God may be all in all" (verse 28). Perhaps what Paul says can appropriately be said only of Jesus Christ as both divine and *human*; in that case it is the incarnate God-*man*, Jesus Christ, who is finally and eternally "subject" to God the Father. (If Paul means that the eternal *Logos*, the second person of the Godhead, will be made "subject" to God the Father, then some of the implications of this may be beyond our ability to explain in the terms of typical, Trinitarian theology. That can be explored at another time.)

Perhaps Paul gives little attention to developing the several elements of this order because he is focusing his attention on the doctrine of resurrection. Regardless, there are some things we can say about the key elements here. For example, regarding the resurrection of believers in (2), as already noted, Paul says nothing about the resurrection of unbelievers, closely matching his treatment of the subject in 1 Thessalonians 4:13–18; see earlier in this chapter. Here in 1 Corinthians 15, Paul will add a note to expand on this: "I tell you a mystery: We shall not all sleep, but we shall all be changed—in a moment, in the twinkling of an eye, at the last trumpet. For the trumpet will sound, and the dead will be raised incorruptible, and we shall be changed" (verses 51–52). In short, that transformation will be a part of the resurrection.

That Paul deals, both in 1 Thessalonians 4 and in 1 Corinthians 15, with the resurrection of the righteous only may be a good enough reason for separating the resurrection (and judgment) of the saved from the resurrection (and judgment) of the lost. The passage here in 1 Corinthians may perhaps be especially helpful in that regard, given that Paul is actually discussing the *order* of things. If this is the case, then the resurrection and judgment of the lost will occur in connection with (3), "the end," when Jesus delivers His kingdom into the hands of the Father, perhaps as the final act of His messianic reign on earth.

It should not be overlooked that Paul opens the door, here, to a kingdom over which Jesus reigns following His *parousia*. This separates "the end" from the resurrection of those who are Christ's at His coming (verses 23–24)—which seems to be the most natural reading of the passage.

There is a prominent biblical background to the idea found in verses 25–27, with its promise that all things will be put under Jesus' feet. I will give this only brief, summary attention. First, from the beginning of God's creation of human beings, He gave mankind *dominion* over that creation; see Genesis 1:28 in its context. This is what David was reflecting on when he composed Psalm 8 (which Paul quotes here). David asked, rhetorically, "What is man? You have made him a little lower than the angels. You have made him to have dominion over the works of Your hands; You have put all things under his feet" (from verses 3–8).

This is not the end of it. Hebrews focuses special attention on this truth, also quoting Psalm 8 (Hebrews 2:6–8a) and making some interesting observations. We do not see this psalm fulfilled yet, he says (verse 8b), but we see Jesus, made a lowly man to suffer and die, now "crowned with glory and honor" (verse 9). In other words, Jesus was made a human being in order that He might bring us to the full measure of our destiny of dominion; in Him now we have that originally intended dominion, and by Him ultimately we will experience that dominion for which we were designed. In fulfilling God's original design for mankind, Jesus was and is the representative man, gaining dominion for us who follow Him. It may be that Philippians 3:21 reflects this same theme in saying—in connection with the coming of the Lord—that He "will transform our lowly body that it may be conformed to His glorious body, according to the working by which He is able even to subdue all things to Himself." There are also reflections of this in Ephesians 1:22 and in Hebrews 10:13, referring to the *present* status of Jesus, seated at the right hand of God.

We learn from 1 Corinthians 15, then, some things we did not see in the teaching of Jesus in the Gospels. There is an order in the resurrection of the dead. It is the Messiah's destiny to reign in order that He, during that reign, may finally conquer all the enemies of God. It may be that we will find some development of this in the book of Revelation.

2 Peter 3:1–13: When the World's on Fire

Paul is not the only inspired writer of New Testament epistles to provide additional information about eschatology. The third chapter of 2 Peter offers a fresh look at the Second Coming and associates with that event a picture of our world in the fires of judgment. Here are the elements of his teaching in this chapter.

(1) We can expect, "in the last days," scoffers who will ridicule the claim that Jesus will return to the earth (verses 1–4). As time goes by without the Savior's return—2 Peter was probably written within a couple of years before or after AD 67—doubts naturally arise and some conclude that the Second Coming is a myth. Peter says they are willfully ignoring some important biblical history: namely, that after thousands of years the world perished once before, under the judgment of God, in Noah's flood. While the Lord said then that He would not destroy the world by water again, He did promise a judgment by fire (verses 5–7). It's interesting that this passage makes a strong contrast between "the then world" and "the now world," thus opening the door for the present world to be destroyed and replaced by yet another to come.

(2) The passing of time has meaning for humans but is not an indicator of what God may or may not be doing. "With the Lord one day is as a thousand years, and a thousand years as one day" (verse 8).

(3) What appears to human beings to be a "delay" in the return of Christ is not really a delay at all; God is allowing time for people to come to repentance; He desires that all take advantage of this opportunity (verse 9).

(4) "The day of the Lord" will certainly come, but unannounced "as a thief in the night" (verse 10a).

(5) When that day comes, there will be a great conflagration (verses 10b-12). The description of this is vivid and compelling: the very elements (perhaps the atomic elements?) melting (stated twice), the heavens dissolving or melting, and all the "works" in the earth being consumed in the flames. These works apparently include all the things human beings have built or other-

wise produced. It would seem that nothing we have achieved will be left; only "treasures in Heaven" will survive (Matthew 6:20).

(4) The present heavens (skies) and earth, being devoured by fire, will be replaced by "new heavens and a new earth" (verse 13). Revelation 21:1 confirms this. Hebrews seems to know about this, quoting Psalm 102:25–27 to say that the heavens, which are the work of God's hands, "will perish," will "grow old like a garment," and "will be changed" (Hebrews 1:11–12). Later we read that the Lord says, "Yet once more I shake not only the earth, but also heaven"—explained by the writer to indicate "the removal of those things that are being shaken, as of things that are made, that the things which cannot be shaken may remain" (Hebrews 12:26–28).

This is an element of eschatology that Peter adds to what we have gleaned from the teaching of Jesus in the Gospels. But Peter does not say just when this conflagration will occur, only that it will be an event that is in "the day of God" (verse 12). I will return to this question after exploring the eschatology of Revelation. For now, I observe that if there is a reign of Christ on earth following His return, this conflagration seems more fitted for the end of that reign than for the beginning. Indeed, that is where Revelation appears to place it. The fire that burns and purges the world would make sense as part of the judgment that falls when Jesus is putting down all enemies on earth, sealing the kingdom for Himself and preparing to turn it over to the Father forever—as we have seen in the analysis of 1 Corinthians 15 above.

The basic elements and implications of the second coming of Jesus are clear enough. But before final conclusions can be drawn, it is necessary to explore the eschatology of the book of Revelation. We will transition to that difficult venture after an extended note.

Extended Note: Will the Second Coming Have Two Phases?

I have referred to the fact that some interpreters divide the second coming of Jesus into two parts: namely, the "rapture" when the saints meet Jesus in the air and the actual coming of Jesus to earth. These two events are separated, they say, by a period of either seven years or half that long.[11] This is the traditional and widespread dispensational view of the Second Coming, and in this view the period between the two phases is specifically identified as "The Tribulation" or "The Great Tribulation."[12]

I have no desire to go into this matter at length, but I do want to make some observations as to why I do not affirm this division. I am reasonably satisfied that all "second-coming" events occur at the same time, at the end of the age. One reason for my saying this is, simply, that I do not find warrant for dividing the Second Coming in the biblical references to the return of Jesus to earth. Even many who are dispensationalists acknowledge that there is no room for a separate rapture in the Olivet Discourse, for example; and some of these will reluctantly agree that the book of Revelation does not seem to provide information about a separate rapture. This is a major consideration against dividing the Second Coming into two separate phases. It seems to me that any reasons given for this division go beyond the text of Scripture.

My second consideration is one I have already mentioned: namely, that the most natural way to take 1 Thessalonians 4:13–18 is that those who are caught up to meet the Lord in the air are simply going out *to meet Him on His way in*. The word *parousia* (*coming, presence*) was often used by the Greeks to refer to the visit of a dignitary or a member of royalty. There would be a welcoming committee of VIPs who would go out to meet the person and his entourage, escorting him back into the city. This passage, therefore, has nothing that needs dividing into two parts.

One of the claims of dispensationalists, in support of dividing the Second Coming, is that the primary word *coming* (Greek *parousia*) refers to the *rapture*, they say, while other words like *revelation* (Greek *apokalupsis*) and *appearing* (Greek *epiphaneia*), refer to the second phase at the return of Jesus to earth to reign. A careful analysis of all the passages where these words occur, in my judgment, shows that such a division will not hold up. This is another consideration that is important to me, and I will spend a few paragraphs providing the evidence without taking time for detailed comments.

All three of the words just identified are used in the New Testament to refer to the Second Coming. (1) The word *parousia*, which means *a coming* or *presence*, is used for the return of Jesus about a dozen times in the New Testament, consistently translated *coming:* Matthew 24:3; 1 Corinthians 15:23; 1 Thessalonians 2:19; 3:13; 4:15; 5:23; 2 Thessalonians 2:1, 8; James 5:7–8; 2 Peter 1:16; 3:4; and 1 John 2:28. Comparing 2 Thessalonians 1:7 and 2:8 sheds light on this. If there are two phases in Jesus' second coming, both of these passages are describing things associated with the second phase, but while 1:7 uses *revelation* (*apokalupsis*), 2:8 uses *coming* (*parousia*).

(2) The noun *apokalupsis* (revelation) appears five times in the New Testament in reference to the return of Jesus: 1 Corinthians 1:7; 2 Thessalonians 1:7; 1 Peter 1:7, 13; and 4:13. To these we can add Luke 17:30 where the verb *reveal* is used instead of the noun. On any reading of these passages, it will not work to think the "revelation" refers to a second phase of Jesus' coming, as distinguished from an earlier phase. The verses tell us that readers are waiting for and ordering their lives in preparation for the *revelation* (not the *parousia*) of Jesus. Luke 17:30 certainly uses the verb *revealed* to refer to rapture events (if the coming is divided) when two will be in one bed or grinding grain and one will be taken and the other left behind.

(3) The noun *epiphaneia* (appearing) refers to the Second Coming five times: 2 Thessalonians 2:8; 1 Timothy 6:14; 2 Timothy 4:1, 8; and Titus 2:13. Paul promises that the Lord will destroy "the man of sin" (literally) "by the appearance (*epiphaneia*) of his coming (*parousia*)"(ESV)—which serves to equate the two words. All of these speak of motivation for living now in the light of Christ's return, which is appropriate only for the rapture if it is separated from the revelation. Furthermore, in the first of these and the last of these, the *epiphaneia* is actually equated to the *parousia* and "the blessed hope."

Interestingly, 2 Thessalonians uses all three words, and all refer to what dispensationalists would include in the category of revelation events. I regard the conclusion as inescapable: the terms cannot be used to distinguish the Second Coming into two events or phases. This does not prove that there will be just one phase, of course, but it leaves the possibility of two phases to be determined on grounds other than the vocabulary. I do not find convincing support for that view, and I do not think Christians, in general, need to think in those terms.

Endnotes

[10] Some interpreters of Paul believe that Galatians was written first.

[11] Those who say seven years affirm a "pre-tribulation" rapture; those who say half that long affirm a "mid-tribulation" rapture. Yet others, who do not divide the Secomd Coming into two phases; affirm a "post-tribulation" rapture, where *post* means *after*.

[12] Some regard the whole seven years as the tribulation, with the last half being the great tribulation.

Chapter 12

ESCHATOLOGY IN REVELATION I: ISSUES IN INTERPRETATION

The interpretation of Revelation is fraught with many difficulties—an understatement of significant magnitude! From one perspective, it may be hopeless to attempt to arrive at a confident reading of the book; at least the morass of diverse readings among Bible-believing interpreters could lead one to despair. Even so, Revelation is part of the inspired Word of God, and we must pay it the respect of trying to understand it. Furthermore, Revelation 1:3 pronounces a blessing on those who read and heed what is written in the book. We ought, therefore, to give it committed attention.

The space of a few chapters will not allow this section to be a full commentary on Revelation. For the purposes of this work, the question is whether Revelation teaches us anything about eschatology—the end of the age—and, if so, what. The purpose of this chapter is to introduce some major issues that are involved in attempting to answer that question. In other words, what are the main issues involved in interpreting this mysterious book?

Revelation as Apocalyptic Literature Using Imagery and Symbols

Here is the first thing we must come to grips with: much of Revelation comes to us in the form of "apocalyptic imagery." This is especially true for the visions in chapters 4–20. Chapters 1–3 and 21–22 are more straightforward, which is not to say that there is no imagery in them at all. But the hardest part of this book is found in the visions in chapters 4–20.

The word *apocalyptic* is originally Greek and means something like "unveiling, revelatory." (In Greek, the book of Revelation is *The Apocalypse.*) When I say that much of Revelation is imagery, I mean that John sees and records visions that are symbolic. Revelation is not the only biblical book that contains such apocalyptic imagery; consider the Old Testament book of Daniel, where—as in Revelation—there are visions of animals with horns, symbolizing or representing the future course of major nations yet to arise. Or consider Zechariah, where much of the first half of the book consists of a series of visions with imagery similar to that of Revelation.

Revelation is that kind of literature; instead of real-world things, John sees "beasts" and other strange—or not so strange—things that *represent* real things. That fact presents a problem for the interpreter, since a given image might easily be interpreted in more than one way. A certain symbol might represent one thing or another. That's what makes Revelation so hard; different interpreters suggest different meanings for almost any given symbol or image in the visions. Indeed, different interpreters not only suggest different meanings for given symbols, they suggest different approaches to the very task of interpreting the book.

Consequently, the reader of Revelation has to keep in mind that what John sees in visions usually *represents* reality rather than being reality itself. It's easy to take something symbolic and view it as reality, a dangerous mistake made even more possible since the visionary scenes in Revelation often get very close to the reality they symbolize. For example, in chapter 5 John sees a *Lamb*, and he describes it thus: "as though it had been slain" (verse 6). Every reader will take this Lamb to be Jesus, and describing the Lamb in the vision as having been slain is so close to the actual reality that this identification is easy and obvious. No problem with that, of course. Even so, readers must discipline themselves to keep in mind that the imagery of the visions is imagery and only *represents* reality. Thus, in chapter 9 there is a horde of what we might call "infernal horsemen." It is not necessary to take this to mean actual horsemen—although some interpreters do. More likely, they *represent* things other than horsemen, and it becomes our task to decide what they represent—*if we can*!

When reading the visions, then, one must ask, What does this refer to? The answer is not always obvious. This is a complex matter. A danger at one end of the interpretive spectrum is to take the symbols as the reality, but at the other end the danger lies in reading *everything* as symbolic. This is such an important matter that I must expand the discussion.

On the one hand, then, one must not confuse symbols with reality, and it is all too easy to fall into the trap of doing this. Symbols represent things in the real world, but the symbols themselves are not in the real world. Thus, for example, the pale horse (6:8) represents death, as the text itself indicates, but there is no real-world pale horse riding forth for people to observe. In chapter 9 John sees a horde of "locusts" whose tails can sting like scorpions, who cause pain to, but do not kill, people who do not have God's "seal" or stamp on them. Does this mean that God-fearing people will have a literal number or name stamped (tattooed?) on them, and that literal, locust-like creatures with biting tails will torment those who do not have this seal? Not necessarily. The vision certainly means something important, but what? Could this represent some sort of plague, like the bubonic plague or a mutated coronavirus? Perhaps. Or could it represent something even less physical, like dangerous false doctrine that infects the world and turns people away from God? Perhaps. That's the sort of difficulty the interpreter faces.

On the other hand, there is the opposite danger of *over* symbolizing. Often in Revelation a particular scene is a mixture of symbol and reality. In chapter 5, for example, John sees God sitting on a throne, holding a scroll with seven seals or ties. Then a Lamb appears and prevails or qualifies to open the scroll. When the Lamb takes the scroll from the hand of God, "elders" sing a song of His worthiness (verses 9–10). The scroll, of course, represents something in the real world, though not necessarily a physical object. The slain Lamb, standing, represents the Lord Jesus, crucified and risen—an apt symbol, given that Jesus is the Lamb of God, fulfilling the typology of the sacrifice of lambs in the Mosaic system (see John 1:29). God on the throne, however, isn't representing anything other than God on His throne, and the worthiness of Jesus, which the elders celebrate in song, is real-world worthiness. Indeed, in Revelation, it becomes so common to refer to Jesus as "the

Lamb" that the symbol is no longer in the consciousness of users or readers. It's not always easy to tell the difference between symbol and reality; one must be careful and discerning.

Add to this the fact that many of the scenes are dramatic, and some of the elements of the visions are like "window-dressing" that magnifies the persons or actions, sharpening the focus of attention on the main elements of the vision. Thus one has to distinguish between the primary elements and the secondary ones that are like staging that heightens the sense of drama or tension and grabs the viewer-reader's attention. Back to the scene in chapter 5, where John hears a voice asking, "Who is worthy to open the scroll?" John himself plays a role in the scene, weeping and lamenting that no one is found worthy. Then comes the reassuring word, "The Lion of the tribe of Judah, the Root of David, has prevailed to open the scroll." I see no good reason to think this very thing has happened or will happen in God's Heaven. It is action that heightens the redemptive drama being portrayed. At the same time, phrases like "the Lion of the tribe of Judah" and "the Root of David" are so pervasively biblical that they are not mere symbols at all; they provide specific identification.

This introduces yet another feature of the scenes in Revelation; namely, sometimes the things depicted in the imagery or symbols *get so close to the reality being depicted that the reality shines through the images and rules out taking what is said as imagery alone.* This is a natural tendency when using imagery of any sort. When people use the symbolism of dramatic visions to represent given truths, they often allow the things symbolized to get so near the surface of what is said that the real-world people and events themselves appear on the stage. This means that not only must we evaluate how convincingly a given interpretation fits a symbol, we must also distinguish between when the descriptive language is *only* symbolic and when it moves from the symbol to what it represents in the real world.

This sort of thing also happens in *analogies* or *parables*, which represent or illustrate truths rather than stating those truths directly. Consider 1 Corinthians 12, for example. Paul is dealing with the variety of gifts in the church and uses an analogy (or extended metaphor) to say, in summary, that a person's physical body has many parts ("members"), with different functions, but all work together in harmony to contribute to the well-being and successful activity of the one person. Thus, every word in verses 14–26 is part of the analogy and refers to the physical parts of any ordinary human body. Every word is symbol in that sense. Yet there are times in those verses when the real-world point of the analogy gets so close to the surface that it shines through and the reader automatically reads Paul to speak the lesson rather than the mere analogy he is using. This tendency is especially likely as Paul draws near the end of this passage before he himself switches over from the analogy to draw the real-world lesson he intends. Thus, in verse 25, when he says, "there should be no schism in the body," he is still talking about a person's physical body; even so, we know he is also talking about the Church as the body of Christ. In verse 26, he means that when one part of one's physical body hurts, all the rest of the person's body suffers with it; and yet the real-world lesson is so close to the surface that we know he means for us to apply this to our lives together in the church.

Similarly, parables are symbolic stories from ordinary life that are used, as a whole, to communicate spiritual truths. This is the reason experienced interpreters warn us not to read too much into parables. Most of the time, the story as a whole conveys one basic lesson. (But not always! Sometimes there are details that add levels to the application.) Regardless, there are times when the teller of a parable, intentionally or not, allows the real-world lesson to get so close to the surface that it shines through clearly. Consider Luke 20:9–16, for example, in the parable of the vinedressers and the son. By the time Jesus gets to the owner's sending his *son*, who is killed, the underlying lesson has gotten so close to the surface that anybody with any discernment at all knows He is speaking of Himself and His hearers. Especially in verse 16, then, the point is obvious: "He [the lord of the vineyard] will come and destroy those vinedressers and give the vineyard to others." The text says his hearers perceived that "He had spoken the parable against them" (verse 19). They were right.

The parable of the rich fool (Luke 12) might be an even better example. Verses 20–21 are actually part of the parable: "God said to him, 'Fool! This night your soul will be required of you; then whose will those things be which you have provided?' So is he who lays up treasure for himself, and is not rich toward God." The real-world application or lesson is so close to the surface that it becomes the obvious lesson.

I have pursued this at length to make sure that what I am saying is clear. Apocalyptic visions may not be in every respect like parables or analogies, but they share this much in common: in the visions of Revelation it is often difficult to discern just where the symbol grows thin and the real-world lesson is so close to the surface that it shines through, loud and clear. This sometimes adds to the difficulty of interpreting the symbolism of Revelation.

Let me illustrate with an example from Revelation, observing also that this phenomenon is much more prevalent than an example or two will show. Consider, again, Revelation 9:1–12, where, when the fifth trumpet-judgment falls, John sees what are sometimes called "infernal locusts." Think of the passage as a video clip that we watch with John. The question is whether *everything* here is symbol—apocalyptic imagery—like a bad dream from which we awaken to wonder what in the world it meant. We watch this clip and say, "OK, here's a video. In it there are these weird-looking locusts and they come flying out of a great bottomless hole through dense smoke. They sting people and cause them great pain, so much that the people wish they could die. Some people have a mark of protection, but those who don't have this protection get stung and suffer the pain. It's weird.[13] Now that we've seen this video, what does it mean?"

That, in essence, is what we must do. Even so, there are places in this passage where the real-world meaning is so close to the surface that the narrative is actually about the real world—which means that some of the "video" is self-explanatory, while the symbolic imagery as a whole is not. We begin to see the real world when we learn that it is *human beings* who are affected by whatever this is; *they* aren't mere symbols. Furthermore, I dare say that in verse 6 the real-world meaning is so close to the surface that it shines through clearly: the *people* who are thus plagued will suffer so much that they will (even if expressed in exaggerated form) "wish they were dead." Whatever this "plague" is, human beings suffer intensely—even if the "suffering" is more mental or emotional than physical, and that's not for sure. At any rate, surely the people and their suffering aren't merely symbols.

I don't think I need to explain this more. What I'm saying is that for many of the instances of apocalyptic imagery in Revelation, one can find references, in with the symbolism, to the real-world persons and events they stand for—not so as to solve the riddles of the symbols, necessarily, but to give a glimpse into their implications. Unless one is aware of this tendency in apocalyptic imagery, he may find himself asking, in reference to this plague of locusts, for example, "What does their inflicting pain on people symbolize?" Actually, whatever the locusts symbolize, they are inflicting pain (whether physical or otherwise) on human beings who are not identified as followers of Christ. That much isn't mere symbol.

In other words, in the various visions and images, there are often, if not always, some hints within the dramatic symbolism that speak to the reality involved. Interpreters need to realize this and watch for the cues. Too many interpreters take a glance at the symbolism and then say, "Here's the lesson for us in our circumstances." Lessons, or applications, as important as they are, are not in themselves full interpretations of the original vehicle of communication. The vehicles themselves mean something by what they represent.

One final observation about symbolism. Sometimes we will not, from our vantage point, be able to tell what a given symbol means. Some symbols, especially if they have future reference, may not be understood until the time of their occurrence. Without taking time to pursue this, I would suggest that there are symbols in Old Testament apocalyptic literature that the original readers, and even the prophets themselves, could not have explained what they represented.

The Numbers in Revelation

It follows from the preceding that many, perhaps most, of the numbers in Revelation are likewise part of the symbolism. Perhaps the seven churches really are, or were, seven specific churches in the Roman province of Asia; I am personally inclined to think so. But numbers within an apocalyptic, symbolic vision are often part of the symbolism and are not intended to be taken literally. If a given disaster, for example, affects one-third of the trees of earth (Revelation 8:7)—and *if* one is satisfied that the whole symbolism represents real-world trees!—that need not be taken as precise. A third of anything is a fraction, and a relatively small one at that (less than half, anyway), and this relative size may be all that is meant. (See also 8:8, 10, and 12.)

Likewise, numerical measures of time, when referring to symbols, need not be taken literally but as pointing to relatively short or long periods. If the "infernal locusts" are active for "five months," that may indicate a very short period of time compared to other amounts of time. In the later chapters of Revelation there are several references to a period of three-and-a-half years (also represented as 1,260 days or forty-two months; perhaps also as "a time, times, and half a time," if the "times" in the middle mean "two times" i.e., two years). This is a relatively short period of time and may not mean anything more specific than that. (But who can tell what period of time is "short" in God's view of time? See 2 Peter 3:8.) It is possible—although I wouldn't say certain—that the number seven represents completion or fullness; if so, one can see interesting implications for half that amount. A time unfinished? A time cut short?

When Revelation 20 speaks of Satan's binding and Jesus' reigning for "a thousand years," this number may only represent a very *long* time. After all, with the Lord one day is as a thousand to us, and a thousand to Him as one to us. In addition to 2 Peter 3:8, see also Psalm 90:4, on which Peter might have been reflecting.

Of course, with any of the numbers I've mentioned, or others in Revelation, it may be that they are literal and exact after all. Who knows? I'm not sure we have a way of knowing. But the fact that the numbers occur in material that is rife with symbols at least raises the possibility that the numbers themselves are intentionally symbolic.

Revelation for Readers Then and Now

Anyone reading this book is probably aware that Revelation is often interpreted as being primarily, if not exclusively, about the future. But only one of four main approaches regards Revelation as being predominantly about, or fulfilled in, the future; any view of this nature is called *futurist*. Another approach is called *preterist*, which regards most of Revelation as having been fulfilled in the past—in the life of the early church, for example, and some would say everything was fulfilled at the destruction of Jerusalem in AD 70. Yet another approach is called *historicist*, which thinks of Revelation as being fulfilled by various events throughout church history, from the time of John the author of Revelation to the end of the age. One more approach is that of the *idealist*, who doesn't think of Revelation as pointing to any one particular time; instead, it symbolically depicts the ongoing battle between God and evil, emphasizing that God and right always or ultimately prevail.

This brief definition is a dreadful over-simplification; there are many varieties within these four main approaches. I do not purpose, in this work, to explain these different approaches in more detail. Neither do I plan to defend either of the four, in general or in particular. As I have indicated, especially in the Preface, this work represents my own thinking and the tentative conclusions I have drawn about how to read Revelation. My approach may not closely match any of the four, although both some futurism and some historicism are involved in how I read the visions in Revelation 4–20. I am considering referring to this approach as *diachronic-futurist*, where *diachronic* means "across (or through) time."

Saying that brings me to the point of this particular section. An important issue, in interpreting Revelation, is what sort of meaning it had for the original readers near the end of the first century when John wrote and it was first distributed to the churches in Asia Minor where he had been ministering. Interpreters who oppose the idea that the visions John saw speak exclusively to the future, to a distant "end of the age," often make the point that what was going to happen 2,000 years, or more, in the future would have had little if any significance for John's readers who were grappling with the power of Rome and the Emperor—Domitian—who lusted after the people's worship. The issue, then, is whether that consideration should affect our way of reading Revelation. Does it matter whether John's original readers could see in this book things in the near future that would have been significantly helpful and encouraging to them?

Frankly, I find myself in sympathy with such objections to a *purely* futuristic interpretation of Revelation. It appeals to me to think that one of John's—and the Lord's—purposes for the book was to reassure the original readers in their painful circumstances, pressured to burn incense to Emperor Domitian by threats on their lives or goods if they did not do so. I think it is important that we view Revelation in a way that fulfilled that purpose.

At the same time, it appears that John and the Lord also purposed that this book be of similar encouragement to any believers at any time in the life of the church. If so, the visions also need to represent realities that will be present at other times when believers need to understand what is transpiring in their world and what the outcome will be.

Is such a dual-sided view possible and realistic? Having studied the book carefully, I am at least tentatively convinced that it is. At any rate, the following chapters will serve to offer such a reading of a very tough book. They will show how I take seriously the impact of the book on the first-century readers in their tense situation. They will show how I also give full weight to the more or less obviously future meanings included in some of the visions. The following chapter should serve to clarify this claim.

Endnotes

[13] It is possible, of course, that the original readers of Revelation, given their cultural outlook, might not have thought anything in Revelation to be *weird*. That could be the case especially for Jewish believers familiar with the apocalyptic literature of the intertestamental period. Thanks to Jackson Watts for reminding me of this. When I use the word *weird* I am thinking from a modern perspective.

Chapter 13

ESCHATOLOGY IN REVELATION II: THE KEYS TO DETERMINING THE TEMPORAL REFERENCE OF THE VISIONS

As I have indicated in the previous chapter, a major issue in interpreting Revelation—perhaps the most important issue—is whether the visions represent past, present, or future events—or even more than one of these. Interpreters over the years have proved it possible to take either approach, and this raises a significant question of methodology: How do we go about determining just when the apocalyptic visions of Revelation were meant to be fulfilled? It is not enough just to choose a temporal setting that one finds appealing; one needs to make this decision with objectivity and sound exegesis.

My purpose in this chapter is to take the reader through the very process I decided to employ in making this determination for myself. My intention was to forget all the arguments I had heard or read—recognizing that one cannot do this completely—and see if I could find a basis in the text itself to settle whether the visions in Revelation reveal the future or the past, or truths not anchored in any one particular time.

First Key: The Temporal Setting of Revelation 4–11

It seems that one must view chapters 4 through 11 as the central or basic vision of the book. These eight chapters describe one single vision that connects from start to finish. That vision can be summarized as the opening of the scroll with seven seals. Chapter 4 sets the stage with the throne of God, and chapter 5 reveals both the scroll and the slain Lamb as the one qualified to break its seals and open it. Then, from chapter 6 on to the end of chapter 11, the Lamb breaks the seals, one after the other, and each breaking introduces a vision (or more than one) that John sees and records.

This opening of the book with seven seals, and the various visions that John sees as it unfolds, is the interpretive key to Revelation. Here is an excellent illustration of what I have said in the previous chapter about symbolic imagery. One does not need to think that there is a literal scroll in heaven, in God's hands, that a slain Lamb, standing, takes and opens by breaking each of the seven seals in turn. Rather, this lengthy and detailed vision, which moves in order from beginning to end, *represents* something. But what?

None of the answers I have encountered over the years seemed to be grounded in the text itself. Nothing in Revelation 4–20 tells what this book and its opening by the Lamb represent. It occurred to me, then, that I should focus on what is said in the text when the last of the seven seals is broken and the singular vision comes to an end; perhaps that would at least provide some clue. So I looked at the final action in this vision and what is said in connection with the opening of the seventh seal.

Anyone familiar with Revelation knows that when the last of the seven seals is broken, the vision that issues from it involves the blowing of seven trumpets and what John sees when each is sounded; that is the final action of this long vision. In 11:15–19, then, when the seventh-seal vision comes to an end with the blowing of the seventh trumpet, here is what we read: "And there were loud voices in heaven [dramatically heightening the expectation], saying, 'The kingdoms[14] of this world have become the kingdoms of our Lord and of His Christ, and He shall reign forever and ever" (verse 15). This voice, in turn, provokes the twenty-four elders to recite or sing praise to the Lord God Almighty, including such affirmations as "You have taken Your great power and reigned"; "The nations were angry, and Your wrath has come, and the time of the dead, that they should be judged" (verses 17–18).

This certainly appears to be a reference to the Second Coming, with its focus on the reign and judgment of Jesus Christ. It seems likely, then, that the vision of the opening of the scroll with seven seals ends with the return of Jesus to this earth to reign and judge—as I have discussed at length in earlier chapters.

Next, I decided to focus again on the *beginning* of this long vision, where the stage for the opening of the scroll is set, in chapters 4 and 5. While chapter 4 only sets the stage, the action begins in chapter 5, where the scroll is introduced in the vision and the Lamb is identified as the One who will open it. What is significant, there, is how the Lamb is presented: He is "the Lion of the tribe of Judah, the Root of David" (5:5), and John sees Him thus: there "stood a Lamb as though it had been slain" (5:6), and this slain but standing Lamb has prevailed or qualified to open the seven-sealed scroll.

This is the One, then, who breaks the seals until the scroll is open, with the recitation cited above: The kingdom of this world has become the kingdom of our Lord, and He will reign forever, and the time of His reign and judgment has come. Who is this unique Lamb? He is Jesus—an identification that probably no interpreter will question. How has He qualified? Obviously, by His redemptive work. He was slain—crucified, in the real world. He was *standing*—this Greek word has the same root as the word for resurrection. It is the crucified and risen Christ who opens the seals and lays claim to the kingdom. Even the titles "Lion of the tribe of Judah" and "Root of David" point to His messianic identity and destiny to sit on David's throne.

What, then, does this seven-sealed scroll and its opening represent? While that question could be answered in more than one way, the meaning seems obvious enough: this long vision represents the bringing in of the fruits of the redemptive work of Jesus to its culmination in His return to reign and judge. I view this as an exegetically justified and sound interpretation of this great vision. The implications are significant.

For one thing, this means that what we see in Revelation 4–11 has a future reference: it won't be finished until He comes to take His throne and reign. Yet this also means that the vision is not solely for the future or the end of the age. It begins at the Cross and the Resurrection and covers everything Jesus has done, is doing, and will do from then until He comes again. He has been about His redemptive work from His passion until now and will continue in that work until He takes His rightful place to reign as messianic King over the kingdom of God.

In other words, there will be things in the vision recorded in chapters 4–11 that have already been, are being, and are yet to be fulfilled. It may even be the case that some things in the visions represent events that will occur more than once. There will be things that John's original readers could see and anticipate in their own lifetimes or near future. There will be things that John saw and recorded that will speak more pointedly to other Christians at other times and places. To all believers there will be things that reveal ultimate realities that all humanity of all time will witness and greet with terror or joy. Most important, the final fruits of Christ's redemptive work will be realized in the form of His coming again, to which all believers of all ages can look with eager anticipation.

It will be my purpose, in the following two chapters, to provide a survey of Revelation and demonstrate how this approach to the book spoke to John's contemporaries and speaks to us.

Second Key: The Relationship of Revelation 12–20:10 to the Central Vision in Chapters 4–11

Of almost as much importance as the preceding is the matter of what we may call the "supplemental" visions beginning at chapter 12 and continuing to the middle of chapter 20. It is not absolutely certain just how many different visions there are in this section; I will attempt to provide some direction in a brief survey in Chapter 15 of this work. At any rate, these visions seem most likely to go back and develop some additional details of what the central vision in chapters 4–11 has already surveyed.[15]

These supplemental visions focus on the conflict between God and His people, on the one hand, and those whose loyalty is to the god of this world, Satan, on the other hand. We see some of the chief characters of this conflict in chapters 12–13, and the outcome of the conflict in chapter 14. There is a vision of seven last plagues (the "bowl judgments") in chapters 15–16. Prominent is the fall or destruction of "Babylon" (whatever that important symbol represents!) in chapters 17–19:10. Then comes a vision that apparently begins with the coming of Jesus and extends to His reign on earth beyond that, in chapters 19:11–20:10.

In a survey of these chapters of Revelation, in the next two chapters of this work, I will attempt to develop this in a little more detail. The issue at this point is how these visions relate to the central vision outlined above. Are there any textual grounds for viewing this section as a further development of things already presented in the vision in chapters 4–11?

I think there are some clues, at least, in this direction. One that catches my attention occurs in 11:7, near the end of the central vision (the opening of the book with seven seals), just before the blowing of the seventh trumpet under the seventh seal. There John sees the vision of the two witnesses and the text notes that "When they finish their testimony, the beast that ascends out of the bottomless pit will make war against them, overcome them, and kill them." But this "beast" has *not yet been referred to* in any scene within chapters 4–11. This beast will be introduced in the supplemental visions in chapters 12–20 and will play a prominent role there. He first appears in chapter 13 and meets his final end in chapter 19, where—at the return of Jesus (19:11–16)—he is "captured … and cast alive into the lake of fire burning with brimstone" forever (19:20). The point is that there is already an awareness of this vision in the central vision, which tends to argue that the supplemental visions will revisit what is introduced in the central vision and focus special attention on some of what is depicted there, giving additional development.

There are other points of contact between the central vision and the supplemental visions. For example, in chapter 5, when the scroll and the Lamb are introduced, a song greets the Lamb (verses 9–10). Among other things, the song celebrates the fact that "You … have made us kings and priests to our God; and we shall reign on the earth." That is exactly what is described in the supplemental vision in chapter 20, especially verses 4–5—"They lived [came to life] and reigned with Christ for a thousand years."

One of the most significant things that ties the supplemental visions to the central vision is the fact that both sections highlight the Second Coming. As already noted, when the last of the trumpets sounds in the course of events connected with the breaking of the seventh seal, so that the scroll now lies open, voices proclaim that "The kingdoms of this world have become the kingdoms of our Lord and of His Christ, and He shall reign forever and ever!" (11:15). Furthermore, the recitation at that point affirms that "The nations were angry, and Your wrath has come, and the time of the dead, that they should be judged" (11:18). This is precisely what the supplemental visions revisit and provide more information about. The nations are angry against God and the Lamb and make war (literal or otherwise) against those "who keep the commandments of God and have the testimony of Jesus Christ" (12:17). God's wrath is poured out—in the form of seven bowl-judgments, which are described as being "full of the wrath of God who lives forever and ever" (15:7). They are also identified as "the seven last plagues" in which "the wrath of God is complete" (15:1).

More detail could easily be provided. This seems enough to establish that the supplemental visions in chapters 12–20 look back on the things seen in the central vision of chapters 4–11 and focus on certain aspects of it in order to provide greater detail. I conclude that this is the very best way to view the material in chapters 12–20:10.

This means, then, that just as the central vision depicts the entire church age from the time of the Cross to the culmination of Christ's redemptive work at His second coming, so the supplemental visions also look at what is true of the same period of time. Even so, it seems likely that in both parts of Revelation there is strong intensification as the present age wears on and approaches its end. The things that characterize the whole become more pronounced as the end of the age nears. The supplemental visions tend to focus more attention on things near the end, and thus in the future, but even these things are connected with the whole church age.

This perspective, or tendency, may well suggest a principle of sorts, one reflected in Paul's teaching in the Pastoral Epistles. In 2 Timothy 3:13, for example, he said, "Evil men and impostors will grow worse and worse, deceiving and being deceived." In verse 1 of the same chapter, he says, "In the last days perilous times will come" and proceeds to describe various forms of wickedness that have always been with us but that will apparently, in the last days, become more open and hostile to the law of God and to those who fear God. In 1 Timothy 4:1–2 Paul warns that "The Spirit expressly says that in latter times some will depart from the faith, giving heed to deceiving spirits and doctrines of demons, speaking lies." As I observed earlier, antichrist is already among us and is yet to come.

Third Key: The Crucial, Connected Scenes in 19:11–20:10

The understanding of this vision—a series of connected scenes—depends on what I have said in reference to the first two key parts of Revelation: namely, on the central vision (chapters 4–11) as culminating in the future but not entirely future and on the supplemental visions (chapters 12–20:10) as representing the same period but focusing attention on certain details that are especially (again, not exclusively) intensified near the end of the age.

There are four "scenes" in this vision: (1) 19:11–16; (2) 19:17–21; (3) 20:1–6; and (4) 20:7–10. What is especially noteworthy about them is that they are consciously connected in the text itself, and each builds, consecutively, on the preceding, showing that they are in order, probably logically and chronologically, as follows.

In the first scene, 19:11–16, the Person on the white horse undoubtedly is (or represents) Jesus; the descriptions cannot be coherently read in any other way. He is identified as "King of kings and Lord of lords," and the action seems surely to depict His coming. Verse 15 contains the textual link to the next scene and promises His reign: "Out of His mouth goes a sharp sword, that with it He should strike the nations. And He Himself will rule them with a rod of iron."

In the second scene, 19:17–21, an "army" gathers to make war against the Person who sits on the white horse, and that Person strikes the army with "the sword which proceeded from [His] mouth." He also captured "the beast" and "the false prophet"—referring to the two apocalyptic images presented in Revelation 13, who have played a prominent role in the supplemental visions—and consigned them to the lake of fire.

In the third scene, 20:1–6, a "thousand-year" time is introduced, and at its beginning the "dragon"—introduced in chapter 12 and identified there as Satan—is bound so that he cannot deceive the nations. This binding comes instead of casting him into the lake of fire with his two servants, the Beast and False Prophet, since he will be released for a final confrontation at the end of "the thousand years." Then Jesus and (at least some of) His servants reign together with Him for this "thousand years." Where the second scene ties to the fact that the Person on the white horse has come to "strike the nations," the third ties to the fact that He has come to "rule them with a rod of iron" (19:15, connected to 19:21 and 20:4). Also, where only the Beast and False Prophet are cast into the lake of fire in scene two, the third member of this unholy triumvirate, Satan himself as the Dragon, is, instead, bound in the abyss. The connection between 16:12–16 and the second scene here should not be overlooked.

In the fourth and final scene, 20:7–10, at the end of the "thousand years," the Dragon, Satan, is released, gathers a group of confederates so large it cannot be numbered, and leads a final rebellion against God and the Lamb. That rebellion, too, can end in only one way. Fire devours the rebels and Satan is cast into the lake of fire and brimstone—"where the beast and the false prophet [already] are," all of them to be tormented forever (verse 10). Thus do the textual links between the scenes tie them together in a neat package.

There is no doubt that these scenes are connected, all by language in the text, to represent consecutive events. *If* the first scene (in 19:11–16) represents the Second Coming, as seems clear, then there seems to be no way to avoid a reign on earth of some duration (regardless how long; as I've said, the one thousand years may not be literal) and a final rebellion at its end.

I suppose one might avoid this view of the events by finding some other representation for the first scene (19:11–16). Can the appearance of the One called "Faithful and True," riding on a white horse, coming to strike the nations and rule them, represent anything other than the second coming of Jesus? This does not seem to me to be a likely possibility.

One other possibility, perhaps a more common one, is to break this passage into two parts, separating 20:1–10 from 19:11–21. This makes the two scenes in chapter 20 a recapitulation of earlier material, with 20:7–10 re-telling 19:17–21. I will include an extended note at the end of Chapter 15 to provide a little more attention to that view.

Meanwhile, this passage is obviously one of the keys to interpreting Revelation.

Endnotes

[14] "Kingdoms" is "kingdom" in the majority of the manuscripts; the meaning is the same either way.

[15] This way of returning to what has been described previously, to give additional detail or a different perspective, is often called *recapitulation*. I will not use that word, given that it has become the name for a specific approach to interpreting Revelation. That approach can easily be over- or under-utilized.

Chapter 14

ESCHATOLOGY IN REVELATION III: READING REVELATION, A SURVEY OF THE CENTRAL VISION (4–11)

Giving serious consideration to the eschatology of Revelation requires dealing carefully with the entire book, and doing so in light of the key issues discussed in the preceding chapters. My purpose in this chapter and the next is to offer a survey of the basic meaning of the major elements of the visions. In this chapter I will briefly mention the preliminary material in Revelation 1–3 and then provide an overview of the central vision (chapters 4–11). In the following chapter I will do the same for the supplemental visions (chapters 12–20:10) and briefly mention the concluding material in Revelation 20:11–22.

Preliminary: Revelation 1–3

Before focusing on the central vision, a brief survey of chapters 1–3 seems appropriate. In chapter 1, John provides an introduction (verses 1–3) and a letter-like greeting to the seven churches in Asia where he had been ministering (verses 4–8). Already the eschatological note is sounded: "Behold, He is coming with clouds, and every eye will see Him, even they who pierced Him" (verse 7a). Then comes a stunning vision of the Lord Jesus who is the true writer of the letter that becomes such a dramatic book (verses 9–20). After all, He is the source of the revelation contained in the book (verse 1). John has been wrenched from the believers in Asia Minor by Domitian, the glory-seeking emperor of Rome; but Jesus, now seen by John in His glory, is present among the churches, observing their strengths and failures in all their trying circumstances.

In chapters 2 and 3, then, "secretary" John takes dictation: a letter for each of the seven churches offering commendations and criticisms, but always providing reassurance for those who will follow their Lord in good faith: namely, those who "overcome." These are apparently straightforward letters about then-present, real situations; there appears no need to interpret them as simply representing different stages of church history. Each of the letters teaches lessons that any church in any age can profit from.

The Central Vision: Revelation 4–11

I have already "introduced" this vision in the previous chapters. Here follows a relatively brief survey in outline, with comments important for the purpose of this work. The chapters move in an orderly and consecutive way through a single vision; this vision may be called "The Seven-Sealed Book and Its Opening."

Chapter 4 sets the stage. It describes what John sees when, in a sense, the curtain rises. Primarily, this is God on His throne, attended by beings strange and familiar, worshiping.

Chapter 5 describes the first action. There is a scroll, rolled up and closed with seven ties or seals. In dramatic fashion a concern is aroused that someone qualified must be located to break the ties and open the scroll. Such a candidate immediately appears, in the form of a slain Lamb, standing. This is, without question, the crucified and risen Jesus, who is hailed in song as the Redeemer who will "reign on the earth." He has prevailed to open the scroll.

As I have suggested in Chapter 12, the opening of this scroll appears to represent the full development, from its beginning on the Cross to its culmination with His return, of the redemptive work of Jesus Christ. As I have suggested in Chapter 13, while this is symbolic imagery, the real-world meaning is often so near the surface that it can't be missed. When this beginning is connected to the ending of the vision (chapter 11), it seems most likely that this entire vision represents the purchase and application of redemption from its inception to its finale with the return and reign of Jesus. What we see will therefore include events between the crucifixion of Christ and His return—and, briefly, beyond that return in chapter 20. There is future in this vision, to be sure, but there is also past and present, as well as some that is timeless.

Chapter 6 unveils what John sees as each of the first six seals (or ties) is broken, often with dramatic staging. There is a pattern in the structure of the various sevens in Revelation: often a break between the first four and the last three, and some additional scenes between one or more of the last three. The first six seals, when broken, unveil the following.

Seal one (6:2): a white horse, whose rider receives a crown and goes forth "conquering and to conquer." The most likely meaning is that this represents Jesus and His gospel.

Seal two (6:3–4): a red horse, representing war.

Seal three (6:5–6): a black horse, representing famine—manifested in the high prices of basic food.

Seal four (6:7–8): a pale horse (pale green perhaps the color of decay?), representing death.

As a group of four (often called "the four horsemen of the Apocalypse"), these may compare to what Jesus promised in the first part of the Olivet Discourse (discussion in Chapter 7). There He described what we may call "signs of the times" that *do not signal the end of the age*. Instead, they characterize the entire present age, between Jesus' first and second comings. These things include wars, famines, and pestilences that cause death. They should not deceive Christians or deter us from our commissioned work of evangelization, preaching the gospel of Jesus, as represented by the white horse.

Painful occurrences like those represented by the second, third, and fourth horses may well intensify and reach climactic proportions as the present age wears on and nears the end. But they are to be expected and should not deceive believers into thinking that they signify the nearness of the end. "The end is not yet," as Jesus said in telling about these things.

Seal five (6:9–11): martyrs. This imagery is presented in dramatic fashion, with John viewing martyrs who cry out to God asking how long before He judges and avenges their blood—implying that such judgment is going to come. The answer is that there will yet be more martyrs before the end. As with the first four seals, then, the fifth unveils what will characterize the entire present age—although, again, the persecution that produces martyrdom may well intensify and reach a new peak not long before Jesus returns to do the avenging spoken of.

Seal six (6:12–17): frightening phenomena in nature. Five specific happenings are mentioned: a "great" earthquake, the sun blackened, the moon becoming blood-red, stars falling to earth, the sky having receded (ESV: vanished) like a scroll rolled up, and mountains and islands moved about. The question is whether this is merely "symbolic." All the features named—like three of the four horsemen and the martyrs—are part of the real world; and if the description here is symbolic, one must ask: symbolic of what? Indeed, there is a frequent scriptural reference to unusual "signs" in nature soon before (and in connection with) Jesus' coming. See the discussion of this in earlier chapters. Most likely, then, these are real-world occurrences, described according to appearance.[16]

The description of the reaction of mankind to these frightening "signs" tends to add confirmation to this understanding. The people described in verse 15 are real-world people, and they realize that what they are observing signals that "the great day of [God's] wrath has come" (verse 17)—and, rather than repenting of their wickedness, they seek to hide.

Throughout the Revelation there is a conscious linking of the eschatological wrath of God that is to be displayed in association with (and beginning even earlier than) the coming of Christ to reign and judge. We have just seen this when the fifth seal was broken, for example, in the cry of the martyrs for the avenging of their blood. When this long vision comes to an end in chapter 11, the celebrating recitation of the twenty-four elders includes that the King, come to reign, will judge the dead and "destroy those who destroy the earth" (verse 18). The wrath of God is mentioned a dozen times in Revelation, and it is one of those themes that ties together the supplemental visions (chapters 12–20:10) and the central vision being analyzed here.

Chapter 7 provides something of an "interlude" between the sixth and seventh seals, with two additional scenes, both of them unveiling groups of God's people. The first group consists of 144,000 who are "sealed" for protection from certain aspects of the judgment that will fall when the seventh seal is broken (verses 1–8). This group includes 12,000 from each of the twelve tribes of the children of Israel.[17] The question is whether this indicates a role for ethnic Israelites in the end times or is a symbolic way of representing new covenant believers in old covenant terms without being meant literally. I will revisit this question in Chapter 16 on eschatology in the Old Testament. Meanwhile, these are apparently God's people (or at least some of them) who will be on earth during the outpouring of God's wrath and who will be protected from the ill effects unveiled when the seventh seal is broken and seven trumpet-judgments immediately follow.

The second group (verses 9–17) consists of an innumerable multitude from "all nations, tribes, people, and tongues" (language-groups). The scene consciously depicts them, anticipatively, in their victorious state with the Lord Jesus, having come there from their time on earth when there was "great tribulation." The description of their new status, especially in verses 15–17, is very much like that of those in the final state in Revelation 21 and 22.

Some interpreters think of these two groups as representing the very same people, although from two different perspectives. They are both God's people, for sure, but it seems unlikely that they are the very same group. Without being dogmatic, I think it likely that these are two views of people involved in that period near the end of the age when God's wrath is being judicially inflicted on the wicked on this earth, leading up to the Second Coming. This would be the period beginning with the frightening phenomena unveiled by the sixth seal and expressly described by the seven trumpet-judgments that immediately follow the breaking of the seventh seal. At the very least, then, the first group reveals that there will be some of God's people (if not all) on earth that will be supernaturally protected from the worst effects of that wrathful judgment—and from the persecution directed against them by the enemies of God who are also enemies of God's people. The second group reveals that there will be many who proceed from that period (perhaps some, if not all, by martyrdom?) to their final reward with the Lamb in His glory and peace.

In saying this, I have almost reduced these two scenes to the *lessons* they teach us: namely, that God protects His people from the severe effects of His judgment, and that those who [wash] their robes and [make] them white in the blood of the Lamb" (verse 14) will be with the Lamb in a blessed state. As I have proposed in an earlier chapter, the *lesson* of a text with symbolism is not quite the same thing as its *meaning*. There must be a reason for the two different descriptions in chapter 7, but the text itself does not say what that reason is nor does it teach us much about the time when God's wrath is being poured out on earth just prior to the Second Coming. Is there a specific role that ethnic Israelites will play? Are those in the second group martyrs? The answers are not clear. This is one of the questions that will apparently have to await the events themselves for answers. Meanwhile, what seems clear is what I have said about the lessons, and that is enough.

If what I have said about the numbers in Revelation is correct, the 12,000 and 144,000 need not be taken literally. At the same time, the innumerable multitude probably is literal.

Chapter 8 begins the longer unveiling that follows the breaking of the seventh seal, describing, in quick succession, the first four of the seven trumpet-judgments. Before the first trumpet sounds, the whole series begins with a dramatic silence (verse 1) and an even more dramatic action (verses 2–6): an angel with a censer (incense censer)[18] burns the incense before the Lord in association with "the prayers of all the saints" and then fills the censer with fire and casts it down to earth accompanied by "noises, thunderings, lightnings, and an earthquake." All of this serves to heighten the anticipation of the judgments about to fall.

Trumpet one (8:7): bloody hail and fire cast to earth, burns up "a third" of trees and grass.

Trumpet two (8:8–9): a mass like a fiery mountain, cast into the sea, turns it to blood; "a third" of sea life dies and a third of ships are destroyed.[19]

Trumpet three (8:10–11): a great, burning star called Wormwood (a bitter plant) falls on "a third" of fresh waters and makes them harmful.

Trumpet four (8:12): sun, moon, and stars go dark for "a third" of their normal shining.

Back in 7:2–3, preceding the vision of the sealing of 144,000, John heard that the "four angels to whom it was granted to harm the earth and the sea" were held back from this until the 144,000 were first sealed for protection. These four trumpet-judgments are those four and now perform their work. It is difficult to determine whether what John sees in these four is to be taken literally or as entirely symbolic. On the one hand, there is no reason to object to judgments that will affect nature—and human beings as a result. But, as I said in Chapter 12 when illustrating the mixture of symbolism and real-world references, using the plagues in Revelation 9, a vision that describes injury to real-world resources, harming human beings as a result, might also be taken to represent spiritual things and matters of truth and falsehood. Consequently, while these four trumpet-judgments seem to refer to harmful effects in nature, it is possible they represent harmful effects in what people believe to be true. I am inclined to the former, but in either case this is divine judgment that is harmful to humanity on earth.

The last verse of chapter 8 (verse 13) is yet another dramatic insertion to heighten the tension and expectation for the final three trumpet-judgments. An angel announces a serious warning about the final three trumpet-judgments; they will be three fearsome "woes."

Chapter 9 offers the fifth and sixth trumpet judgments, which are the first two of the three fearsome woes. These will consist of two strange "plagues."

Trumpet five (9:1–12): "infernal" locusts. Verse 1 dramatically introduces this, beginning with an angel from Heaven who unlocks the "bottomless pit" (the abyss), from which the locusts arise. We are not told their size, but they are not "normal" locusts. Their tails sting like scorpions' tails, causing not death but severe pain, enough that people wish they were dead. Their "king" is none other than the Destroyer himself. This plague lasts "five months."

Trumpet six (9:13–21): "infernal" horsemen or cavalry, released from bondage in the "great river Euphrates"—the latter a symbol with much the same meaning as the abyss. Like the locusts, these are not "normal" mounted troops, as the description shows, and there are "two hundred million" of them. Unlike the plague of locusts, these kill "a third" of mankind; they do so with fire, smoke, and brimstone from their mouths or with the bites of serpent-like tails.

As already noted, this is one of the best illustrations in Revelation of the difficulty in deciding whether to take a symbol literally or as representative of something else. While I leaned toward a more literal view of the effects in nature described under trumpet-judgment four, above, here I lean toward taking both of these plagues as representing the warfare of ideas, the battle between falsehood and truth. The description of both of these appears to mean that the source of the harm is demonic, but that works as well for falsehood as for physical pain and death. Ultimately, in the spiritual realm, lies are much more serious than physical hurts, even deadly ones, since they destroy the soul. I am inclined to connect this directly to what Paul says in 2 Thessalonians 2:11–12, regarding the end-times: "God will send them strong delusion, that they should believe the lie, that they all may be condemned who did not believe the truth but had pleasure in unrighteousness." This "sending" is judicial, and it consists in allowing Satan and his associates (whether demons or humans) the freedom to sow their falsehood in the world.

Interestingly and significantly, the description of the second of these two "infernal" plagues ends by reporting that, even after these two fearsome woes, the rest of the people of the world "did not repent." They continued in their idolatry, murdering, sorcery, sexual immorality, and theft (verses 20–21). That fits precisely with the spirit of 2 Thessalonians 2.

Chapter 10, following a pattern we have found in the series of sevens, interrupts the trumpet-judgments to present additional scenes, one in chapter

10 and another in chapter 11. These two scenes add dramatic detail, and John himself gets involved in the action.

The scene in chapter 10 we may divide into two parts. In the first part (10:1–7), John sees yet another "mighty angel" whom he describes in such a way that we can hardly avoid recognizing Him as Jesus Himself. We remember that the word *angel* literally means "messenger." With much dramatic accompaniment, this angel places one foot on the land and one on the sea, raises his right hand (perhaps as if in an oath), and announces that there will be no more delay; instead, during the time covered when the seventh trumpet sounds, "the mystery of God," as told to the prophets, will be "finished." In other words, when the seventh seal of the scroll is finally broken and the scroll is fully open, this age will end.

At this point, John gets involved, and that is the second part of this scene. He is instructed to take the "little book" held by the "mighty angel"; then he is told to eat it, that it will be sweet in his mouth but bitter in his stomach. That is exactly what happens, and verse 11 provides the only explanation of the meaning of this scene.

The meaning of the whole is relatively obvious. At this point in the larger vision, we are nearing the end of the age. Only one trumpet-judgment (the third woe) remains; there will be no more delay. Even so, there is much yet to be written by John.

Chapter 11:1–14 unveils the other scene that holds back the final trumpet-blowing; it is about two witnesses, and it is difficult to interpret. First, John gets involved again (verses 1–2), being given a surveyor's measuring rod and told to measure the temple precincts and the people who worship there. At the same time, he is not to measure the court of the Gentiles, since "it has been given to the Gentiles" to occupy for "forty-two months" (verse 2). This appears to refer to what is called elsewhere *the times* (or "fullness of the Gentiles")—as in Romans 11:25, for example. Such "measuring" as John is instructed to do apparently represents preparation for occupying; this may have bearing on the issue I have raised, earlier, as to whether ethnic Israel (the Jews) will have any special role in end-times events, an issue to be discussed subsequently. Whatever the case with that, this measuring is a dramatic device to heighten tension in introducing the vision of the two witnesses. Whether the forty-two months is meant to be literal or symbolic is not certain; as I have indicated earlier, I do not think the numbers in Revelation are necessarily literal, especially in referring to periods of time in symbolic descriptions.

The vision of the two witnesses begins in detail in verse 3 and continues through verse 14. In summary, the two witnesses give their witness (or testimony) in Jerusalem, apparently, for a period of 1,260 days—also equal to three and a half years (of 360 days each). Although they are the objects of hostility (from those who do not obey God), they are impervious to attempts to kill them; they are able to perform various miracles, including belching out fire to devour those who would assault them. But when they have "finish[ed] their testimony," they are slain by "the beast that ascends out of the bottomless pit." This person (or power, if not a person) has not yet been introduced but will appear in chapter 13—where I will devote more attention to this. Whatever the identity of this "beast," it represents a source of evil in the world, hostile to all that is good and godly. When the two witnesses are slain in Jerusalem (verse 8), all of wicked mankind rejoices over them. But after "three-and-a-half days" they are restored to life and ascend to God, to the consternation of those who hated them and rejoiced in their demise.

At this point the scene ends with a great earthquake that causes the death of "a tenth" of the population of the city—apparently still the city of Jerusalem (verse 13). The record notes that the "second woe" (meaning what occurred when the sixth trumpet sounded) had passed, and the "third woe" was about to follow. As will be noted, that "third woe" apparently refers to the pouring out of the seven bowls of wrath on the earth, depicted in the supplemental visions soon to follow.

The question, of course, is what or whom the "two witnesses" represent. The text does not identify them beyond describing what John saw. There may be a hint regarding this identity in verse 4, which says "These are the two olive trees and the two lampstands standing before the God of the earth." This citation apparently refers to a similarly apocalyptic vision in Zechariah 4.

In that ancient vision, the prophet saw two olive trees on opposite sides of a single lampstand. There the lampstand may represent Zerubbabel, but the answer to Zechariah's question about the two olive trees is that "These are the two anointed ones, who stand beside the Lord of the whole earth." This does not offer much help to us in determining the meaning of the two witnesses in Revelation 11.

Some interpreters, especially dispensationalists, tend to think the two witnesses are two Old Testament prophets—Moses and Elijah, for example—brought back to life on earth during this period. My approach to Revelation does not lend itself to that view. At the same time, I acknowledge that there is nothing in this chapter that offers help in identifying the two. I suspect that this is still a mystery that will not be revealed until the time comes. Meanwhile, the scene reassures us that even in the dark hours of the next-to-last of the final "woes" on earth, there will be witness to the truth, a witness that will be temporarily stopped but cannot finally be overcome and will prevail in the end.

Chapter 11:15–19, provides an abbreviated conclusion to the vision of the opening of the scroll with seven seals. All that remains is the blowing of the seventh trumpet, and the vision concludes with a simple but dramatic notice of the outcome of the whole vision. We already know that when the seventh trumpet sounds, there will be the dreaded third "woe." But that is not described here; instead it will be saved for what I have called the "supplemental" visions in chapters 12 and following.

What is recorded here, instead, is the meaning of the whole vision: namely, that "The kingdoms of this world have become the kingdoms of our Lord and of His Christ, and He shall reign forever and ever!" (verse 15). I have already commented about the significance of this and of the recitation of the twenty-four elders that follows this momentous announcement (verses 16–18). The "Lord God Almighty," who is the Christ (Messiah), has "taken [His] great power and reigned" (entered into His reign) (verse 17). The time of God's wrath has come, the time for even the dead to be judged and the wicked destroyed; but it is also a time when those who fear the Lord will be rewarded—that, too, being a part of judgment (verse 18). Following this is a dramatic note; John sees the heavenly temple opened and the ark of the Lord's covenant there—probably symbolizing that God has fulfilled His Word in every way and has brought redeemed people into His unhindered presence. The "lightnings, noises, thunderings, an earthquake, and great hail" conclude the vision with dramatic flourish.

Endnotes

[16] It is clear, of course, that a single star, colliding with planet Earth, would consume and utterly destroy the planet. I take the language to be phenomenal, using words the way people typically use them. People often call everything visible in the heavens "stars," even when they aren't true stars but are comets or other pieces of rock flying in the heavens.

[17] It is not clear why the tribe of Dan is left out, while both Joseph and one of his two sons, Manasseh, make up for that omission. There are various speculations about this offered by any number of interpreters. I am inclined to think this is not significant.

[18] It might have been the "censer" used for the incense that was burned on the altar where incense was burned before the Lord.

[19] According to most manuscripts, a third of earth burned up.

Chapter 15

ESCHATOLOGY IN REVELATION IV: READING REVELATION, A SURVEY OF THE SUPPLEMENTAL VISIONS (12–20:10)

In the previous chapter I have provided a survey of the central vision of Revelation, recorded in chapters 4–11 of the book. This survey continues, now, covering the supplemental visions in chapters 12–20:10. These visions provide additional information about the matters revealed in the central vision.

Supplemental Visions: Revelation 12–20:10

As noted earlier, this part of Revelation—about the same length as the central vision—offers additional visions that revisit and fill in some of the details of the central vision. In other words, for the most part, they cover the same period of time as the central vision—although they are not necessarily consecutive. They often overlap, and some focus on different aspects of what we have already seen, in outline, in the central vision. Indeed, there is repetition in what they unveil.

These visions, like the central vision, represent things that span the entire church age. However, even though they are anchored in the present age and offer some understanding of the whole age, they are more focused on "the last days" of the present age and have more to say about outcomes. As I noted earlier, there are connections between things in the central vision and things in the supplemental visions: the reference in 11:7 to a certain "beast" who will be introduced, as though for the first time, in chapter 13, for example. That "beast" will play an important role in these supplemental visions. Also, the fact that the third (and apparently most dreadful) "woe" was not unveiled when the seventh trumpet sounded in chapter 11, even though 11:14 solemnly warned of it, leaves open the door for the supplemental visions to provide the details of that "woe" in the vision of the seven last plagues of God's wrath.

As I have done for the central vision, then, I will do for the supplemental visions in these chapters of Revelation. I observe, up front, that markers separating the section into distinct visions are not always present. I had hoped, at first, that there would be some words to serve as transitions between visions—as in John's use of "I saw," perhaps—but a careful analysis along those lines proved fruitless. It would be possible, then, to subdivide the section differently; nonetheless, I think the divisions I will use are reasonable and practical for our use.

Vision 1: Introduction of Characters in the Conflict (Chapters 12–13)

Although the two chapters could be treated as two visions, it seems best to take them together. The main point is that there is conflict during the period represented, and the major characters in the conflict are unveiled in the vision. Those characters are, in the vision, a woman, a Dragon, a male child, the woman's seed (chapter 12), and a Beast and a False Prophet (chapter 13). The period of this conflict is, in the broadest possible sense, the whole history of the world, but here in Revelation the focus is on the entire church age. Furthermore, the conflict of this period intensifies and reaches its most contested state as the present age wears on and the coming of Christ approaches. I will comment on each of the characters in the vision.

(1) *The woman* (chapter 12, especially verses 1–6, 13–17). There are two women who are prominent in Revelation's symbolism, each representing one side of the conflict; see 17:3–6 for the other side. This one represents the forces of good, those who fear God, the people of God in whatever form they may have at any given time: Israel in the Old Testament, the church in the present

age. That she wears "a garland of twelve stars" (verse 1) probably identifies "her" with both Israel's twelve tribes and the twelve apostles at the foundation of the New Testament Church. But at the time of Jesus' birth; "she" is the righteous remnant of Old Testament Israel, from whose line Messiah comes forth.

We will focus on her "Child" below, who is Jesus, and on her "seed," made up of those who fear God. That she flees into the wilderness in God's protection (verse 6), apparently for the same 1,260 days as in 11:3 (commented on in the previous chapter), represents her as the object of wicked hostility, a condition that is always true but intensifies and becomes more virulent shortly before the second coming of Jesus. This three-and-a-half-year period could be a precise measure of time but seems more likely figurative, representing something like a relatively short but significant period of time. (Even "short" might not fit *our* idea of short!)

(2) *The Dragon* (chapter 12, especially verses 3–4, 7–17). We do not have to guess who is represented here, since verse 9 identifies this one as the devil himself, the archenemy of God and His people, at "war" (spiritual conflict) with them. Verses 7–10, and following, refer to a war between him and God's archangel Michael, which shows that the conflict is cosmic and of long-lasting duration. This passage may be taken in either of two ways: as a "flashback" to the original conflict in Heaven that resulted in the expulsion of Satan and his fallen angels (demons); or as suggesting a "new" warfare that comes about with Satan's failed attempt to "capture" the Christ. I am inclined to the first of these, especially if the conflict of this entire section of Revelation is the conflict that has raged since before (or beginning with) creation.

(3) *The "male Child" of the woman* (chapter 12, especially verses 2, 5) has been interpreted by some to represent the Christian Church, but the image is far too much like Christ to be taken any other way. Thus, His being "caught up to God and His throne" (verse 5) refers to the ascension—or at least to Jesus' victory over Satan's efforts to overcome Him—and His destiny to "rule all nations with a rod of iron" (verse 5) precisely fits what will be said about Jesus at His return to earth. Like the description of the cosmic battle in verses 9–10, this failed attempt of Satan to "devour" the Christ may be taken as a

"flashback"; but since the conflict described here occupies at least the entire church age, it may be a more direct reference to the historical birth of Jesus. I am more inclined to the latter.

(4) *The woman's "seed"* (chapter 12, especially verses 13–17). In his antagonism Satan has first focused his attention on the woman herself, but this effort has been thwarted by a supernatural protection of her—for that same three-and-a-half years ("a time and times and half a time") (verses 13–14). In frustration Satan attempts to wash her away as with a flood of water, perhaps representing a flood of falsehood, but he is unsuccessful (verses 15–16). In consequence, he focuses his attention on making war with "the rest of [the woman's] offspring," identified as those "who keep the commandments of God and have the testimony of Jesus Christ" (verse 17).

This chapter, then, unveils the nature of the conflict not just of the end times but of all times and especially of the present age. We are expected to understand that all who follow Jesus will be targets of Satan and those who identify with him. Such hostility will reach its peak shortly before the second coming of Jesus.

(5) *The Beast* (chapter 13, especially verses 1–10). In his vision, John sees this "beast" "rising up out of the sea" (verse 1); in apocalyptic literature such a "sea" typically represents the world of peoples, especially those who are in rejection of God. It seems clear that this beast represents a person or power that is hostile to God and serving Satan's purposes in his "war" against the people of God. Just as the "dragon" has seven heads and ten horns (12:3), representing earthly powers under his sway, so does this beast (13:1).

Other references in Revelation 12–20 to "the beast" are to this character, even when it becomes less symbolic and refers to a real-world power. (Later in this chapter "another beast" will appear, subsequently wearing the name of "the false prophet.") This "first beast" (as in 13:12) is obviously the same as was mentioned in 11:7 that targeted the two witnesses and succeeded in killing them. There he is identified as "the beast that ascends out of the bottomless pit (the abyss)"; that is his source, as confirmed for this beast in 17:8, which does not contradict that John sees him arising out of the sea in this vision. (It does fit with what is said about the abyss later in Revelation 20.)

This "beast" will play a prominent role in the supplemental visions of this section of Revelation; the "mark of the beast" is his, as is the mysterious number 666; see chapters 13, 14, 15, 16, 17, and 19 of Revelation. The description here in 13:2–10 includes significant elements. His power comes from the devil (verse 2). He blasphemes God (verses 5–6). He seeks and gets worship as though he is God (verses 4, 8). He "make[s] war with the saints" (verse 7). He exercises authority over the nations (verse 7). All of this more or less interprets itself as spiritual warfare against God and the people of God.

Verse 3, however, is not so easy. One of his seven "heads" receives an otherwise mortal wound but instead of death there is healing, furthering the worshipful response of the peoples. The seven heads represent the kings of nations that affiliate with this figure in power, as chapter 17 will clarify. This recovery—of a given nation, apparently—is regarded as a miracle and gets mentioned again in chapter 17; I will save further interpretation of the heads and horns for analysis of that chapter. We may say, already, that this "beast" represents, in some way, a confederacy of nations and a combining of their power in the cause of rebellion against God.

Significant, here, is the fact that the description of this beast and his "false prophet" (verses 11–18) matches closely what Paul says about "the man of sin (or lawlessness)" in 2 Thessalonians 2. In Chapter 11 of this book I have drawn a comparison between that passage and this one and will not take space to repeat the comparison here. I am convinced by this similarity that the "beast" John sees here is the same as "the man of sin (or lawlessness)" described there. In other words, this beast represents antichrist, which I also introduced in Chapters 3 and 11. I will make some additional observations about antichrist now.

I emphasize here what I suggested there: namely, that antichrist is *both* a recurring influence—in the world and throughout church history, against God and His people—*and* a specific power or person (or both) that will arise and actively make war against all that is good not long before Jesus comes back to earth. Thus John's original readers, near the end of the first century AD, could see antichrist in the power of the Roman government and in the person of Emperor Domitian, who was causing them great pressure and distress. In chapter 17 of Revelation, as we will see later, there is a distinct reflection of the city (and empire) of Rome in the unveiling of this beast-antichrist. No doubt antichrist has been seen often, and correctly, throughout church history; the Reformers, for example, tended to see the pope and the papacy as antichrist. Various interpreters through the ages have attempted to find ways to identify antichrist by the mysterious number 666, and they have settled on specific persons, like Adolph Hitler, for example, or Joseph Stalin. It would not be surprising, in our current state of affairs, to hear that the name of Russia's Vladimir Putin or China's Xi Jinping or North Korea's Kim Jong Un can be represented by 666! This effort is misguided, but seeing antichrist in circumstances where powerful persons target God or His people is justified.

At the same time, the final and fullest manifestation of antichrist is yet to appear; Paul's observations in 2 Thessalonians 2 evidently require that this must be true before the Lord Jesus returns. Even so, that does not settle, for sure, whether antichrist will be a single person, or an office such as centers in a government or other organization; one cannot rule out the possibility that a *church* organization may be the final expression of antichrist. After all, in 2 Thessalonians 2 Paul associates "the man of sin" with a great apostasy or rebellion.

(6) *The False Prophet* ("another beast"; chapter 13, especially verses 11–18). John sees this character arise "out of the earth"; he is a close associate of "the beast" just described, receives authority and power from that beast, and leads the campaign for submission to and worship of antichrist. If there is antichrist at various times and places in the present age (or even before), then there will also be persons or institutions that exercise his power. That this beast "had two horns like a lamb and spoke like a dragon" may well indicate that, though he is linked directly to Satan (the Dragon), he is in some way a religious figure. If the pope were, indeed, the Antichrist, the Roman church might be the False Prophet—as this second beast is called in 16:13; 19:20; 20:10. Indeed, the Dragon (Satan), the Beast (antichrist), and the False Prophet form something of an

"unholy trinity" aiming, apparently, to overthrow God and take His place and deceive the world; see 16:13, especially.

The description of this False Prophet is such as to identify him as antichrist's "right hand man"—whether representing a person or institution or both. He aims to influence people to worship the Beast as God (verse 12). He performs supernatural "signs" with this purpose in view (verse 13). His deception of mankind includes the erection of an image to represent the Beast (verse 14). He makes the image appear to be alive and—like Nebuchadnezzar of old—kills those who will not worship (verse 15). He institutes a measure requiring people to have a mark or take the name of the Beast in order to carry on regular commerce (verses 16–17).

All of this is presented in dramatic imagery and may be taken more or less symbolically rather than literally; regardless, the point is that antichrist and the False Prophet, whether persons or powers, oppose God and by falsehood deceive people on a large scale into at least the idolatry of trusting in something or someone other than Almighty God for their welfare and security. This has always been the work of Satan and his followers, a universal and timeless effort that is part of what the Beast and the False Prophet in this chapter of Revelation represent. But as the end nears, such an effort will be intensified and reach its peak, setting the stage for the King to come in glory and judgment and to reign.

Verse 18 adds a puzzling detail: namely, the number of the beast—perhaps the "mark" people will wear?—is 666. Whether literal or not—and either is possible—those who follow the antichristian campaign will be identified with it, in distinction from those who follow Jesus. I suspect that we are not intended to know the significance of this number or the end-time identity of the two "beasts" until the time for their unveiling comes, a time referred to by Paul in 2 Thessalonians 2.

Vision 2: Glimpses of the Outcome of the Conflict (Chapter 14)

It would be possible to regard this chapter as part of the same vision as chapters 12 and 13, with that vision introducing the characters of the conflict and this one giving a preview of the outcome for both the righteous and the wicked. At any rate, this chapter provides three scenes that look forward to the end of the time of intense conflict that culminates and ends with the return of Jesus.

Scene 1 (14:1–5): The 144,000 with God and the Lamb. It seems obvious that this is the same group that we saw "sealed" for protection in 7:1–8, in the interlude between the breaking of the sixth and seventh seals in the central vision. John sees them again, now, in the presence of the Lamb to whom they have been faithful. Perhaps verse 1b indicates the nature of the seal mentioned in 7:3. The point is that they have firmly identified themselves with God, they have resisted the influence of Satan and his servants—whether demonic or human—and so they have avoided all falsehood. In other words, they are overcomers, victors—the category entitled to reward mentioned in every one of the seven letters to the churches in chapters 2 and 3.

As I mentioned in analyzing chapter 7, it is possible that this group represents an ethnic Israelite component in the people of God during the last days and/or beyond the Second Coming. I will discuss this in a little more detail in Chapter 16 on eschatology in the Old Testament.

Scene 2 (14:6–13): Three angel proclamations. These announcements relate especially (but not exclusively) to the outcome for those who have resisted God and followed Satan's influence. (1) The first angel announces that "the hour of [God's] judgment has come" (verses 6–7), apparently referring to the judgment that will fall just prior to and at the return of Jesus to the earth. This announcement includes an appeal to worship the true, creator God, which appears to be the reason this angel is described as "having the everlasting gospel."

(2) The second angel announces that "Babylon is fallen" (verse 8), a theme that a subsequent vision will develop in chapters 17–18; see the subsequent discussion of those chapters.

(3) The third angel announces that the wrath of God is being poured out in full measure, and any who worship "the beast" or receive his "mark" are warned of the eternal torment that awaits (verses 9–11).

Then a closing observation (verses 12–13) confirms the outcome for those who keep the commandments of God and maintain faith in Jesus Christ. They are the blessed dead and will have eternal rest.

Scene 3 (14:14–20): The final "harvest." The outcome of the conflict introduced in vision 1 (chapters 12–13) continues, with special focus on the gathering of humanity for judgment at the second coming of Jesus. Verse 14 indicates that a Person, one "like the Son of Man," comes to reign and gathers humanity for the judgment that He will administer. We have seen, in our survey of eschatology in the Gospels and Epistles, that when Jesus returns He will judge both the righteous and the wicked—as in Matthew 25, for example, discussed earlier. Here it is primarily, perhaps entirely, the judgment of the wicked that is in view, and this may provide yet another reason for separating the judgment of the wicked from the judgment of the righteous.

In dramatic fashion, this takes the form of representing King Jesus as having a "sharp sickle" in His hand, ready to cut and bind the sheaves of grain. Then the vision takes a different form, representing this as a grape harvest, with the "grapes" placed in a "winepress" which is driven by the wrath of God. Verse 20 depicts this in dramatic fashion.

The vision in chapter 14, with its three scenes, is basically anticipatory, pulling back the curtain to let us know that God's people will not be destroyed or defeated in the "war" with Satan and his followers, and that the destiny of the forces and followers of evil will be eternal torment. This revelation covers—in a summary manner—what subsequent visions will reveal in more detail, both for the righteous and for the wicked. Essentially all the ideas in these scenes will be revisited in later supplemental visions.

Vision 3: The Seven Final Plagues—the "Bowl Judgments" (Chapters 15–16)

This is a distinct vision that reaches back to "finish" what was referred to but not described when the seventh trumpet was blown—the trumpet-judgments that came when the seventh seal of the scroll was broken. In 11:14, this word appeared: "The second woe is past. Behold, the third woe is coming quickly." These bowl judgments constitute the third "woe."

Preliminary and Introductory (chapter 15). Verse 1 confirms that this will be about "the seven last plagues," in which "the wrath of God is complete (ESV: finished)"; this Greek word (*teleō*) indicates that something has reached the full measure of its nature, its intended goal or end. The chapter proceeds to prepare for this by unveiling yet another glimpse of the outcome of the conflict for "those who have the victory over the beast, over his image and over his mark," all of which has been described in the preceding supplemental visions. They are at peace before God's throne, with harps and on the "sea of glass" (compare Revelation 4:6; 5:8); and they sing a song appropriate for the occasion: the God of judgment is holy and His ways are just.

Then John sees a dramatic vision designed to focus attention on what is about to transpire: namely, seven angels receive, from the hands of one of the four living creatures, "seven golden bowls full of the wrath of God who lives forever and ever" (verse 7). Foreboding phenomena accompany and heighten the expectation (verse 8).

The Seven Final Plagues (chapter 16). While the visions in Revelation cover the entire church age, some of them unavoidably represent the last days before Jesus returns. These "bowl judgments" fit into that category; they are the *last* plagues in which the wrath of God is *completely finished*. I will survey them quickly and then discuss them all as a group.

Bowl 1: Sores (verse 2), described as "foul and loathsome" (ESV: "harmful and painful").

Bowl 2: Seas turned to blood (verse 3), causing the death of all things living in the seas. Compare Revelation 8:8–9 and the second trumpet-judgment, where only "a third" (a significant part, but relatively small compared to a whole) of the seas and marine life were thus affected.

Bowl 3: Fresh waters likewise affected (verses 4–7). An angel voice confirms the justice of this judgment.

Bowl 4: Scorching fire and heat (verses 8–9). But people, instead of repenting, curse God.

Bowl 5: Darkness and pain (verses 10–11), perhaps bitter cold with no sun shining. This plague is focused on the kingdom of "the beast" (antichrist), which I assume is very broad if not worldwide. Again people, though chewing their tongues in agony, blaspheme God.

Bowl 6: The Euphrates dried, making way for "the kings from the east" to gather for a great, final resistance to God and His people in "battle" at "Armageddon" (verses 12–16). This bowl-judgment takes a different course, but it is a judgment still. Verses 13–14, in typical imagery, show that the kings are deceived by the "unholy trinity": the Dragon, Beast, and False Prophet. This "battle" (not necessarily literal) will be referred to again in 19:17–21, where I will comment further. In the meantime, it is not clear that these place names should be taken literally; the identity of "Armageddon"—Mt. Megiddo?—is uncertain anyway. For that matter, the entire description may not be literal; more about that below.

Bowl 7: Great earthquake and severe hail (verses 18–21). The earthquake is so severe that the earth's features, like mountains and islands, are changed. The large hail is deadly. Once again, the record indicates that people do not repent but blaspheme God. The description includes the fact that "the great city was divided into three parts" and other cities fell into ruins. That this "great city" apparently means Jerusalem may be confirmed in 11:8; compare also the earthquake in the city mentioned there (11:13), where the effect was not as widespread. Again, as in 14:8, the doom of "Babylon" is announced—which the next vision will describe in detail. The voice proclaiming, "It is done!" (verse 17), like the fact that with these bowl-judgments the wrath of God is finished, implies that the things represented here are very near the end of the age and the return of Jesus.

The first question about these bowl-judgments is when they occur. That they come under the seventh trumpet of the seventh seal seems clear enough and tends to point to their being late in the present age and only shortly before the coming of Jesus back to earth. There is a broad lesson in them that applies to all of human history and especially to the church age (including the present): namely, that God must judge sin. The cup of His wrath can become full, and He will bring painful judgments. Even so, that same principle will be at work in a highly intensified way near the end of the age and leading up to the Second Coming. The prominence of references to God's wrath in the supplemental visions, and here with these seven bowls of wrath, is significant and sobering.

The other question is equally important and more difficult to answer: namely, whether the descriptions of these bowl judgments are meant to be taken literally or as symbolic and representing something other than what is said—judgment still, but in a different form. Either approach to interpretation is possible. If we take the judgments literally, such occurrences and effects could come to pass in the real world, just as described. All seven descriptions—with the possible exception of the sixth bowl-judgment—are not fantastical or weird.

By the same token, it would also be possible to take the descriptions as purely symbolic. In that case, the things John sees (mostly in the natural realm) represent some other kinds of hurtful judgments. All of them could possibly represent the infliction of spiritual "plagues," as in various kinds of falsehood, including both untruths and deceptive signs. The sixth bowl-judgment seems especially open to this kind of interpretation, with "three unclean spirits like frogs coming out of the mouth of the dragon, out of the mouth of the beast, and out of the mouth of the false prophet" (16:13). These seem most likely to represent lies that God deliberately allows to go forth, deceiving the nations; compare "send them strong delusion" in 2 Thessalonians 2:11. Even the "battle" described could just as easily be a war of truth and falsehood; I will return to this briefly in discussing chapter 19.

My own inclination, with regard to the first five judgments in particular, is to take them, broadly and primarily, to refer to physical judgments on mankind but not necessarily in exactly the forms used in the imagery. These judgments might come in any number of forms that cause great suffering by people on earth, whether originating in disease, natural disasters, or unusual phenomena. Some of the events of our recent years—including a pandemic virus, hurricanes, tornadoes, mudslides, earthquakes, raging forest fires, severe climate change, and others—at least impress us with great possibilities for suffering and death in the world. God has all sorts of things at His disposal, including things beyond anything we would presently comprehend. No one but Noah and his family believed a great flood was coming.

Vision 4: The Fall of "Babylon" (Chapters 17–19:10)

This event has already been signaled, and thus placed in our consciousness, at least twice: in 14:8 and 16:19. This vision doubles back to focus primarily on that. It can easily be subdivided into five parts, each with its own contribution to the whole, as follows.

Introduction of "Babylon" as a woman-harlot (17:1–6). She rides on a scarlet beast with seven heads and ten horns (verse 3), thus identifying the source of her influence or power. This scarlet beast is apparently the same beast that appears often throughout these supplemental visions after being anticipatively mentioned in 11:7 and introduced in chapter 13. Of course, the power behind the beast, also having seven heads and ten horns, is Satan himself (compare 12:3; 13:2).

Her attire is gaudy and expensive (verse 4). The name on her forehead (verse 5), "Babylon," is a code-word (note "mystery") indicating that this image does not represent the literal city by that name. That "the kings of the earth committed fornication" with her (verse 2) appears to refer to the "spiritual fornication" that was involved in commerce and trade, calling for alliances of various kinds.

The most significant thing about her is seen in the repetition in verse 2, "the inhabitants of the earth were made drunk with the wine of her fornication"; verse 4, "a golden cup full of abominations and the filthiness of her fornication"; and verse 6, "drunk with the blood of the saints and with the blood of the martyrs of Jesus." Babylon is wickedness personified, the enemy of God and persecutor of His people, the cause of much martyrdom in the ranks of followers of Jesus.

I will say more about what this image represents as the vision develops. For now I would urge that "Babylon" (like antichrist, as discussed earlier) is a broad image, representing more than a single person, institution, or place. In the history of the interpretation of Revelation, she has been identified with a number of actual cities, including a literal (restored) Babylon, Rome, Jerusalem, and others. All of these may have some truth to them, but Babylon is not a city as such—at least not primarily.

Interpretation of the "mystery" (17:7–18). This is one of the few times when Revelation undertakes to explain some of the symbolism of the apocalyptic imagery being used. In the Bible, a *mystery* is something that is known only by a revelation from God. That "Babylon" is a mystery (verse 5) leads to the revelation provided here, adding identification to both the "woman" Babylon and the scarlet beast which carries her.

This inspired interpretation is itself somewhat puzzling. In summary, the main points are as follows.

(1) The beast is the one "that was, and is not, and yet is" (verse 8), referring back to chapter 13 where "the beast" was introduced as having been mortally "wounded by the sword and lived" (13:3, 14). This is therefore antichrist, but there is little if anything to separate between antichrist and the Satan who empowers antichrist. Here verse 8 indicates he "will ascend out of the bottomless pit and go to perdition," which indicates his source and looks forward to his final destiny as described in 19:20.

(2) The seven heads of the beast represent seven mountains on which the woman-city rests (verse 9).

(3) The seven heads also represent seven kings, of whom five have already fallen, one is presently in power, and another will arise subsequently—all from the temporal perspective of John, apparently (verse 10).

(4) The beast represents an eighth king, yet to arise (verse 11).

(5) The ten horns represent "ten" kings, also yet to arise and to be in power for a short time ("one hour") with the beast; they confederate with the beast (verses 12–13), and God Himself is in control, deliberately permitting their motivation to do this (verse 17).

(6) This confederacy (of the beast and kings) will make war against the Lamb (Jesus), who will prevail over them (verse 14)—another reference to things to come as described in Revelation 19:17–21.

(7) The waters (on which the harlot sits) represent peoples (verse 15).

(8) The confederacy also turns against the harlot "Babylon" and contributes to her downfall (verse 16); this, too, is by God's active prompting (verse 17).

(9) The woman represents "that great city" that "reigns over the kings of the earth" (verse 18). Given that the woman herself rode the scarlet beast (verse 3), this means that there is a sense in which the power of Satan and antichrist are "divided against themselves," which is not surprising to us who know something of the ways of God. One wonders if Jesus might have had this very future in mind when He said, "And if Satan has risen up against himself, and is divided, he cannot stand, but has an end" (Mark 3:26). Indeed, at this point in Revelation, Satan's end is at hand.

Not everything about these identifications is certain, but some observations seem justified. Political power and intrigue are involved in Satan's campaign against God and His people, and the structures of the world that are ultimately used by Satan are active in his cause. As long ago as Psalm 2, the sacred canon took note of the fact that "the nations rage, and the people plot a vain thing," that "The kings of the earth set themselves, and the rulers take counsel together, against the Lord and against His Anointed [One]." Someone has said, "This world is not a friend to grace," and the power structures of the world often, if not always, represent the attempt of fallen mankind to declare independence from God and "run the show" without Him. It may well be that Paul had this in mind when he wrote that our spiritual warfare is against "principalities, against powers, against the rulers of the darkness of this age" (Ephesians 6:12).

In a sense, then, "Babylon"—like antichrist—is always with us, manifesting the malignant influence of Satan in high, political circles and other places of worldly power. The original readers of Revelation probably read this chapter and saw "Babylon" as Rome and antichrist as the then-current Emperor Domitian who was attempting to force them to bow to him as their god or to burn incense as an expression of worshipful submission to him. They were right if they thought this way. Some of the imagery of this chapter seems deliberately selected to suggest such a conclusion. After all, Rome famously sat on seven hills, and many other nations were confederate with the Empire and enriched themselves in trade with her.

In the history of the present age, there have been other candidates for Babylon, well deserved. New York City, the site of the United Nations main offices, might qualify; or Washington, DC, in the thinking of some. I wouldn't rule out the possibility that every great city in our world is, in some ways, Babylon—yet not in its final form.[20]

Even so, this does not eliminate the implication that near the end of the present age, and shortly before Jesus comes, there will be a place and powerful people and institutions—including a government or governments—that will serve as a central collection of the forces of evil heading up hostility to God and His people "in the latter days." This has always been the tendency of mankind in independence of God—going all the way back to ancient Babel, from which the name Babylon derives—and that tendency is sure to come to a head before the end.

Christians in John's day, then, as with Christians of any age—including ours—can rejoice in knowing that "Babylon" will fall before the coming King of kings and Lord of lords.

Announcement of the fall of "Babylon" (18:1–8). As the vision continues John sees and hears an angel—perhaps Jesus Himself, like the one in 10:1—declaring the destruction of Babylon: that is, of whatever place and power-structure qualifies when Jesus is about to return. The descriptions are somewhat abbreviated: her desolation (verse 2b), her spiritual harlotry with the nations (verse 3, repeating from chapter 17), an appeal to God's people to come out from her (verse 4), and an imprecatory appeal for her just punishment (verses 5–8). Most of this is dramatic enforcement of the reason for and nature of her judgment. She will be utterly destroyed in the hands of a holy God who judges recalcitrant wickedness.

Mourning over the ruins of fallen Babylon (18:9–20). The scene is pure drama, depicting the peoples of the earth who had done business with Babylon as being in mourning for her demise. These are in two main groups: the kings who—in the terms of chapter 17—committed spiritual fornication in being confederate with her (verses 9–10); and the merchants who enriched themselves in trade with her (including the masters of trade vessels, verse 17), thus complicit in her wickedness (verses 11–20).

Verse 20 seems a little strange to be in the mouth of the same mourners as verse 19. The solution to this lies in the fact that all of verses 4b-20 constitute a lengthy quotation of what is said by "another voice" (verse 4) within the vision, describing the scenes, rather than being scenes John himself saw. Then verse 20 is the concluding observation of that voice and stands in contrast to what the kings and merchants have been quoted as saying. They lamented Babylon's destruction; this voice calls for God's people to rejoice in Babylon's fall.

Pronouncement of the finality of Babylon's fall (18:21–24). Praise to God for Babylon's destruction is about to begin, in the spirit of verse 20. First, however, the coming fate of Babylon must be sealed by a final word. A dramatic action symbolizes the suddenness and completeness of Babylon's death (verse 21). Her desolation will be complete (verses 22–23). The reason is stated again to emphasize the justice of her judgment (verse 24): namely, Babylon is guilty of the death of those martyred for their faith in Jesus.

All of this, it appears, serves to confirm what I have said about the nature of "Babylon" as more than a single city at a given moment in history. Babylon is wickedness, active against God and His people. Shortly before Jesus returns, this evil will culminate in a great manifestation of this hostility and power, and the coming of Jesus will bring its destruction.

Praise to God and rejoicing at the destruction of Babylon (19:1–10). The fall of "Babylon" is rewarded with a great outburst of praise—a doxology—to God, presented in appropriate dramatic detail. The praise recognizes the justice of God's judgment of "Babylon," described again in the form in which she was introduced earlier. Her judgment is just, because of her "fornication" and her martyrdom of saints (verse 2). "Alleluia," as in the Old Testament, literally means "praise to Yahweh" (verse 3). The twenty-four "elders" join in (verse 4). A voice calls for praise, and such praise resounds (verses 5–6).

Then comes an invitation to "the marriage supper of the Lamb" (verses 7–9), where the bride of Christ—the Church made up of all saints of all time, apparently—is described as clothed in her wedding garment of fine linen, representing righteousness as expressed in actions (plural in the original). The dramatic staging of this vision concludes with John's own involvement again, falling at the feet of the angel guiding him—perhaps in deep emotion because of what he has seen—but being rebuffed for misguided worship.

For the most part, all the description of chapter 18 is dramatic staging and offers very little if anything toward identifying what the symbolism represents. As often, the real-world meaning is close enough to the surface to be recognizable. Once it has been established that "Babylon" is the final expression of a broad, powerful force that has been active throughout the church period (indeed, throughout human history), chapter 18 serves specifically to show that Jesus Christ, leading up to and culminating with His second coming, will defeat "Babylon" finally and completely. All the raging of the heathen and the vain plotting against God and His Son, led by persons or institutions hostile to Him and inflamed in their hatred by Satanic influence, will be put down. If the final form of this centers in a world power and its leader, headquartered in a great city, so be it. When Jesus returns He will reign and put all enemies under His feet (1 Corinthians 15:25).

Vision 5: The Second Coming and Beyond (19:11–20:10)

We come now to the last of what I have called the "supplemental visions" of chapters 12–20; I call them this because they supplement the central vision of the opening of the scroll with seven seals (chapters 4–11). This last vision unveils the climactic event of history: namely, the second coming of Jesus. It also briefly surveys what follows that coming.

This vision unveils in four consecutive scenes, with each clearly linked to the preceding by elements of the text. I have listed these in brief, survey fashion in Chapter 13. I revisit them now for final details.

Scene 1: The Second Coming (19:11–16). The primary question about this is whether it does, in fact, represent the still-future second coming of Jesus to earth. There is no question about the identity of the Person on the white horse; all the description leaves no doubt. Words like "eyes ... like a flame of fire," "name is ... the Word (*logos*) of God," "out of His mouth ... a sharp sword," and "rule ... with a rod of iron" are borrowed from previous descriptions of Jesus in His glory, given earlier in this book. His name is "King of kings and Lord of lords" (verse 16).

Furthermore, as the following, connected scenes will show, this One on the white horse comes to do things that involve final and eternal dispositions. Even here it is said He "treads the winepress of the fierceness and wrath of Almighty God" (verse 15). The next scene indicates that He slays wicked rebels with the sword that proceeds from His mouth (verse 21) and commits the Beast and False Prophet (of the earlier visions) to eternal torment in the lake of fire (verse 20). This makes it difficult, if not impossible, to interpret this scene as only symbolically representing earlier times when Jesus rescues His people from hostilities and persecution.

Scene 2: The defeat of those in rebellion (19:17–21). This is connected to the preceding, textually linked by the fact that it is the Person on the white horse who is acting (compare verse 11) and that He destroys by the sword proceeding from His mouth (compare verse 15). Rebel forces, under the leadership of the Beast and False Prophet, are defeated and these two are consigned forever to the lake of fire. This rebellion does not necessarily refer to a typical, physical warfare.

I observe again that the event described here is the same as that which is described in 16:12–16. In that earlier passage, there were three who sent out word to "the kings of the earth" (as here in verse 19) to gather for battle: namely, the unholy trinity of Dragon (Satan), Beast, and False Prophet. In this scene only two of these are captured and cast into the lake of fire, which ties directly to the next scene.

Scene 3: The binding of Satan and the reign of Jesus and His followers (20:1–6). Although the Beast and False Prophet, who were operating in the power of Satan (as previous visions indicated), were consigned to the lake of fire, the Dragon was not (as verse 10 will clarify subsequently). Instead, he is bound in the abyss for a "thousand years"; perhaps meaning a long period of time on earth. Because he is bound, he is no longer able to "deceive the nations."

For the same duration as Satan is bound, Jesus and His followers reign on earth. Whether those reigning with Him are *all* the saints, living and dead, who join Him in the air at His return, or are only the martyrs mentioned here depends on the antecedent of the pronoun "they" in the last sentence in verse 4. Does it refer back only to the martyrs just mentioned? Or does it look back to the earlier "they" at the beginning of verse 4? I am strongly inclined to the latter, and part of the reason is the emphasis on the "first resurrection" that follows. In other words, as we have seen in 1 Thessalonians 4, when Jesus returns, all saints living and dead will be resurrected or transformed (which has the same effect as resurrection) and go to meet Him in the air. This is, indeed, the "first resurrection" and the context here appears to justify us in concluding that all those in the first resurrection reign with Jesus. Furthermore, passages in Revelation like 3:21 and 5:10 indicate that the saints will reign with Jesus.

Scene 4: The final rebellion and disposition of Satan (20:7–10). My immediate reaction on reading this is to ask an incredulous "Why?" It seems such an unnecessary and surprising thing for Satan to be released to gather yet another rebellion against God and His people. Even as I ponder this, however, I realize that the Word of God is accurate and our Lord has His reasons (which I don't need to know). Perhaps the answer is as simple as recognizing that mankind must always be tested by God, and that need must apply also to the generation at the end of Jesus' reign.[21]

Regardless, Satan is released at the end of Jesus' messianic reign, ruling earth "with a rod of iron." He immediately spreads his lies to deceive the nations and foments another uprising. People who have perhaps conformed outwardly to the law of the King but whose hearts have not yielded to Him are easily enlisted by the prince of demons and by those whom he uses. A huge following assembles and marches to "the camp of the saints" and surrounds them. But fire from heaven falls and destroys them, Satan is taken prisoner, and he is consigned to the lake of fire and brimstone—*where the Beast and*

False Prophet already are (as in 19:20)—another note connecting these scenes. This is the final defeat of all rebellion against God.

Concluding observations about this entire vision. As already noted, the several scenes are closely connected, so that this is one consecutive vision. The glorified Messiah comes to reign, gathering to Himself (in the air) saints both living and dead at the time. Proceeding to earth, He puts down the pretenders—antichrist and "false prophet"—and those who have joined them to resist Jesus' rule, consigning the two leaders to eternal torment in the lake of fire. The powerful one behind them, Satan, is bound for the duration of Jesus' rule, which begins immediately, and the resurrected and transformed saints reign with Him. That this is for "a thousand years" is not necessarily literal, given that the numbers in Revelation are often symbolic; regardless, a time of significant length is meant. At the end of that time, when Satan is released and gathers a final following that would take the throne violently, they too are slain and the rule of Jesus continues unchallenged. At this point, then, Jesus has put down all enemies except for death itself, and that will come shortly.

I find it interesting that so little space is given to this "thousand-year" reign of Jesus. Apparently it is not the purpose of Revelation to provide much information about that except for the fact that it will be. Some interpreters of the Bible, and of Revelation, do not believe that there will be such a reign of Jesus on this earth; indeed, that may seem as unlikely as the release of Satan at the end of that reign. Many interpreters suggest that if it were not for this last vision, there would be no need for this reign. I myself have sometimes said that if it were not for Revelation 20 I could hold to a judgment of both righteous and wicked at Jesus' second coming, followed immediately by the eternal state that is described in Revelation 20:11–22:5. At the end of this chapter, I will include an extended note regarding the possibility that Revelation 20:1–10 is not connected to 19:11–21 but is, instead, an instance of recapitulation.

Yet, even in studying the entire New Testament in preparation for writing this volume, I have come to the conclusion that the reign of Jesus on this earth is a biblical (and logical) necessity. That is the reason I have focused on the fact that Jesus is coming to reign in Chapter 4. As the Davidic Messiah, it has always been Jesus' destiny to reign.

I realize that Christ's kingdom is not just for "a thousand years" (literal or otherwise) but is forever. Paul speaks of a time when Jesus has put all enemies under His feet and hands the kingdom over to God the Father, having completed His mission. That must come immediately after Revelation 20:10; and it seems certain that when He has turned the kingdom over to God, He will rule it forever, jointly, with the Father.

Final Judgment and Eternal State: Revelation 20:11–22:21

These last two and a half chapters in Revelation provide the conclusion of the story that the book has told. It would be possible to include them, or at least 20:11–15, among the "supplemental" visions just surveyed. Indeed, the last half of chapter 20 proceeds naturally from the account in 19:11–20:10 and seems to indicate what John saw next in that series of scenes.

The main reason I have not included the remaining part of Revelation with the section from 12:1–20:10 is that from this point on there is not much disagreement about the temporal setting. While not all interpreters will agree with the way I have viewed that vision (Vision 5, above) as being primarily future, beginning with the Second Coming, most interpreters will agree that once we reach 20:11 everything revealed will be in the future. (One need not hesitate to mark a new start in the middle of chapter 20, given that the chapter divisions are not part of the original, inspired text.) Since there will be significant agreement about this final section, I will provide only brief comments about it.

We may divide this final section into three parts.

(1) *The Great White Throne Judgment* (20:11–15). Apparently this judgment includes the wicked of all time, dead or alive at the end of Jesus' reign on earth, as well as the righteous who have died during His reign or are alive at this time. The righteous, dead or living, at the time of Christ's return to earth have probably already been judged at the Second Coming; but it is possible

that their judgment, also, takes place at this time at the end of His reign. (See the discussion of the time of judgment in Chapter 5.)

This is a judgment of works, on the one hand (verses 12–13), and a judgment between eternal life and death on the other hand (verse 15). The basis of the latter is whether the individual's name is written in the Lamb's Book of Life, which is determined by whether the individual is in saving union with Christ by faith.

At this judgment, Death itself is cast into the lake of fire, along with Hades. This is the "last enemy" to be put in total subjection to Christ, as in 1 Corinthians 15:26.

That "there was found no place for them"—that is, for "the earth and the heaven" of the natural cosmos—probably means that immediately prior to this judgment and in connection with 20:9b-10, the great conflagration of which 2 Peter 3 speaks will occur; what John sees immediately after this, in 21:1—"a new heaven and a new earth"—appears to confirm this timing.

(2) *The New Jerusalem and the New Heaven and Earth* (21:1–22:5). The eternal state of the righteous is described in beatific terms. This, too, is a vision John sees; like all the visions in Revelation, it may be a mixture of symbolism and real-world description. Knowing no more about the eternal state than we do, it probably is not possible for us to determine, in every word, which elements of the vision are to be taken literally and which are symbolic. We don't need to be able to do that, given that the entire description is meant to thrill us with what the eternal future holds.

Interestingly, the "New Jerusalem" is described both as a *city* with measurable dimensions (21:16–17) and as a *people*, the bride of Christ, the Church (21:2, 9)—I assume the "Church" of all time.

Among the most important elements of this blessed state is the fact that God and the Lamb are finally and forever "with" His covenant people (21:3); the wording of this verse is deliberately in the standard covenant terminology that runs through the entire Bible. As 1 Corinthians 15:28 expresses this, God will be "all in all"; there is therefore no need for temple or light in the eternal state of the righteous.

The earthly reign that ended with the final rebellion and destruction of Satan now becomes the eternal reign of God and the Lamb—and of the Holy Spirit, I assume; they share the throne (22:3). Indeed, even the saints will "reign forever and ever" with Jesus (22:5).

It should not escape notice that there is apparently an intentional reflection of the original state of the creation, before the fall, in this vision. Revelation 21 and 22 provide the restoration-culmination of God's purpose: namely, restoration to what was lost in the fall as a result of the sin of Adam and Eve. What seems clear is that "Paradise Regained" will be far superior to "Paradise Lost," and there will be no possibility of its being lost again.

(3) *Conclusion of Revelation* (22:6–21). It is helpful to read this final portion of Revelation immediately after reading 1:1–8; John picks up on his words to the churches in Asia about this book he is sending them. Again, the eschatological note sounds and in effect ties the whole together. Jesus is quoted as saying, "Behold, I am coming quickly" (verse 7), then again (verse 12), and yet again (verse 20). John, on behalf of all of us in the church, responds, "Even so, come, Lord Jesus" (verse 20).

Following the next chapter, a final chapter will bring together all the elements of eschatology that we have surveyed. Doing that will allow a comprehensive picture of biblical eschatology. The chapter will not answer every possible question or provide every possible detail, but it will provide a framework that answers the basic questions about the future according to a biblical perspective.

Extended Note Regarding Revelation 19:11–20:10

As I have indicated, some interpreters do not agree that there will be a messianic reign on earth following the Second Coming. Given the apparent tight connectedness of this entire passage, then, the question is how this connectedness can be avoided. There may be more than one way of accomplishing this, but one that I am aware of is the view that 20:1–10 does not follow, in time, 19:11–21 but is a separate vision.

I will not take the space to set this forth in detail or to argue against it; I have engaged in very little defense of my understanding in this book, since that would go well beyond my purpose. However, given how important this issue is, I wish to inform the reader where a thorough presentation of that view can be found. The writer is G. K. Beale, and his book is *The Book of Revelation: A Commentary on the Greek Text*, in the *New International Greek Testament Commentary* series (Grand Rapids: Eerdmans, 1999). In addition to his comment on the passage, he devotes a lengthy section to "Arguments for a Nonsequential Temporal Relationship between 20:1–6 and 19:11–21" on pages 974–84.

In summary, Beale regards 20:1 as beginning a new vision, one that recapitulates (re-tells for added information or perspective) what has been given before. In his view, verses 1–6 look back to an earlier period, and verses 7–10 describe again the same event as is described in 19:17–21. This way, the casting of Satan into the lake of fire (20:10) is at the same time as the casting of the Beast and False Prophet into the lake of fire (19:20); and the destruction of the rebels by fire in 20:9 corresponds to the execution of "the rest" with the sword that proceeds from the mouth of the coming Christ in 19:21. (Beale holds, as I do, that 16:12–16 refers to the same event as 19:17–21.)

This view seems to me to be indifferent to the connectedness of 19:11–20:10 that makes it a single story that develops from beginning to end, with each scene developing the story step by step. It does allow the interpreter to affirm that the Second Coming is followed immediately by the Great White Throne Judgment and the eternal state, without a so-called millennial reign of Christ on earth. My understanding of how 20:10 relates to 19:20, as explained above, will not allow me to take this approach.

Endnotes

[20] Jeff Blair—helpfully, I think—reminds me that even our own political U.S.A. can be Babylon, especially when Christians confuse the nation with the kingdom of God. He wisely observes that the church must always keep free to speak truth to power.

[21] Jackson Watts suggests the possibility that God will give this final generation on earth what they most want—a recurring biblical theme.

Chapter 16

ESCHATOLOGY IN THE OLD TESTAMENT, A SAMPLE FROM JEREMIAH

My purpose in this book does not include a thorough treatment of Old Testament eschatology, for more than one reason. (1) To analyze all passages in the Old Testament that may look to the end of the present age, and beyond, would require another volume. (2) One sample from the Old Testament will serve to introduce the main consideration in eschatology. (3) My main reason for dealing with the Old Testament at all is to pursue the question whether there is any defined role for ethnic Israel in the eschatology that has taken shape in the previous chapters devoted to the eschatology of the New Testament.

While the Old Testament will not change the basic outline found in the New Testament, it adds its own perspective, and that perspective largely speaks to the possibility of a place for Israel in the end-time events unveiled in the New Testament. The Old Testament might add details to the situation during the reign of Jesus on the earth, but that, too, is beyond the purpose of this book.

The sample I will use in this chapter will be the book of the prophet Jeremiah, focusing primarily on the part of that book that is often called the "Little Book of Comfort."

Old Testament Prophecy: Some General Observations

Before turning to Jeremiah, however, I think it helpful to offer some general observations about Old Testament prophecy, a literary genre where eschatology may be found. One should realize, first, that biblical prophecy is not merely revelation of the future. Prophets were, simply, people who spoke for God: that is, they received revelation from Him and were responsible to pass that revelation on to the people. Only at times did that revelation look to what was future—whether near or distant—for them. If one studies the prophets—both the major and the minor prophets, from Isaiah to Malachi, specifically—he or she will notice several themes common to them all, or at least common to them as a group.

A *major* theme in the prophets is the exposure of Israel's sins—and when I use *Israel* in this chapter I will usually be referring to the nation as a whole, not just to the northern kingdom in the days when Israel was divided from Judah, extending from the reign of Rehoboam to the captivity. The reader should usually be able to discern, in context, the sense of *Israel* as I use it.

Some of the prophets spoke primarily to those in Israel as the northern kingdom; Hosea was one of these. Some spoke primarily to those in Judah, the southern kingdom; Zephaniah was one of these. But nearly all of them revealed the sins of ethnic Israel. A great part of the prophetic message focuses directly on the nation's sins as the reason for the impending judgment of God and as the condition from which they needed to repent. When you read any of the prophets, you won't have much difficulty reading the larger part of their message, which was an exposure of sin and of impending judgment.

As a result, a commensurate part of the focus of the Old Testament prophets was on that judgment—future to them, not so much to us—that was to fall. For the northern kingdom, that judgment culminated in their conquest by Assyria in 721 BC. For the southern kingdom, it was the conquest by Babylon in 586 BC. In both cases a major portion of the people were carried away into captivity by the conquerors. Many of the prophets warned about this coming judgment in God's providential government of the affairs of humanity. You won't have any difficulty, usually, in recognizing when a given prophet is speaking about this; and you'll realize how gracious God was in revealing this in a way that allowed for repentance and the possibility of avoiding such judgment—which both branches of the ethnic Israelites finally failed to do.

A few of the prophets speak primarily to issues different from these. Jonah and Nahum preached primarily to Nineveh in Assyria and to Assyria itself, respectively. Obadiah spoke directly to the Edomites, descended from Esau. Daniel ministered as much to the Babylonian royalty as to Israel, during the days when the Jews were settled in Babylon. Haggai and Zechariah ministered to Israel, but after the people had returned from captivity to the Holy Land, primarily to promote the rebuilding of the Jewish Temple. Malachi also ministered to Israel, but even later than that. By and large, however, the Old Testament prophets exposed Israel's sins and pronounced the judgment that was to come. In looking to coming judgment, of course, they were "eschatological" from their own temporal perspective, but that was in reference to a relatively near future.

In some cases the Old Testament prophets looked farther down the road than that, often seeing a more distant future that was foreshadowed by then-present or near-future events. Thus Isaiah spoke of the birth of an "Immanuel" to a virgin (7:14) and of a Child who would bear on his shoulder a government and peace that would not end (9:6–7). Micah prophesied about a ruler that would come from Bethlehem (5:2). Daniel prophesied about four kingdoms, including three that would take Babylon's place (2:36–45), and also about the length of the period between his own time and the appearance of "Messiah the Prince" (9:25–26)—a prophecy not so easy to pin down—and beyond the scope of this chapter. There are others, and among the prophecies of the Old Testament were many that, like Daniel, looked several hundred years ahead to the coming of Messiah.

Finally, in some cases the prophets apparently looked beyond the first coming of Messiah—prophecies now fulfilled, of course—to things beyond that first coming. In a general way, these prophecies speak of a restoration of Israel to the land God promised them and to a state of blessedness in relation to God that would amount to a full renewal of the covenant relationship between Israel and God.

This is where problems of interpretation arise. No one would question that the prophets often said, under divine inspiration, that God was yet going to bless Israel in special ways. In the history of interpretation, two radically different approaches to such prophetic utterances have developed. One is that at least some of these prophecies promise a future blessedness for ethnic Israel that has not yet come about; this means that ethnic Israel has yet to play a role in eschatology, specifically in the kingdom over which Jesus Messiah will reign.

The other approach is to interpret such prophecies to apply to the people of God of the future, in which Gentile believers and the Christian Church are viewed as the "Israel of God" in the days near the end of the present age. This way, "Israel" (as in Romans 11:26) does not mean ethnic Israel; instead, it means the Church—which has *replaced* Israel in the program of God. According to this approach, then, any Old Testament prophecies that promise a blessed future for Israel must be understood to speak, not of a renewal of the covenant relationship between God and ethnic Israel but of a new covenant relationship between God and all who are in the true Church of God by faith in Jesus Christ, regardless whether they are ethnic Gentiles or Jews.

One of the things that plays a part in this approach to interpreting the Old Testament prophecies is that such prophecies usually take the form—or *genre*—of poetry. (If you have a Bible that formats poetry differently, you can see this in much of Old Testament prophecy.) The reason this is involved is simple: poetry often relies on imagery, conveying truth by means of literary images that evoke truth less directly than in ordinary prose. (This is not just true for Old Testament poetry; it is true for poetry in other languages, including English.) I sometimes say that poetry is intended to be *felt* and not just told and understood. In poetry—whether in English or Hebrew—one may convey truth in an evocative image that is not meant to be taken literally.

This is not necessarily *limited* to poetry, by the way. If someone says, "I'm walking on air," he or she shouldn't be taken literally. The expression originated as an image that conveys the idea of being elated. The reader will no doubt understand this, but it is important to take it into account when interpreting Scripture, especially poetry in Scripture. Here is where the "problem" of interpretation often arises: namely, shall we take the language at full face value, or is it meant to convey a truth that isn't quite the same thing as the language literally communicates?

As a fairly obvious example take Isaiah 11:6–8, which describes a beatific future in appealing, poetic language, including: "The wolf also shall dwell with the lamb, the leopard shall lie down with the young goat, the calf and the young lion and the fatling together; and a little child shall lead them." Also: "The weaned child shall put his hand in the viper's den." This description evokes strong and appealing emotions. Should it be taken literally to refer to animals and children in an idyllic state? Or is it intended to paint a picture of a blessed state—of peace and harmony, perhaps in a more ordinary state of affairs?

Dispensationalists have attempted to teach us the following hermeneutical principle: Always interpret a passage literally unless it is impossible to do so. That's not a principle that the Bible itself teaches, and it isn't fully justified. It is better to say, always interpret a passage literally or figuratively as the passage itself, in its context, appears to require.

I'm not trying to say that Isaiah 11:6–8 should be interpreted literally or figuratively. I am saying that the language itself doesn't tell us which way to interpret it. An objective interpreter must weigh the possibilities and, being as honest as possible—within himself and with the text in its context—assess the intended teaching of the passage. If the Spirit of God, in inspiring Isaiah or any other biblical writer, meant for a passage to be taken literally, take it literally; if He meant for it to be taken figuratively, take it figuratively.

So how do we decide this? By carefully studying the text itself, in the immediate context and in the larger context of the whole document. It isn't easy to do this. It's all too easy to be influenced by the opinions of others.

To restate my point: When biblical prophecy is written as poetry, there will sometimes be imagery that can possibly be taken literally at full face value, or that can be taken (like the apocalyptic imagery we have encountered in Revelation!) as representing a real-world truth that isn't exactly the same thing as the language of imagery expresses. This caution—and it is a call for caution—affects our understanding of Old Testament passages that are eschatological, that look to a future linked to the second coming of Jesus to this earth and beyond. The Old Testament sample that I have chosen for this book will provide occasion for dealing with this issue.

Jeremiah and the "Little Book of Comfort"

The prophecy of Jeremiah provides a helpful study of an Old Testament contribution to our present-day, New Testament eschatology. Jeremiah's ministry extended from 627 to about 580 BC. According to the prophet himself (1:1–3), he ministered to Judah during (and beyond) the reigns of the last five kings of Judah before the Babylonian Exile. His ministry began in Josiah's thirteenth year (628/27 BC; see 1:2) and continued under Josiah's progeny, as follows: Jehoahaz/Shallum (609); Jehoiakim (609–598); Jehoiachin/Coniah/Jeconiah (598–597): and Zedekiah/Mattaniah (597–586). Jeremiah was among the Jews who were left behind (when the Babylonians carried most of them to Babylon). He then ministered to the others who remained in Palestine for an undefined period of time (see 39:11–44:30).

For Jeremiah's call and commission, see 1:4–19. For the way he was received, see (in probable chronological order): 11:18–23; 18:18–23; 20:1–18; 36:1–32; 29:24–32; 28:1–17; 37:11–21; 38:1–28; 39:11–14; and 42:1–44:30. No information about his death appears in the record.

The Major Message of Jeremiah

The proclamation of Jeremiah that dominates the book is two-fold: (1) Judah and Jerusalem are guilty of great wickedness; (2) God is about to judge them severely at the hands of the Babylonians.

(1) For the first of these, 7:1–10 provides a good overview and names Judah's most outstanding sins. These are then brought up again and again throughout Jeremiah's prophetic proclamation. These sins included: *rapaciousness*: namely, greed manifested in the unjust seizure of others' belongings and including *oppression, covetousness,* and *false dealing* (see also 5:26–29; 6:7, 13; 8:10; 21:11–12; 22:3, and 13–17); *violation of the Sabbath* (see also 17:21–27); *adultery* (see also 23:10, 13–14; and 29:23); *lying* and *deceit* (see also 9:3–6); *false prophets* (see also 5:12–13; 14:13–15; 23:16–17, 21–22, 25–27; and

27:16–18); and *idolatry*, represented as *spiritual adultery* (see also 2:4–8, 11, 20, 26–28; 5:7–9; 10:2–5; and 19:2–5). This provides a general picture of what life was like in Judah during these years of spiritual apostasy, especially after the death of Josiah, the last God-fearing king of Judah.

(2) The second major element of Jeremiah's message was the certainty that God was going to judge Judah and Jerusalem for their wickedness. Yahweh had provided some postponement of judgment, first during the reign of good king Hezekiah (715–686) and finally as a result of revival under Josiah (640–609). But Jeremiah insisted that God's judgment, using the Babylonians as his instrument, was now both impending and inevitable. Avoiding it was no longer possible—if for no other reason because there would be no repentance. Among many elements of this condemnation to doom were: *coming destruction (*4:5–8—note the poetic elements; 5:15–17; 32:26–36); *resulting lamentation and bitterness* (7:29–30, 33–34); *the broken flask* object lesson (19:10–15); *the ruined sash* object lesson (13:1–11); *even Moses and Samuel could not intervene* (15:1–9); *a captivity of 70 years* (25:8–12; 29:10); and *safety only in submission to their conquerors* (21:1–10).

If you master these two themes in Jeremiah—Judah's wickedness and Yahweh's impending judgment—you will thereby master probably two-thirds of the book.

Promises of Hope Under a Pall of Impending Doom

Relieving the dominant and distressing message of Jeremiah—about wickedness and judgment—is a message of hope sprinkled here and there among denunciations. This is especially true of chapters 30–33, at the heart of Jeremiah's work, sometimes called the "Little Book of Comfort." But the promises are not limited to that important section. There are invitations to repentance sprinkled throughout the work, accompanied by promises of blessing if that invitation should be heeded. This offer of grace does not mitigate the certainty of impending judgment, since Yahweh knows that Judah for the most part will not respond to the invitation; but it stands as a pointed reminder of God's mercy and provision for forgiveness. As Keil urged long ago, "It was no longer possible to turn aside the judgment. … Yet the faithful covenant God, in divine long-suffering, granted to His faithless people still another gracious opportunity for repentance and return to Him."[22]

Before undertaking a closer analysis of key passages, then, I list here a broader selection of passages that promise blessing. This yields a better understanding of how widespread the offer of hope is.

3:12–18; 4:1–4—A call to Israel, then also to Judah, to return to Yahweh.

7:1–7—A call to Judah to amend her ways, with an attendant promise.

22:1–4—An appeal to restore justice in the land, with an attendant promise.

23:1–8—Judgment on the "shepherds," to be followed by restoration.

24:4–7—Yahweh's good purpose for those taken into captivity.

29:10–14—After the 70-year captivity, Yahweh will restore and bless.

30–33—The "Little Book of Comfort."

50:4–5, 17–20, 33–34—When Babylon is judged, Israel and Judah will be restored.

These passages (with a few others, less extensive) show that even when the Divine Judge's sentence had been formally and irrevocably pronounced, there was always a door of hope. It could open right away if God's people would repent and mend their wicked ways. There was definite hope for the future, found in Yahweh's covenant promises.

Analysis of Selected Key Passages

From those listed above I have selected the most informative ones for a brief analysis, without detailed exegesis; the reader will need to read carefully each passage along with this analysis. Most of what is promised is clear enough and not controversial. I will emphasize the elements of each passage that speak more directly to my purpose.

23:1–8—The shepherds (kings and other leaders, as in chapter 22) have scattered Yahweh's sheep (verses 1–2). But He will regather the sheep, make them fruitful, and give them good shepherds (verses 3–4). "Days are coming"[23] when He will raise up to David a Branch to reign and restore justice, save Judah and Israel, and be known as "The LORD [Yahweh] Our Righteousness" (verses 5–6).[24] Those restored will swear by Yahweh as the One who brought them back from all the lands where He had driven them, and they will dwell safely in their land (verses 7–8). It seems likely that Jesus Christ is the fullest expression of this messianic "Branch."

29:10–14—Jeremiah sends a letter to those already exiled in Babylon, assuring them that this was Yahweh's doing and that they should settle down there and seek the welfare of that city (verses 1–9). He promises that after 70 years Yahweh will visit them, fulfill His promise to them, and cause them to return to the homeland, for He purposes "a future and a hope" for them (verses 10–11). They will call on Him in prayer and He will listen, and they will seek Him with all their hearts and find Him (verses 12–13). Yahweh will be found, will bring them back from captivity in "all the places where I have driven you," and will restore them to the place from which they had been carried away (verse 14).

Verses 12–13 apparently refer to their seeking Yahweh, wholeheartedly, while yet in captivity—probably reflecting Deuteronomy 4:29–30; verse 14 likewise summarizes Deuteronomy 30:3–5.

This paragraph is "bookended"[25] at the beginning and end by the promise to "cause you to return to *this place*" (verse 10) and "bring you to *the place* from which I cause you to be carried away captive" (verse 14). I will refer to the significance of this below.

30:3, 8–11, 17–22—Chapter 30 begins the "Little Book of Comfort." Intermingled with pointed reminders of the sins that have brought exile to Judah are these marvelous promises of hope. "Days are coming" (cf. 23:5, 7) when Yahweh will bring both Israel and Judah back from captivity and restore them to possession of the land he gave to their forefathers (verse 3). "In that day" (apparently the day described in verses 5–7) their yoke and bonds will be broken and foreigners will no longer enslave them. They will serve Yahweh, instead, and David their king whom Yahweh will raise up for them (verses 8–9)—most likely meaning the messianic Branch of David, as in 23:5. They need have no fear, for Yahweh will save them and their descendants "from afar" (their place of exile). They will return in peace and Yahweh will be with them and, though He must discipline them, He will not "make a complete end" of them as He will of their captors (verses 10–11). He will bless them in many ways (verses 17–22): He will heal them (verse 17); their city and palace will be rebuilt right where they had formerly been (verse 18); they will be thankful and rejoice and be honored (verse 19); their people will thrive (verse 20); their leader will be one of them and will draw near to God (verse 21); and the historic covenant affirmation will be reaffirmed: "You shall be My people, and I will be your God" (verse 22).

31:1–40—This passage is at the very heart of the promises of hope in the "Little Book of Comfort." "At the same time" (verse 1) apparently connects with "in the latter days" (30:24) and means the messianic future. Yahweh makes promises of covenant and restoration (verses 1–6), for "all the families of Israel" (that is, Israel and Judah). As in 31:22, the covenant language will apply (verse 1) and be manifested in their experience of grace, rest, love, rebuilding, natural planting and eating, and desire for Zion and Yahweh himself (verses 2–6).

Specifically, the promises are meant for Israel, the ten tribes (verses 7–21). Yahweh will bring them from the North and from the ends of the earth (verse 8), lead them "in a straight way" as Israel's Father (verse 9), and regather them as their Redeemer (verses 10–11). They will come in song, prosperity, and joy (verses 12–13); be satisfied with Yahweh and His blessing (verse 14); grieve no more (verses 15–16); and have hope for the future return of their children (verse 17). Yahweh will have mercy on Ephraim (Israel) as the son of His love (verses 18–20) and they will turn back to their cities (verse 21).

The promises are also specifically for Judah (verses 22–26). Yahweh will call her back to Himself (verse 22) and they will again speak of their land as a place of justice, holiness, and God's blessing (verse 23). Farmers and shepherds will again flourish there (verse 24), and Judah will be satisfied and replenished (verse 25). Jeremiah awakes and finds this vision sweet (verse 26).

"Days are coming" when Israel and Judah will be fully inhabited again, characterized by rebuilding and planting (verses 27–28). The old saying about fathers and children will be replaced by a recognition of each person's individual responsibility (verses 29–30).

Indeed, "days are coming" when a new covenant will be established (verses 31–34). It will include both Israel and Judah and will be unlike the former (Sinaitic) covenant which they had broken (verses 31–32). God's law will be written in their hearts (verse 33a)—internalized, in other words—and the covenant formula ("I will be their God; and they shall be My people") will be renewed (verse 33b). They will know God apart from having to teach knowledge of Him to one another (verse 34a), and their sins will be forgiven (verse 34b).

Finally, Yahweh certifies His promises to them (verses 35–40). They are as sure as the ordinances of nature (verses 35–37). The seed of Israel will not cease "from being a nation before Him forever" (verses 36b, 37b) and Jerusalem will be permanently rebuilt (verses 38–39). All of it will be "holy to the LORD" forever (verse 40).

32:37–44—Leading to the substance of this passage, in verses 1–36, Yahweh instructs Jeremiah to buy a field in his home area of Anathoth, which he does. But he prays to ask why, given the impending certain destruction. Yahweh responds and reiterates His promises of restoration. He will gather them from all countries where He has driven them and bring them back to dwell in safety (verse 37). The covenant commitment will be reaffirmed: "They shall be My people, and I will be their God" (verse 38). They will have "one heart and one way": to fear Yahweh forever (verse 39). He will make "an everlasting covenant" with them—apparently another way of referring to the new covenant (verse 40)—and will put the fear of Yahweh in their hearts—through His Spirit—so that they will not depart (verse 41). Yahweh says, movingly, that He will do them good and plant them in the land "with all My heart and with all My soul" (verse 41). Fields will once again be bought (thus Jeremiah's action) in all the land because the exiles will return (verses 43–44).

33:6–26—In yet another message to the prophet (verses 1–5), Yahweh rehearses His promises of hope. He will give them healing and peace (verse 6) and cause the exiles—both Israel and Judah—to return and rebuild (verses 7,

11b). He will cleanse and pardon them from their sins (verse 8) and they will be known among the nations as a testimony to God for their joy, honor, and prosperity (verses 9–11), with shepherds and flocks (verses 12–13).

Furthermore Yahweh certifies the performance of His promises (verses 14–26). "Days are coming" when He will do all He has said for Israel and Judah (verse 14). He will raise up a Branch of righteousness to David (verse 15), and Judah and Jerusalem will be safe and known as "The LORD Our Righteousness" (verse 16). Both the Davidic covenant (verse 17) and the Levitical covenant will be fulfilled (verse 18), as surely as the ordinances of nature are established (verses 19–21), and the descendants of both David and the Levitical priests will be multiplied (verse 22).[26] To repeat: the promises are as sure as the ordinances of nature; Yahweh will not cast away the descendants of Jacob and David, and the descendants of David will rule over the descendants of Abraham, Isaac, and Jacob (verses 23–26), for He will cause the captives to return (verse 26b).

Key Elements Common to the Passages Promising Hope

I proceed now to enumerate key elements that appear throughout these (and the rest of the) positive passages that promise hope for Israel's future in spite of the condemnation of sin and sentence of judgment on Israel, Judah, and Jerusalem.

1. The promised future is for both Israel (the ten northern tribes) and Judah (with Benjamin) and includes the tribe of Levi. This important element appears several times throughout most of the passages. See 23:6; 30:3; 31:27, 31; and 33:14. Typical is 31:31: "I will make a new covenant with the house of Israel and with the house of Judah." In 31:1, "all the families of Israel" likewise speaks of all the tribes.

2. In all the passages, the first element is the promised return from captivity. This is where the hope for the future begins, even though it does not end there. Without this, there would be no promises and no comfort. Interestingly, several passages appear to use this basic promise to wrap the rest of the promises in, a literary technique typically called by the Latin word *inclusio*:

23:3—"I will gather … out of all countries where I have driven them."

23:8—"from all the countries where I had driven them."

29:10—"I will … cause you to return to this place."

29:14—"I will bring you to the place from which I cause you to be carried away."

32:37—"I will gather them out of all countries where I have driven them."

32:44—"I will cause their captives to return."

33:7—"I will cause the captives of Judah and the captives of Israel to return."

33:11b—"I will cause the captives of the land to return as at the first."

33:26b—"I will cause their captives to return, and will have mercy on them."

3. Closely related to the preceding and necessarily involved in it is the ancient covenant promise of the land, to which Israel and Judah will return:

23:8—"They shall dwell in their own land."

29:10—"I will … cause you to return to this place."

30:3—"I will cause them to return to the land that I gave to their fathers."

31:17—"Your children shall come back to their own border."

31:21—"Turn back to these your cities."

In a number of places this promise becomes highly specific:

30:18—"The city shall be built upon its own mound."

31:5—"You shall yet plant vines on the mountains of Samaria."

31:12—"They shall come and sing in the height of Zion."

31:38–40—"The city shall be built … from the Tower of Hananel to the Corner Gate." (Additional specific details follow.)

32:43–44—"Fields will be bought in this land"; "Men will buy fields for money, sign deeds and seal them, and take witnesses." (Specific locations are named.)

33:10–11—"There shall be heard in this place … in the cities of Judah, in the streets of Jerusalem … the voice of joy."

4. The promises include a Davidic king, who will be raised up as a branch or sprout of righteousness:

23:5—"I will raise to David a Branch of righteousness; a King shall reign and prosper."

30:9—"They shall serve the LORD their God, and David their king, whom I will raise up for them."

33:15—"I will cause to grow up to David a Branch of righteousness." (See also verses 17ff.)

5. The promises emphasize the fixing of God's law in hearts and not just on tablets of stone:

29:13—"You will seek Me and find Me, when you search for Me with all your heart."

31:33—"I will put My law in their minds, and write it on their hearts."

32:40—"I will put My fear in their hearts so that they will not depart from Me."

As already observed, this indicates an internalization of God's revealed will, resulting in obedience from the heart as the expression of the fear of God.

6. The promises likewise emphasize the forgiveness of sins and cleansing that will be part of the hope for the future, closely related to the internalization of God's law:

31:34—"I will forgive their iniquity, and their sin I will remember no more."

33:8—"I will cleanse them from all their iniquity … and I will pardon all their iniquities by which they have sinned."

7. The promises include what is apparently a renewal of the covenant relationship between Yahweh and His covenant people. This is immediately obvious in the repeated expression of the traditional covenant formula:

30:22—"You shall be My people, and I will be your God."

31:33—"I will be their God, and they shall be My people."

32:38—“They shall be My people, and I will be their God.”

This covenant emphasis, however, is not merely a renewal of the covenant put in force at Sinai. Instead, it will involve the establishment of a “new covenant,” as found in 31:31–34. Indeed, this new covenant includes the very same elements brought out in this section. (a) Both Israel and Judah will be involved (verse 31); (b) God’s law will be in minds and hearts and not just on tablets of stone (verse 33); (c) the originally intended covenant relationship will be realized (verse 33); (d) individuals will know God personally (verse 34); and (e) there will be forgiveness of sins (verse 34). (That this passage is quoted in Hebrews 8:7–13 will be discussed below.)

As I have noted, Yahweh’s promise to “make an everlasting covenant with them” (32:40) is yet another reference to this new covenant.

The Fulfillment of These Promises: Implications for Eschatology

Almost any reader of these sections of Jeremiah, including especially the “Little Book of Comfort” (chapters 30–33) will ask the question *when*, and so in what way, these promises were to be fulfilled. There are implications for our eschatology and the way we do our hermeneutics.

My study of Jeremiah, with results summarized in this chapter, was undertaken before beginning this work on eschatology. I intended to determine what Jeremiah says, and means, without any prejudice toward any given school of thought on the subject. Here, then, are my observations about some things that seem important for understanding Jeremiah.

1. All of Jeremiah’s passages that contain promises of hope for the future, in the face of then-present condemnation and impending judgment, should be seen as a single “package,” with all of them referring to the same content. This includes not only the passages I have surveyed above but a number of other lesser statements in the book, including (for example) 16:14–15. In all the passages the language is similar and the same threads appear, as the survey above tends to demonstrate.

Whatever time and manner of fulfillment one of the key passages has, then, all of them have. Nor should this be surprising, since the same commonality applies to the many passages exposing Judah's sins and pronouncing doom. These passages are even more lengthy and repetitive, and all of them refer to the same basic diagnosis and prognosis.

The phrase "days are coming when …" occurs some fifteen (or more) times in Jeremiah, and about half of them are in passages promising Israel's conquest and exile at the hands of the Babylonians, with the other half being promises of hope. This usage means that the phrase itself cannot be seen as any indicator of how far off those "days" are, even though they were definitely future when Jeremiah spoke of them. Even so, the phrase serves as yet another affirmation that binds all the promises together as one package: see 23:5; 30:3; 31:27, 31; and 33:14.

From here on, then, I will be identifying the elements that I think must be included in this "package" of promises.

2. Whatever else may be included, the return from Babylonian captivity to "the promised land" (which began in 539 BC with Cyrus's decree releasing the Jews from Babylonian exile) is the foundational element in this package of promises. I say this for more than one reason. First is the clear emphasis, throughout, on that return. I am impressed with the *inclusio* I have mentioned above, wrapping the package in this promise to bring the captives back just as they went away. In 31:21, for example, Yahweh tells the people, in effect, to mark well the route by which they go so that they can follow it back to the homeland. Jeremiah makes clear that the captivity will last 70 years, specifically (29:10), and then they will return. I have noted the emphasis on the land, and the specificity with which that emphasis is developed: they will build on the very mound of Jerusalem's ruins (30:18).

I am not suggesting that all the promises in this package were completely fulfilled when the Jews returned from captivity under Zerubbabel and Joshua, or in the days of Ezra or Nehemiah. I'll return to this shortly. But we must not underestimate the importance of that return for this package of promises. Nothing else would have followed had it not been for that. Everything begins with that and builds thereon. The return is of primary importance, and everything else that happens to fulfill the promises has its foundation in the return from Babylonian exile in 539 BC and the years following.

3. Even so, there are some promises that do not seem to have been adequately or completely fulfilled when the Jews returned to Palestine at the end of the exile in Babylon. To some degree, deciding this is subjective and the stuff of disagreements. But that is not entirely the case, and each individual will have to weigh this to decide for himself or herself. Here are the most important possibilities.

a. It is a question whether Israel and Judah have been reunited to participate in the fulfillment of the promises. I suppose two extreme views are possible here. One would say that Israel—that is, the ten northern tribes—became wholly estranged from the Jewish community during and following the exile and that they remain the "ten lost tribes" to this day. The other extreme would be to say that the two branches did, in fact, become fully reunited following the captivity in one way or another: either in literal reality or at least in a "spiritual" sense in the New Testament people of God, the Church—if, indeed, this last sense can be thought of as the reunion of Israel and Judah.

I will not attempt to judge between these possibilities here, except to suggest that the truth probably lies somewhere between these extremes. On the one hand, I am satisfied that the old and persistent idea that there are still "ten lost tribes" is not justified. I would especially reject suggestions that they are to be identified with the British (British Israelism) or with Native Americans. I think, instead, that representatives from the ten northern tribes made their way back into Palestine along with those of Judah and Benjamin who returned from Babylon; today's "Jews" probably include some from all of the original tribes of Israel. From the beginning of the division, "Judah" (used broadly) included Benjaminites and many Levites. The biblical text describing the return from exile tends to support the fact that they thought of themselves as representing the whole of Israel. But I will not take the space to develop or argue this now.

What I think is true, however, is that the reuniting of Israel and Judah, and the participation of both in the restoration after the exile, plays but a very small part in the post-captivity literature: namely, Ezra and Nehemiah, as well as Haggai and Zechariah—not to mention 2 Chronicles. In that light, it seems to me that the Bible does not support the idea that this particular promise in Jeremiah was truly fulfilled in the return from exile.

b. It seems clear that Jeremiah's promises about the heart and knowing God were not fulfilled in the return from captivity. The promises included having God's law written in the heart and such knowing of God that they would not have to teach the knowledge of God to one another. It is difficult to believe that this was true of the Jews after their return.

No doubt they had learned *some* lessons fairly well. In particular it appears that they had learned to avoid traditional idolatry. Apart from that, however, the record of Ezra and Nehemiah appears to point to a religious outlook that was only a little better than before the exile. The reformers had to deal with mixed marriages, Sabbath breaking, and failure to support the Levites, for examples, and not just once. To be sure, there was some spiritual renewal, such as followed the long reading of the law under Ezra, but it apparently lasted no longer than such renewals under the pre-exilic kings.

Indeed, the picture I get of Judaism in the first century (the time of Jesus) is that of a false religion, one where external observance was substituted for internal righteousness.[27] I won't pursue this at length, but it may well be that the widespread rejection of Jesus the Messiah is ample evidence of what I am saying. The internalization of the law and knowledge of God promised by Jeremiah seems a far thing from the dominant mindset of Judaism in the time of Jesus. It is difficult to reconcile the internalization of the law of God with the Jewish leaders' hostility to Him who was the very incarnation of that law.

At least until the crucifixion of Jesus, then, it does not seem that Jeremiah's promises of the internalization of the law and knowledge of God had been fulfilled.

c. The same can be said for the promise of a Davidic king to reign. It is true, of course, that Zerubbabel was descended from David, but it is likewise true that he did not reign as king over the returning Jews. From the fall of Jerusalem in 586 BC until the present, there has not been a king for the Jews of any lineage, much less that of David, or a continuing kingly rule.[28] It seems clear that one must look beyond the return from captivity to find any fulfillment for this element of Jeremiah's promises.

4. There are important elements of the "new covenant" (31:31–34) that are clearly fulfilled in the new covenant inaugurated by the redemptive work of Jesus Christ and celebrated in the Lord's Supper. This is perhaps the most outstanding feature of Jeremiah's promises. I could have listed this, with the three elements above, as something obviously not finally fulfilled in the days of the Jews' return from the Exile; but these are important enough to be treated separately.

The single most significant thing about this, as regards its fulfillment, lies in the fact that it is quoted, essentially verbatim, in Hebrews 8:8–12. It is quoted, in that context, in a way that makes one thing clear: namely, that this promise is being fulfilled, in a significant way, in the present Christian faith and experience. While this does not have to be the *only* fulfillment of the promises, it is at least *one* very important fulfillment of them—and therefore of the promises in all these passages in Jeremiah. I say this last because I think I have already shown that there is so much in common in all these passages, wrapped in *inclusio* as they are, that they must be seen as a unified package.

So if 31:31–34 (and the same elements in other passages in Jeremiah) is being fulfilled in the new covenant we celebrate at the Lord's Table, what specifically does this mean? Here are three all-too-brief observations about fulfillment in the life of the Christian Church.

a. Certainly, some of the more "spiritual" elements of the promises—like the law written in people's hearts, the knowledge of God that in some sense does not have to be taught, and the forgiveness and cleansing from sin—are easily viewed as fulfilled in the new covenant in Christ.

b. The identity of Jesus Christ as the truest fulfillment of the Davidic covenant can likewise be seen as fulfillment of Jeremiah's promises. There is a sense in which the kingdom of God has been established in the hearts of those who exercise saving faith, and Jesus is the greater David who reigns over that kingdom now and forever.

c. This *could* mean, then, that the Christian Church is *the* reality in which *all* the promises of Jeremiah are fulfilled. In that case, *the* fulfillment is primarily "spiritual" or figurative. Yes, there was fulfillment of the promise that the Jews would return from captivity to the land, and this promise was fulfilled in the days of Zerubbabel, Ezra, and Nehemiah. But perhaps most of the rest of the promises waited for the coming of the Messiah and are fulfilled in the church He bought with His blood and is "building" even now (Matthew 16:18). Some interpreters make this move. To do so includes the implication that the true Christian Church (considered organically, not organizationally) *replaces* Israel as the people—the Israel—of God. In that case, the Jews as a people have no more place in God's eschatological program.

5. But there are some elements of the promises in the total "package"—at least implied in the new covenant (31:31–34)—that do not appear to lend themselves well to an entirely "spiritual" or figurative fulfillment in the present Christian church. Among these are the following, recalling points I have cited above.

a. A great deal of the language regards the status of Israel, and of Judah, as descendants of Abraham, Isaac, and Jacob who will return to the land of their forefathers. When Yahweh says they will not fail to be a people before Him forever, that promise seems to require something more than replacement by the Church.

b. Closely connected is the very specific language about the land itself, the city of Jerusalem, and the blessings and prosperity to be enjoyed under the hand of God. These promises include many references to specific places in Palestine, and to what Israel will do in those places, and this seems to go well beyond the pattern of poetic imagery that borrows language from an emotionally appealing realm and applies it to a different realm.

c. Also closely connected is the language describing the reign of "David"—certainly messianic—as king, instituting justice and righteousness in the land. As I have shown in an earlier chapter, the New Testament itself gives considerable attention to the messianic reign that will attend the return of Jesus to earth.

6. I should also make some observations about Jeremiah's use of *forever* or *everlasting*, given that this may be important to discussions about fulfillment. Here are instances I refer to:

31:36—"If [the sun, moon, and stars] depart . . . then the seed of Israel shall also cease from being a nation before Me *forever*."

31:40—The city of Jerusalem, with very specific geographical boundaries named, "shall not be plucked up or thrown down anymore *forever*."

32:39—"I will give them one heart and one way, that they may fear Me *forever*."

32:40—"I will make an *everlasting* covenant with them, ... I will put my fear in their hearts so that they will not depart from Me." (As noted, this is the same as the new covenant in 31:31–34.)

The question is obvious: Does this word (translated by various English words) always mean something like "throughout eternity"? The answer is that it does not. The two Hebrew words used in these verses, however, typically refer to something more than a specified period of time. They can indicate something *permanent* or *perpetual* or even *of indefinite duration*. Regardless just how they are taken, they seem to promise, together, (1) the place of Israel as a nation before God; (2) the city of Jerusalem to have specific boundaries in Palestine; (3) a heart for God that is expressed in walking in one way and characterized by the fear of God; and (4) such a fear of God that does not turn away from Him—and all of these with no marked termination.

At this point, then, I raise the questions we need to ask—and seek to answer. Are all the promises in these passages meant to be a single "package"? Are they all meant for the Church? Are they all meant for Israel as an ethnically defined people? When are the promises fulfilled?

A Proposed Approach

In conclusion, I suggest—relatively briefly and in outline form—what seems to be a probable set of answers to these questions.

1. I repeat that it is important to view all the passages as a unified "package" of interrelated promises of hope for the future.

2. The fulfillment of this package *began* (but did not finish) with the return of the Jews from exile, beginning in 539 BC. They were restored to the land, rebuilt the Temple and the city, and came to enjoy a relatively stable, albeit temporary, existence in the land. This occupation of the homeland varied somewhat from time to time but at best lasted only until AD 70 when Jerusalem was destroyed again by the Romans.

3. Growing out of this, the fulfillment *continues* with the redemptive work of Jesus Christ, the Messiah. He inaugurated the new covenant which Jeremiah promised in 31:31–34 (and which is quoted in Hebrews 8). In the administration of this new covenant, all who exercise faith in Jesus Christ, whether Jewish or Gentile, are brought into the true people of God and made a spiritual kingdom. Over this kingdom, Jesus as the greater David, the Branch of righteousness, rules even now. The knowledge of God and the law of God are internalized, written on the hearts of those who make up this people, rather than on stones.

4. Growing out of all this, again, the fulfillment *will continue* with the genuine repentance of a significant segment of the Jews, recognizing and exercising faith in Jesus as their Savior, Messiah, and rightful King. In consequence, God will restore them to the land in faith, and Jesus as the Davidic King will come and reign over them and over the world. (This is not necessarily connected to the creation of "Israel" in 1948.)

5. Finally, still growing out of the preceding, the fulfillment *will reach its final and permanent completion* with the truly eternal state in the New Heaven, New Earth, and New Jerusalem.

These are the basic elements of the view I am suggesting for consideration, and as I look at this approach it seems somewhat complicated. Even so, it may well be that these different aspects of the fulfillment are needed to cover all of Jeremiah's wonderful promises of hope, restoration, and a new covenant. I do not see this as *multiple* fulfillments but as one package of promises that incorporates *progressive* fulfillment in stages. Each new stage grows out of the preceding and yields more and more complete fulfillment—including the incorporation of Gentile believers into the people of God—until all the promises are perfectly and permanently fulfilled in eternity.

Concluding Observations About Eschatology in Jeremiah and the Old Testament

The view I have suggested will at least *allow* a role for ethnic Israel in the eschatological, messianic reign of Jesus on earth. If this is adopted, then what we have seen in Romans 11:26 and its context, discussed earlier, can be taken at face value: "All Israel will be saved." "Israel" can still mean ethnic Israel and not a spiritualized "Israel of God" that is equal to the Christian Church. Likewise, the 144,000 sealed in Revelation 7:1–8 can be understood as ethnic Israelites, even though the numbers—12,000 each of the twelve tribes (Dan omitted)—do not necessarily need to be taken literally.

This does not address the question as to just when or how a significant population of Jews will be converted to faith in Jesus and become available for a role as Israelites in the reign of Jesus at His return. One can speculate that such a thing might happen during the period leading up to Jesus' coming: that is, when the great apostasy and outpouring of the wrath of God come to pass. But this is speculative, after all; none of the passages we have examined in the New Testament provide information to confirm or deny it. We will learn about the timing and nature of this great turning to God when it comes about.

This should not be understood to reestablish an old separation between Jews and Gentiles. One of the biblical teachings often given too little attention in dispensational theology is the fact that Gentile believers and Jewish believers are "made one" by Jesus through the blood of His cross. Ephesians 2:11–22 is an important resource in understanding this. Although I will not provide a thorough exegesis of the whole, I recommend it for further analysis. I call attention to some of its key elements.

Paul notes that Gentile believers *were* "aliens from the commonwealth of Israel and strangers from the covenants of promise, having no hope and without God in the world" (verse 12). "But," he says, "now in Christ Jesus you who once were far off have been brought near by the blood of Christ" (verse 13). This means that "He … has made both [Jew and Gentile] one" (verse 14); He has "abolished in His flesh the enmity" . . . so as to create in Himself one new man from the two" (verse 15). In this way He was able to "reconcile them both to God in one body through the cross, thereby putting to death the enmity" (verse 16). This does not suggest that there are two entirely distinct peoples of God but that we Gentile believers have joined with those of faith among the Jews in one body.

Paul develops something like this in Romans 11, when he observes that Gentile believers have been "grafted in" among Jewish believers and "with them became [partakers] of the root and fatness of the olive tree" (verse 17). Indeed, he continues, "they also, if they [Israelites] do not continue in unbelief, will be grafted in, for God is able to graft them in again" (verse 23). There is *one* body or olive tree—to use Paul's metaphors—not two; and in some very fundamental sense both Jewish believers (of any age) and Gentile believers (of any age) participate in that body.

The view of things, and of eschatology, that I am suggesting should not be confused with the popular form of dispensational premillennialism expressed in the notes in the Scofield Bible, for example, or in the writings of men like Harry Ironsides and Clarence Larkin, or as represented in the teaching associated with Dallas Theological Seminary. If it is to be called *premillennialism*, it is more like "historic premillennialism," which does not ground eschatology in a dispensational view of Israel with its postponed kingdom. It looks forward to the second coming of Jesus to this earth, at which point He will establish His rightful reign on earth. In that sub-final expression of "the kingdom of God"—the final expression being the eternal state—ethnic Israel may play a role, but we will not know just how (or when) they are converted to faith in Jesus or what role they have until such things are revealed as they occur. Perhaps the Old Testament prophecies can fill in some of this detail, but doing so now goes beyond my purpose in this book.

If one chooses to leave ethnic Israel out of his or her eschatological framework, let that be so on the basis of careful interpretation of all the scriptural teaching on the subject. Other elements of the approach I am suggesting need not be changed for that reason alone. One may indeed object to the idea that ethnic Israel, as part of the people of God, will once again enjoy special blessedness under God. Grounds for that objection may be found in the fact that restoring ethnic Israel to the people of God would be to turn back from a higher spiritual level to a former, lower level. But true spirituality never was, and never will be, determined by physical descent from a common ancestor. God's use of ethnic Israel was never intended to make spiritual reality secondary or to negate the need for faith. It has always been true that "the just shall live by faith." If there will be a "not yet" kingdom on earth—whether literally for a millennium or not—and if ethnic Israel will be in some way part of that, we can be sure God knows how to make that even greater and more spiritual than the "already" kingdom of God that is now present in the hearts of true believers in Jesus, Gentile and Jew alike. There is more we do not know about the messianic kingdom of the future than what we do know.

The following chapter will provide a concluding outline of a biblical eschatology.

Endnotes

[22] C. F. Keil and Franz Delitzsch, *Old Testament Commentary*, vol. 5 of 6 vols. (Grand Rapids: Associated Publishers and Authors, n.d.), 520; the comment is in the "introduction," §2.

[23] This expression occurs fiften times (or more) in Jeremiah, about half promising judgment and half restoration. It appears to heighten the contrast between the present condition and the hope (or judgment) promised.

[24] It seems clear that this Branch-Messiah will be called "Yahweh Our Rightesouness." In 33:16 the same name is applied to Jerusalem in the future.

[25] Such "bookending" is a literary device called *inclusio*.

[26] For the Davidic covenant referred to, see 2 Samuel 7:8–16; the Levitical covenant is apparently that made with Phinehas in Numbers 25:12–13.

[27] I am aware that the so-called "New Perspective on Paul" makes a case that first century Judaism was more spiritually minded than has traditionally been thought. I don't want to reject such claims entirely, but at the same time I find that the New Testament perspective of Judaism under the influence of the Pharisees and the rabbinic school, as depicted in the Gospel (which I trust), suggests a largely legalistic and externally oriented religion.

[28] It would be a stretch, indeed, to view the Maccabean "kings" as fulfillment of this promise. For that matter, the biblical record makes no attempt to establish them as such.

Chapter 17

MERE ESCHATOLOGY: A CONCLUDING OVERVIEW

The purpose of this final chapter is to provide a survey of the biblical eschatology I have developed in this volume. This overview will not focus primarily on details but on the main elements we are to expect. My intention is to give primary attention to these key elements. I will deliberately avoid the use of charts and timelines, heavily used by many Bible teachers in the past to stress dispensational themes and distinctions.

Focus One: The Times Leading to the Second Coming

The Christian concept of the present age is eschatological by definition. We are already in "the last days" and have been ever since Jesus ascended to the Father (Hebrews 1:2; 1 Peter 1:20). The Christian experience of the new birth and the indwelling Holy Spirit is, in a definite way, a taste of the age to come in the present age. Hebrews 6:5 includes, in the passage's description of genuine Christian conversion, having "tasted … the powers of the age to come"—and in Hebrews *taste* reveals a genuine experience.

There is an aspect of our present reality, then, that speaks of a greater reality to come. We are caught in this age temporarily, tasting and looking for the final dawning of the age that is already breaking in on us.

What the New Testament teaches us, as I said earlier, is that we are disciples-in-waiting. We see already the "signs" that this age is not the end of things, that there is—as Jesus said in passages like Matthew 12:32 and Luke 18:29–30—an "age to come" in which we will experience eternal life. It is the very nature of a Christian, therefore, "to be waiting for His Son out of the heavens … Jesus, the One who will be delivering us from the wrath that will be coming" (1 Thessalonians 1:10, my translation).

Apostasy and Antichrist

But there will be some increasingly dark times on this earth before Jesus sets foot on it again in His glory. Paul spoke briefly of this prospect: "In latter times some will depart from the faith" (1 Timothy 4:1); "In the last days perilous times will come" (2 Timothy 3:1); "evil men and impostors will grow worse and worse" (2 Timothy 3:13). These are general observations, but they anticipate an ever-growing power of the evil one in the present age. His power and influence will only increase as we approach the end of the age.

Especially in 2 Thessalonians 2, Paul speaks pointedly of two things that must precede the Second Coming: namely, "the apostasy" (falling away, rebellion) and "the revelation of the man of sin (or lawlessness)." Paul does not describe the first of these any more than to name the phenomenon. The second he describes in some detail. This "man of sin" is (at least when Paul wrote) hindered from being fully revealed; but he is already at work. When he is revealed, in the providential government of God, he will attempt to usurp the worship of people that ought to go to God alone. If the two things Paul names are closely related, as seems most likely, then this one is the Antichrist, leading the apostasy from or rebellion against God.

The book of Revelation, especially in chapter 13 (and beyond) has much to say about this "beast," this antichrist figure who in one form or another is at work throughout the present age (the last days) and will be fully manifested near the end of the age, shortly before Jesus returns. "Every spirit that does not confess that Jesus Christ has come in the flesh is not of God. And this is the spirit of the Antichrist, which you have heard was coming and is now already in the world" (1 John 4:3).

The career of this figure is not limited to an end-time person or even to one or two people of wicked influence in the past or present. Antichrist, in the days of Revelation's first readers, was Domitian, the Roman Emperor who tried to force the Christians to burn incense to himself as a god. Some Reformers, breaking away from the Roman church's grip on the Christian faith in the sixteenth century, identified the pope, or the Roman church itself, as antichrist, and with good reason. Wherever there has been or will be an institution, government, or person leading resistance to the Trinitarian God of the Bible, there has been or will be antichrist at work. The visions in Revelation that portray this "beast" include within the scope of their fulfillment any and all appearances of "the spirit of the Antichrist" at any time during the present age.

At the same time, these visions likewise foretell that there will be a figure or institution (or both), not long before Jesus returns, who will be the last and fullest embodiment of antichrist. This final version of antichrist "the Lord [Jesus] will consume with the breath of His mouth and destroy with the brightness of His coming" (2 Thessalonians 2:8; compare Revelation 19:20–21).

Tribulation

In association with this apostasy and antichrist, we expect a time of great trouble on earth, especially for the wicked, brought on by the judicial wrath of God poured out on the world. The "coming wrath" that Paul spoke of in 1 Thessalonians 1:10 will not be limited to eternal punishment in hell. There is a long-standing, biblical emphasis on the fact that God will visit the earth with a judicial punishment for sin.

Again, we need not think of this exclusively in terms of a single period of time just prior to the coming of Jesus. God's hatred for sin has been demonstrated in natural calamity ever since the original sin, in response to which God cursed the natural order. More than two millennia after the fall, God was exercised by the fact that "the wickedness of man was great in the earth, and that every intent of the thoughts of his heart was only evil continually" (Genesis 6:5). In response, He sent a flood that covered the whole earth and destroyed all mankind except for Noah and his family. When that was over, He promised that "the waters shall never again become a flood to destroy all flesh" (Genesis 9:15); at the same time He appointed the present natural order as "reserved for fire until the day of judgment" (2 Peter 3:7). His wrath will fall again.

Indeed, the wrath of God against sin finds expression throughout the present age. In His mingled wrath and grace, He provides punishments that ought to serve to make mankind wary of sin and careful to obey Him. This is, at least in part, the reason for "evil" in the world, in the form of natural calamity. Local floods, earthquakes, wildfires, tornadoes, hurricanes, landslides, and all the rest, including plagues of disease and death—these are the results of the curse and expressions of God's judicial wrath against sin. They have as their purpose to warn us away from the worst expression of evil imaginable—eternal hell—and so they are expressions of grace, too.

In the Olivet Discourse, Jesus said that such natural calamities would characterize the present age; and the implication is that they will grow worse and worse as the end of the age and the return of Jesus to earth approach. Revelation, if it depicts anything at all, depicts this. Three of the four horsemen ride to signal war, famine, and death—throughout the present age and intensifying in the last of the last days. The trumpet-judgments appear to focus, at least partly, on the geographic features of earth and skies. The seven last plagues repeat but intensify such trials. The visions in that strange book picture hurts and death that go beyond our imagination. Again, all these have their precursors throughout the present age, but not long before Jesus returns to earth they will reach their peak and serve as the penultimate expressions of God's wrath—the last expression being the eternal lake of fire itself.

Even during these tribulations, there is still opportunity to repent. Sadly, Revelation notes more than once that men and women—for the most part, at least—refuse to repent even in the face of God's terrible wrath and their own crippling fear; see Revelation 9:20–21 and 16:9, 11. Instead, they double down on their hatred for and blasphemy of God, even in their awareness that this is a tribulation of judicial wrath on account of their sins. They are, after all, deceived by the great deceiver himself, and that too is a manifestation of the judicial wrath of God, who sends or permits—the two words say the same thing—the delusion to come on them as a result of their prior rejection of the truth (2 Thessalonians 2:11–12).

Bible students often ponder whether the Church will "go through the tribulation." No need for argument about that: for one thing, God protects His people, and, for another, we are already in the tribulation, and it will get worse before it is done. Nor do we need to try to define "the tribulation" as seven years, and "the great tribulation" as the last half of that. As I have indicated, the measures of time in Revelation are symbolic. No other parts of the New Testament tell how long the most severe outpouring of God's wrath will last before Jesus returns to earth. We do not now and will not then know the time of His appearing—although I suspect that the spiritually informed will sense that their final redemption draws near.

All of this suggests, as I have indicated in the earlier chapters, that there already is and will continue to be increasing hostility against God and God's people at the hands of those under the sway of the evil one—including the principalities and powers that hide behind the visible powers of the world and the present age. The supplemental visions in Revelation 12–20:10 depict the long-standing, cosmic conflict between God and Satan that we are caught up in. That conflict, too, will intensify and will be part of the trial or tribulation of the days before Jesus arrives. Revelation 12:17 describes this ongoing warfare: "The dragon was enraged with the woman, and he went to make war with the rest of her offspring, who keep the commandments of God and have the testimony of Jesus Christ." That is now, and that will be even more the case during the tribulation of the last of the last days.

Focus Two: The Second Coming

Jesus is coming again, coming to the very world from which He ascended forty days after His triumphant resurrection from the dead. This visit to earth will stand in sharp contrast to His first coming. That was the time of His humiliation; He will return in power and great glory.

It appears that, either shortly prior to or coincident with the return of Jesus, there will be a pronounced turning to God by faith in Jesus Christ on the part of at least a significant segment of ethnic Israelites. We have been given no information as to how or when this comes about, but it comes in fulfillment of wonderful promises found in the writings of the Old Testament prophets, like Jeremiah. In the New Testament, both Paul (Romans 11) and John (Revelation 7), apparently speak of this, though without detail. More about this below.

Meanwhile, Jesus' coming will be unannounced. Only His shout of command, the voice of an archangel, and the trump of God (1 Thessalonians 4:16—are all three different ways of expressing the same event?) will serve to signal His arrival. His coming will likewise be publicly visible and glorious. "Every eye"—at least everyone where He arrives—"will see Him" (Revelation 1:7).

He will raise the believing dead and transform the believing living and forcefully lift them to meet Him in the air to descend with Him and be with Him permanently. There will be no interruptions of personal fellowship with God such as those that are caused by our sins. There will be no sin for those transformed fully and finally into the image of Jesus Christ.

Jesus will destroy the man of sin, antichrist (2 Thessalonians 2:8), and consign him and his "prime minister"—the False Prophet—to the lake of fire (Revelation 19:20). At the same time He will slay all those who have supported the Antichrist in his rebellion against God (Revelation 19:21), apparently to await final judgment (Revelation 20:12).

He will take His rightful throne as the Branch of David, the messianic King of kings and Lord of lords (Matthew 25:31), perhaps ruling from a restored Jerusalem and a restored Israel. As Paul expresses this, "He must reign till He has put all enemies under His feet" (1 Corinthians 15:25). As a simple fact, all Christians can agree with this, whether they think of it as initiating a reign on earth or as entering into His eternal reign. From any perspective, His reign is eternal. I will return to this below in the section entitled "Focus Three," where I will make clear that a reign on earth that consummates in an eternal reign with the Father seems the more likely view.

As reigning King, Jesus' return will also result in His judgment (Matthew 25:31–46). His judgment of those caught up to meet Him may occur at the meeting in the air. In the main, however, *if there is a reign of Jesus on earth fol-*

lowing His return, this judgment will occur at the end of His messianic reign; at least the wicked and those converted during that earthly reign will not be judged until then.

Regardless of the details of judgment and a possible reign on earth, the Second Coming is the blessed hope of all believers. Paul might well have thought that he would be among those still living at Jesus' coming; in 1 Thessalonians 4:17 he says, "*we* who are alive and remain." Indeed, all of us belong in that *we.* Although the time will remain unannounced, we should expect His coming soon, and even though there will be a final manifestation of the spirit of antichrist and severe tribulation, He may come while we live. Waiting eagerly and expectantly for that coming helps define us as Christians.

Focus Three: The Reign of Christ

If I have interpreted both 1 Corinthians 15:25 and the vision John describes in Revelation 19:11–20:10 correctly, Jesus will fulfill His messianic destiny with a reign on earth—not necessarily for a thousand years but for a significant length of time—perhaps more or less than a thousand years. At the end of that reign, He will have put all enemies under His feet and will put the Kingdom in the hands of His Father, with whom He will be co-regent for eternity. In doing this He will bring to its final and fullest confirmation the Davidic covenant.

During this reign on earth, Satan will be "bound" (Revelation 20:2) and his access to human beings will be thus limited. At the end, he will be released and gather a mob of people, beyond number, for a final resistance to God. That rebellion will be immediately put down and the rebels slain. Satan will join his companions, the Beast and False Prophet, in the lake of fire for eternal torment (Revelation 20:7–10).

The New Testament gives us little information about this reign; we cannot tell how life will function and be governed. Some things seem clear.

(1) Those who were caught up to meet Him at His coming—which includes all saints living and dead up to that point—will reign with Him in one

way or another. There are hints that they will reign and judge on earth as His agents.

(2) There will be an immense population of people living their natural lives on earth, entering the period of His reign. They will apparently live longer than is customary on earth now, possibly reminiscent of the patriarchs before the great flood of Genesis 6. How their daily lives will be conducted is not described, but they will marry and give birth as before. There will be peace and prosperity on earth, and wickedness will be forcibly curtailed. Under Christ's government people will at least outwardly submit to His authority. Some will be converted, but many will not and will join Satan's resistance at the end.

(3) Given the nature of Old Testament prophecy, as exemplified in Jeremiah's "Little Book of Comfort," it appears that there will be a wide-scale turning to God among those of ethnic Israeli descent. This does not necessarily mean that we can take all the details of Old Testament poetry-prophecy literally; whether there will be a physical temple during the reign of Jesus, for example, is debatable. (There seems to be no good reason against that idea; after all, even in the days of the Tabernacle and Temple, God has been worshipped in spirit and truth.)

What seems likely is that, *if there is a messianic kingdom on earth following the Second Coming*, these Israelites will enjoy the fulfillment of those Old Testament promises and experience a faith that is written in their hearts. In this they will enjoy a reality akin to that of New Testament Christians, and both they and Gentile believers will be one people of God together. If this is correct, it suggests that God has not yet finished making special use of ethnic Israel in His program. There is as good reason to think this will be true as there was for Him to use Israel under the old covenant.

Focus Four: The Final Judgment and Eternal State

When the reign of Jesus is done and Satan and his followers are vanquished for the last time, the final judgment (Revelation 20:11–15) and the eternal state (Revelation 21–22) will follow. There is much wider agreement about the meaning of this final part of Revelation.

At this "Great White Throne Judgment" will be all of mankind, dead and living, wicked and righteous—the only possible exception being those caught up to meet Jesus at the Second Coming, if indeed they have already been judged—which is not certain. At this final tribunal, judgment will be according to two standards: (1) by whether their names appear in "the Lamb's book of life" as having genuinely committed themselves in faith to Jesus as their Lord and Savior; and (2) by their works. Among both the righteous and the wicked there will be some differences depending on the second of these. We do not know enough to describe what those differences will be.

All those whose names are not in the Lamb's Book will join Satan, the Beast, and the False Prophet in the lake of fire for eternal punishment. No wicked persons will sully the fellowship of the saints forever; instead they will be eternally separated from God and everything good in "the second death" (Revelation 21:8), forever "outside" (Revelation 22:15).

Those whose names are found in the Lamb's Book are variously identified in the Bible in general and in Revelation in particular. The most important designation is that they have committed themselves in faith to Jesus and have thereby become His disciples or followers. In Revelation they are—among other things—the "overcomers" (chapters 2–3; 21:7), the ones who "keep His commandments" (12:17; 14:12; 22:14[29]) and who "have the testimony of Jesus" (1:9; 12:17; 19:10). Such are the evidences of saving faith.

The last two chapters of Revelation describe the eternal blessedness of these whom the Lamb acknowledges as His. The mixture of symbol and literal reality is so close that we cannot fully discern what our forever lives will be like. It appears that the new Heaven and new earth will be our range, with our "place" in "the Father's house" (John 14:2–3) there somewhere, perhaps in the capital city.

But the "New Jerusalem" is in fact the people of God, the bride of Christ—Jew and Gentile without distinction (Revelation 21:9–10). How we will occupy ourselves—beyond joyous expressions of worship to the Triune God:

Father, Son, and Spirit—is not clear; it may be that the new life will offer some of the same joys and pleasures that the present life does: experiences like achievement, learning, knowing, serving, but all to the glory of God.

Some things are clear enough. We will have no lingering tears, no sorrows, no pain, no night, no darkness, and no death (Revelation 21:4). We will have unfettered access to the Tree of Life and the River of Life (Revelation 2:7; 22:1–2, 14); if those are symbolic, what they represent is obvious and far better than the symbols themselves. Most of all we will have access to God Himself and to the Lamb and His Spirit. In that direct fellowship with God, the words of His covenant relationship with His people, which run throughout the Bible, will be established forever: He will be our God, and we will be His people (Revelation 21:7).

Amen. Even so, come, Lord Jesus!

Endnotes

[29] Some manuscripts have "wash their robes" instead of "do His commandments" in Revelation 22:14, an equally apt identification of a Christian; compare Revelation 7:14.

Postscript

I first thought to write an appendix with suggestions for individuals, pastors, and churches to heighten expectation for the Second Coming. On second thought, I think this is not a good idea.

I do think it is a good idea for us to whet our appetites for Jesus' appearing, of course—and that this is a biblical thing to do. But I suspect we will be more successful at this if each of us, both for ourselves and for others with whom we have influence, will sit down and consider just how we might go about keeping the truths of the Second Coming before us in a way that enhances our excitement about Jesus' return—and perhaps even hastens His coming.

I therefore simply challenge every reader to ponder this seriously and decide on some practical things to do to keep the Second Coming fresh in our awareness. Those who have influence over others, especially pastors, may think of some things to introduce regularly into the life of the churches they serve, things that will help the people in the churches to think more about the Second Coming and about watching and being ready for it.

It may be very soon. I hope it is.

Scripture Index

Daniel

Acts

Romans

1 Corinthians

2 Corinthians

Galatians

Ephesians

Philippians

Colossians

1 Thessalonians